VOLUME 483   JANUARY 1986

THE ANNALS

of The American Academy *of* Political
and Social Science

RICHARD D. LAMBERT, *Editor*
ALAN W. HESTON, *Associate Editor*

RELIGION AND THE STATE:
THE STRUGGLE FOR LEGITIMACY AND POWER

Special Editor of this Volume

ROBERT J. MYERS

President
Council on Religion and International Affairs
New York City

Ⓢ **SAGE** PUBLICATIONS   *BEVERLY HILLS   LONDON   NEW DELHI*

THE ANNALS

© 1986 *by* The American Academy *of* Political *and* Social Science

ERICA GINSBURG, *Assistant Editor*

Editorial Office: 3937 Chestnut Street, Philadelphia, Pennsylvania 19104.

For information about membership (individuals only) and subscriptions (institutions), address:*

SAGE PUBLICATIONS, INC.
275 South Beverly Drive
Beverly Hills, CA 90212 USA

From India and South Asia, write to:

SAGE PUBLICATIONS INDIA Pvt. Ltd.
P.O. Box 4215
New Delhi 110 048
INDIA

From the UK, Europe, the Middle East and Africa, write to:

SAGE PUBLICATIONS LTD
28 Banner Street
London EC1Y 8QE
ENGLAND

SAGE Production Editor: JACQUELINE SYROP

**Please note that members of The Academy receive THE ANNALS with their membership.*

Library of Congress Catalog Card Number 85-072100
International Standard Serial Number ISSN 0002-7162
International Standard Book Number ISBN 0-8039-2539-5 (Vol. 483, 1986 paper)
International Standard Book Number ISBN 0-8039-2538-7 (Vol. 483, 1986 cloth)
Manufactured in the United States of America. First printing, January 1986.

The articles appearing in THE ANNALS are indexed in *Book Review Index; Public Affairs Information Service Bulletin; Social Sciences Index; Monthly Periodical Index; Current Contents; Behavioral, Social Management Sciences;* and *Combined Retrospective Index Sets.* They are also abstracted and indexed in *ABC Pol Sci, Historical Abstracts, Human Resources Abstracts, Social Sciences Citation Index, United States Political Science Documents, Social Work Research & Abstracts, Peace Research Reviews, Sage Urban Studies Abstracts, International Political Science Abstracts,* and/or *America: History and Life.*

Information about membership rates, institutional subscriptions, and back issue prices may be found on the facing page.

Advertising. Current rates and specifications may be obtained by writing to THE ANNALS Advertising and Promotion Manager at the Beverly Hills office (address above).

Claims. Claims for undelivered copies must be made no later than three months following month of publication. The publisher will supply missing copies when losses have been sustained in transit and when the reserve stock will permit.

Change of Address. Six weeks' advance notice must be given when notifying of change of address to insure proper identification. Please specify name of journal. Send change of address to: THE ANNALS, c/o Sage Publications, Inc., 275 South Beverly Drive, Beverly Hills, CA 90212.

THE EIGHTY-NINTH ANNUAL MEETING OF THE AMERICAN ACADEMY OF POLITICAL AND SOCIAL SCIENCE

APRIL 18 AND 19, 1986
THE BELLEVUE STRATFORD HOTEL
PHILADELPHIA, PENNSYLVANIA

The annual meeting of The Academy is attended by many distinguished scholars, statesmen, authors, and professionals in diverse fields, including representatives of many embassies, academic institutions, and cultural, civic, and scientific organizations.

This 89th Annual Meeting will be addressed at each session by prominent scholars and officials and will be devoted to the topic of

REVITALIZING THE INDUSTRIAL CITY

Members of the Academy are cordially invited to attend and will receive full information. Information on Academy membership can be found in each volume of THE ANNALS.

- Proceedings of the 89th Annual Meeting will be published in the November 1986 volume of THE ANNALS.

- All members and attendees who have published a book may participate in the exhibits at the hotel. Contact Harve C. Horowitz & Associates, 10369 Currycomb Court, Columbia, MD 21044, tel. (301) 997-0763.

FOR DETAILS ABOUT THE ANNUAL MEETING WRITE TO
THE AMERICAN ACADEMY OF POLITICAL AND SOCIAL SCIENCE
BUSINESS OFFICE ● 3937 CHESTNUT STREET
PHILADELPHIA, PENNSYLVANIA 19104

CONTENTS

BOOK DEPARTMENT CONTENTS

PREFACE

The struggle between religions and states has been a long one. For much of human history the ruler has played both a temporal and a priestly role, and the dualism was, in those times, resolved. At other times, however, political leaders have needed religion as a popular motivating force to legitimize their power. Religious leaders, in turn, have extracted from political leaders, and from society as a whole, whatever price they could in favor of their beliefs. This mutual dependence—or exploitation—has led each to sacrifice a measure of power, sometimes to the point where religious and political leadership have become, once again, identical.

Religion being by definition concerned with God and the supernatural, and belief being the evidence of things unseen, there is always room for the creation of new religions and for reinterpretations of the old. Politicians, on the other hand, are committed to the stability of their rule. Consequently the conflicts between the religious impulse and the state's conservative power are perennial, as is the tension between competing religious ideologies.[1] The situation at any moment remains in flux.

It is the work of political scientists and theologians, respectively, to clarify the role of politics and religion in a given society.

RELIGION AND SOCIETY

For many Westerners, the classic statement on relations between religion and the state is found in Matthew 22: 21: "Render therefore unto Caesar the things which are Caesar's; and unto God the things that are God's." This neat division, however, did not settle the matter for all Christian societies, as some of the articles in this volume illustrate, and the relationship between religion and the state is equally unsettled in other parts of the world, whatever the dominant religion. Even in states where the Muslim religion is the established, state religion, these kinds of tensions continue to arise.

For Alexis de Tocqueville, the American method of dealing with this relationship seemed the surest and most felicitous. The United States' founding fathers, mindful of the history of Europe, had said in the First Amendment to the Constitution that "Congress shall make no law respecting an establishment of religion, or prohibiting the free exercise thereof." By 1835, Tocqueville believed, this arrangement was working smoothly and had actually strengthened religion in America:

> When a religion seeks to found its sway only on the longing for immortality equally tormenting every human heart, it can aspire to universality; but when it comes to uniting itself with a government, it must adopt maxims which apply only to certain nations. Therefore, by allying itself with any political power, religion increases its strength over some but forfeits the hope of ruling over all.[2]

1. See, for example, Mircea Eliade, *A History of Religious Ideas* (Chicago: University of Chicago Press, 1978), p. 321.

2. Alexis de Tocqueville, *Democracy in America* (Garden City, NY: Doubleday, Anchor Books, 1969), pp. 294-301.

It is not, to be sure, inevitable that the separation of church and state will favor religion; separation alone neither strengthens nor fosters aspirations toward universality. Lenin quotes Engels: "Complete separation of the church from the state. All religious communities without exception are private associations. They are to be deprived of any support from public funds and of all influence on public schools." Lenin adds, "And nothing else!"[3]

The question remains, What people and what ideology control the power of the state? The difficulty of resolving the question is compounded by the fact that no concept of the state is value free; the values inherent in the prevailing concept of the state determine the parameters of political, social, and cultural engagement within a society. Religions often have a great deal to say about what values are incorporated into such a concept of the state; religions most often attempt to assure that those values are compatible with their own priorities for this world. Within the religious community itself there is tension between those who wish to concentrate on the spiritual aspect of their religious teachings and those who prefer to work for the application of those precepts through the extant political community. Professor Kenneth W. Thompson's article provides an informative update on the religious question in the United States some 150 years after Tocqueville made his observations.

The principal unifying thread of these articles is that each examines the way religion both uses the state for its own purposes and, in turn, is used by the state for the state's ends. Here is the natural tension, between the competition for ideological superiority—legitimization—on the one hand and the necessary accommodation and compromise, on the other.

In the daily press, one can see the ongoing competition of religious groupings, in all parts of the world, with one another and with other institutions, as each struggles to define the purposes and role of the state in its own terms. Often, a religious belief reinforces an ethnic group in its attempt to carve out a position of influence or independence. The shifting lines of such struggles define, to a large degree, contemporary world politics. The countries selected for study here cover the major religious traditions and exemplify the current condition of religion and state around the world.

Religions do not have identical ways of making an impact on their societies. "The great religions of the East, Hinduism and Buddhism, which stretched human vistas into vast and endless cycles far beyond the seasons and the years of an individual life or a generation, brought a refuge from these cycles by helping the individual merge into the All."[4] The promise of these religions is escape from the endless reiterations of earth by transcendence into the Universal. These religious concepts may have less influence on the political and social priorities of the average believer than they do on the religious leadership. Professor Ralph Buultjens argues, in his article on India, that the ideals of democracy—which, through the vote, may be said to emphasize the individual and the temporal—have so far been the legitimizing agent for the Indian state, despite its Hindu majority.

3. Lenin, *Marxism on the State* (reprint ed., Moscow: Progress, 1974), p. 18.
4. Daniel J. Boorstin, *The Discoverers* (New York: Random House, 1983), p. 566.

It is not my intent, however, to summarize these articles, which, I believe, will be read with considerable pleasure and profit. They offer valuable insights by providing political analysis from the perspective of the role of religion in particular societies—a perspective too often overlooked or taken as an afterthought, despite daily evidence of religion's often central significance in the current dilemmas of international relations.

My sincere appreciation goes to the contributors of these articles, who did this work out of personal dedication and commitment. I would also like to thank John Tessitore and Linda Griffin of the Council on Religion and International Affairs for their editorial assistance.

ROBERT J. MYERS

Religion and Politics in the United States: An Overview

By KENNETH W. THOMPSON

ABSTRACT: This article seeks to examine the relationship between the sacred and the secular in the United States historically and in the present. It probes what the founding fathers intended and how church-state relations have changed over time. The tendency of contemporary leaders to inject their religious views into public policy positions is analyzed in some detail, and perils of abridging the principles of church-state relations that are enshrined in the Constitution are reviewed. Also treated is the perception of leaders and opinion makers at home and abroad. An effort is made to draw on the thought of both classical and recent interpreters of the problem. The shifts in the positions of American leaders in response to the demands of partisan politics are noted.

Kenneth W. Thompson is director of the Miller Center of Public Affairs at the University of Virginia and former vice-president of the Rockefeller Foundation. He is the author of Morality and Foreign Policy; The Moral Issue in Statecraft; Christian Ethics and the Dilemmas of Foreign Policy; Moralism and Morality in Politics and Diplomacy; Ethics, Functionalism and Power; *and editor of* American Moral and Political Leadership in the Third World, *all books related to the subject of this article.*

T HEOLOGIANS and political philosophers through much of the twentieth century have found that the separation of church and state provides a unique source of strength in the U.S. constitutional system. Yet friends abroad are puzzled by the American justification for a division between the secular and sacerdotal worlds. Muslim, Confucian, and other non-Western thinkers would unite and bring together what American religious and political thinkers keep separate. Even in Western countries such as England the existence of a state church draws church and state closely together. In a recent monograph, Don K. Price, of Harvard University, traces the interconnection between a religious establishment in England and the existence of a political establishment.[1] He finds that because the political establishment derives from the religious establishment, its credibility is enhanced. In the United States, science and administration have been substitutes for the trustworthiness of religiously acknowledged leaders.

THE FOLLOWING

Whatever questions outsiders may raise, the intention of the founding fathers seems clear. They believed in religious and political freedom. The political edifice they sought to build was dualistic in conception, balancing religion and politics. Not only Thomas Jefferson but also his most respected political allies feared an established religion and religious tests for political office. Nor did the author of the Declaration of Religious Freedom stand alone among presidents. In 1815, John Adams wrote to Jefferson, "The question before the human race is whether the God of nature shall govern the world by his own laws, or whether priests and kings shall rule it by fictitious miracles." This most balanced system has not prevented fear of abuse arising from the convergence of religion and politics. Writing to Adams six years after his second term, Jefferson described "this loathsome combination of church and state." Earlier he had warned that history provides no example of a clergy-ridden people maintaining a free civil government. The lack of such a government, he felt, marks "the lowest grade of ignorance," of which political as well as religious leaders will always "avail themselves for their own purpose."

Fear of the abuse of religion by political leaders reflected deep-seated underlying doubts concerning human nature. To keep lesser mortal motives within bounds, religion and politics were to exist in an equilibrium ordered by an intricate network of checks and balances. Not Hamilton but Jefferson declared, "Free government is founded on jealousy and not confidence which prescribes limited Constitutions to bind down those whom we are obliged to trust with power: that our Constitution has accordingly fixed the limits to which and no further our confidence may go."[2] Jefferson was more emphatic about human nature in the debates over the Kentucky Resolutions of 1798, saying, "In questions of power then let no more be heard of confidence in man, but bind him down from mischief by the chains of the Constitution."[3]

1. Don K. Price, *America's Unwritten Constitution: Science, Religion and Political Responsibility* (Baton Rouge: Louisiana State University Press, 1983).

2. Last article of the Kentucky Resolutions of 1798.

3. Ibid.

Thus the outlook of the founders on human nature was grim. With certain contemporary philosophers, they believed in the mutually reinforcing quality of the two independent forces, religion and politics. Indeed, that reinforcement constituted for them the genius of American society. With a few tragic exceptions, notably the Civil War, the United States has escaped the fierce and destructive conflicts that have torn other societies asunder. In that war, a sitting president was forced to speak of warring factions who read from the same Bible, prayed to the same God, and invoked His blessings on their cause. They went to war for principles, not politics or possessions. For the most part, however, Americans within territorial boundaries have been spared those conflicts that stem from crusades for righteousness. Ordinary citizens have not rallied to fight holy wars or wars of religion; those who have fallen have not been helpless victims of *jihad*s conducted in the name of religion.

The different aims of religion and politics

The cornerstone on which the separation of church and state rests, then, is the belief that religion cannot be equated with politics or politics with a particular religion without threatening their mutual destruction. Each has its own imperatives. Historically, every attempt to substitute the pursuit of one for the realization of the other has been doomed from the start. The ends of religion are not the ends of politics. The claim that religion and politics are interchangeable will not stand scrutiny, especially in the long run.

The end of religion is to discover a purpose beyond all human purposes, according to Nikolai Berdyaev[4]. Men and women yearn for a perspective that transcends all the fragmentary purposes of human existence. Politics and nationalism remain fragmentary endeavors; when a political regime crowds out a higher religion, a religion is made out of politics, nationalism, or science. Societies will not long tolerate a spiritual vacuum.

Yet religion is more than a political necessity. It is the ground of man's being, as Paul Tillich has maintained,[5] and religious faith stands above and beyond religious practices.[6] Faith is a matter of a person's ultimate commitments, while religion expresses itself largely in ceremonies, practices, and institutions. To place every person's faith in a single doctrinal straitjacket is to trivialize that faith. Religious faith is above politics and institutions. It is not exhausted in observances or procedures. Ideologies and political religions are, at best, approximations—at worst, corruptions—of religion. Religion's province is human life and the cosmos, good and evil, judgment and salvation. Even in its most noble expression, politics' ends are not the same as religion's.

To be more specific, the ends of politics are order and justice. Whether through social compacts or conquest, we seek to bring nature and the war of each against all under control. We strive for justice, which John Dewey described as giving each man his due. Hans J. Morgenthau

4. See, for example, Nikolai Berdiaev (*sic*), *Solitude and Society,* trans. George Reavey (1938; repr. ed., Westport, CT: Greenwood Press, 1976).

5. See Paul Tillich, "Reinhold Niebuhr's Doctrine of Knowledge," in *Reinhold Niebuhr: His Religious, Social and Political Thought,* ed. Charles W. Kegley and Robert W. Bretall (New York: Macmillan, 1956), pp. 35-43; see also idem, *Systematic Theology* (Chicago: University of Chicago Press, 1967).

6. Rom. 14:5-12.

wrote of "equality in freedom" as the distinguishing characteristic of American politics.[7]

Politics is not allegiance to a single moral principle but the ability to coordinate and adjust multiple principles such as order and freedom, justice and equality, or peace and national security. It was Justice Oliver Wendell Holmes, with his eye on politics, who explained, "Some people admire the man of principle. I admire the man who can find his way through a maze of conflicting principles."[8] The art of politics is that persons who hold convergent and divergent purposes and interests work together. Toward certain of these goals and interests, legitimate resentment may be felt, a resentment that moral sentiment alone cannot sweep away. The constituents of a religion are the faithful, but the constituents of most politicians are not members of a single religious faith. For example, along with voters of many religions, some 100,000 Hindus helped elect Senator Daniel Patrick Moynihan of New York. It is deception, therefore, when the leader of a religiously diverse constituency presumes to speak for his or her acts in the name of one God.

Looking back, we remember leaders who displayed cosmic humility concerning the will of God. At the time of the Civil War, Abraham Lincoln was visited by a group of Presbyterian ministers bearing a petition calling for the emancipation of all the slaves. He replied saying that in every great contest each party claims to be following the will of God. Though God cannot favor two opposing causes, proponents of both believe they act in his name. Lincoln went on to ask why, if God had revealed His will to others, He would not have revealed it to him, the president, accountable to all the people. He said he was anxious to learn the will of God and to follow it, but this was not the day of miracles. In politics he had chosen as his guide "to study the plain physical facts, ascertain what is possible and learn what is wise and just." In practical affairs, he had to balance the desirable with the possible.

In defining the role of church and state, constitutionalism speaks from two historical traditions. One of them is the Judeo-Christian legacy, which is the source of the higher law and the moral and political standards on which the Bill of Rights in the Constitution is based. Love and its approximation in justice are the guideposts of higher religion. Such a religion drives the individual in the direction of what Reinhold Niebuhr called "the impossible possibility," which is the law of love.[9]

Within the most intimate communities, and especially the family, the law of love is at least a tenuous possibility. In politics and business, love is almost always beyond reach. Great collectives such as political parties and nation-states do not love one another. For them, not love but respect is a practical possibility. Yet political leaders and nations, whose moral possibilities are of a lower order than the Judeo-Christian ethic, tend to justify themselves in the highest moral terms. Within the Ameri-

7. See John Dewey, *Philosophy and Civilization* (Magnolia, MA: Peter Smith, n.d.); Hans J. Morgenthau, *The Purpose of American Politics* (1960; repr. ed., Washington, DC: University Press of America, 1982).

8. See Paul A. Freund, *On Law and Justice* (Cambridge, MA: Harvard University Press, 1968); see also Oliver Wendell Holmes, *The Common Law,* ed. Mark DeWolfe Howe (Cambridge, MA: Harvard University Press, 1963).

9. This concept appears in many of Niebuhr's writings; see, for example, his *Justice and Mercy,* ed. Ursula M. Niebuhr (New York: Harper & Row, 1974).

can constitutional system, they translate the practical politics of limited policies and programs into the language of moral absolutes. They sanctify their pragmatic actions as though they were universal truths and, in the process, hamper those who search for political compromises and agreements. We know that moral principles resist compromise. It is interests that yield in the political process.

The second historical tradition undergirding the constitutional order is the Graeco-Roman inheritance. Its focus is on politics and law. As the University of Chicago poet-philosopher T. V. Smith was wont to say, politics brings relations among people down from the heavens. Politics means the harmonization of interests and differences. The seamy side of politics is bargaining and horse trading in smoke-filled rooms. A political agreement means settling for half a loaf. John F. Kennedy observed that Lincoln was a sad man because he learned that in politics one cannot get everything one wants. Hard-boiled politicians know, as did Boss Tweed, that "this God-business" may have little to do with politics.

However, both traditions in politics—the Judeo-Christian and the Graeco-Roman—when carried to their logical conclusion are imperiled by certain excesses. Put too simply, the one suffers from moralism, the other from cynicism. Religious men and women can be excessively moralistic in defending the righteousness of their cause but singularly ineffective in reaching positions of consensus in a sinful world. Perhaps this is why Harold Nicolson described religious people as the worst diplomats.[10] They cannot escape the illusion that morality is bound up in a single moral principle. Yet we know that our versions of good and evil are almost always colored by the taint of self-interest. Dean Acheson once complained, for instance, that for Nelson Rockefeller stealing was the only sin. Politics, on the other hand, struggles with an opposite vice: an excess of hubris in putting means before ends, procedures ahead of purpose, and success above virtue.

The signal accomplishment of the founders was in achieving balance and proportion in the relationship between religion and politics, between church and state. Because they recognized that each must have its place, they sought for each a position of independence. Neither was to rule the other, both were to serve in accustomed and well-understood constitutional spheres. How the ordering of that relationship and the accepted definitions of the constituent roles has been challenged, if not upset, in the 1970s and 1980s is the theme of the section that follows.

THE CHALLENGE

The challenge to the separation of church and state has come in the last quarter of the twentieth century. The causes are both immediate and long-term. The more immediate causes are social and political. The long-term reasons for the challenge stem from religious changes.

The Indonesian social philosopher Soedjatmoko, who is currently president of the United Nations University, directed attention to one of the deeper causes of change when he wrote of mankind's loss of an unquestioning faith in the afterlife. Soedjatmoko argued that this change has transformed people of faith into people in a hurry. The perspective from which they view social problems is radically altered. Their

10. Harold Nicolson, *Diplomacy* (1939; repr. ed., London: Oxford University Press, 1955), p. 50.

time frame has shifted and they pursue salvation here and now. Political goals have become infused with religious fervor. Utopianism has replaced survival. The motivating force of political movements on both the Right and the Left is social transformation in the reformer's image.

At one level, the struggle is being waged within religious bodies themselves. Denominations in which opposing trends have long coexisted find themselves locked in self-described holy wars. Fundamentalists and theological moderates face one another across a deep spiritual chasm, as in the Southern Baptist Convention. Religion writer Ed Briggs quotes Baptist moderates as saying that "fundamentalism is not so much a doctrinal position as it is a style of life that is negative, judgmental and suspicious of anyone who doesn't agree with the way they see things."[11] A seminary president denounces "unholy forces . . . at work in our midst" and "campus subversives" recruited and indoctrinated by the fundamentalists. Conservative leaders call for a reversal of the drift into biblical liberalism and predict a takeover of all the church's institutions in less than 10 years.[12] Church factions are at war.

As viewed by the public, the more visible manifestation of the change in church-state relations is in the political arena. Religion and politics appear to be merging in what one church historian— George Marsden, of Calvin College— calls "shallow folk religion." Thirty years ago, the United States was witnessing the greatest surge of churchgoing in its history. A record-level 49 percent of the population attended weekly church services. That level has dropped to 40 percent. Liberal Protestantism and the National Council of Churches were in the ascendancy, symbolized by President Dwight D. Eisenhower's laying the cornerstone of the council's building in New York City. Today fundamentalists and conservatives alone have access to the White House. *New York Times* columnist Kenneth A. Briggs describes the changing patterns of religion and politics as follows:

Armed with moral agendas, some conservative Christians who once felt excluded from the centers of political power are seeking to regain public backing for values they believe were wrongly stripped away by legislative and court action.

At the same time, liberal Protestants, many of whom enjoyed close ties with official Washington in the past, are pushing a set of such issues as disarmament and improved social services that they consider neglected.

Roman Catholics, meanwhile, have found a new, independent voice through their bishops that is measuring United States nuclear arms strategy, domestic social programs and foreign policy in a more sharply critical manner.

These developments stem from a common perception among Christian groups that the civil authorities no longer offer sufficient support for their beliefs and moral standards. Often their interests overlap as they separately seek to gain a stronger hearing in shaping public policy. The situation is urgent, they believe, because America is morally floundering and its values are up for grabs.[13]

Religion's influence on the political process

On the extent of the renewal of the public's commitment to religion, the

11. Ed Briggs, "Fundamentalist-Moderate Showdown Drawing Near," *Richmond Times-Dispatch,* 1 Sept. 1984.

12. Ibid.

13. Kenneth A. Briggs, "Political Activism Reflects Churches' Search for a Role in Secular Society," *New York Times,* 9 Sept. 1984. Reprinted by permission.

debate goes on. Most observers see it in terms of mixed signals at best. The religious reawakening has done little to narrow the gulf between religion and morality. "People can feel spiritual and still indulge their secular yearnings for wealth and power."[14]

On the reemergence of religion as a factor in politics, more consensus exists. Two decades ago, Harvard theologian Harvey Cox prophesied an irreversible tide of secularism in politics. Now, in his latest book, he discovers a religious revival. At the forefront of religious groups striving to seize a firmer foothold in public affairs are the fundamentalists, many of whom turn to the Reverend Jerry Falwell of the Moral Majority for guidance and direction. Briggs writes, "Fundamentalists and their somewhat more moderate evangelical brethren believe that moral degeneracy and court decisions, especially those against school prayer and Bible reading and in support of abortion, have undercut America's divinely sanctioned mission."[15]

To turn back moral degeneracy, the Reverend Falwell claims to have registered 8.5 million new voters since 1978. In 1984, the focus of the group's efforts was the reelection of President Ronald Reagan—called an "instrument of God"—and Senator Jesse Helms of North Carolina, whom Falwell once described as "a national treasure." In an interview following the election, he revealed that the Moral Majority employed a full-time coordinator for North Carolina for a year before the election. He added, "We worked on a daily basis with 2,400 pastors and churches in that state."[16]

The Moral Majority also campaigned for senatorial and congressional candidates who opposed abortion and favored a strong national defense. In preparing for the 1988 presidential election, it plans to register a million new voters each year.

If the Moral Majority represents a more or less direct form of religious intervention into the political process, the leader of conservatism within the Roman Catholic hierarchy in the United States, Archbishop John J. O'Connor of New York, recently named a cardinal by the Vatican, stands for a more ambiguous interventionism. He spearheaded the church's more subtle initiative during the 1984 presidential election centering on a litmus test for candidates on the abortion issue.

O'Connor, who was the major dissenter to the bishops' pastoral letter "The Challenge to Peace," joined conservatives Archbishop Bernard Law of Boston and Cardinal John Krol of Philadelphia in seeking to make abortion the paramount issue of the campaign. According to United Press International columnist David E. Anderson, "O'Connor publicly questioned whether Catholic officeholders such as Democratic vice-presidential nominee Geraldine Ferraro and New York Governor Mario Cuomo could remain good Catholics without actively joining the bishops' anti-abortion campaign."[17] By indirection, he questioned their acceptability as candidates. Governor Cuomo, himself a Catholic, responded that "the church has never been this aggressively involved in politics," adding, "You have the Archbishop of New York saying that no Catholic can vote for Ed Koch, no Catholic can vote for Jay Goldin, for Carol Bellamy, nor

14. Ibid.

15. Ibid.

16. *Daily Progress* (Charlottesville, VA), 11 Nov. 1984.

17. Ibid., 10 Nov. 1984.

for Pat Moynihan or Mario Cuomo."[18] Representative Ferraro, who had earlier stirred controversy by expressing skepticism about the Christianity of President Reagan's social policies, answered the archbishop through an aide, "I am amazed at how times have changed. Twenty years ago people were afraid that John Kennedy would impose his religious beliefs on his decisions in government. Now some people are afraid that I won't."[19] Archbishop O'Connor replied that Mr. Cuomo had misinterpreted his views, but approximately 55 Roman Catholic theologians, some belonging to Catholics for Free Choice, cautioned bishops against trying to penalize priests or politicians who disagreed with them. Besides, Catholics, whether in theory or practice, were not of one mind on abortion.

Whatever the judgment of historians may be on the intentions of bishops or politicians, it seems clear even in the minds of its own members that the Catholic Church in the 1984 elections was walking a fine line that threatened the separation of church and state. Daniel Callahan, head of the Hastings Institute of Society, Ethics, and Life Science and a former editor of the liberal Catholic journal *Commonweal* has commented,

The tradition [of the church] has been to speak to broad themes and let individuals reach their own judgments about how to apply church teachings to specific elections. But as the church gets more and more specific about the policies it supports and [as] it asserts that Catholics should consider its moral guidance as they decide how to vote, the people can pretty much deduce whom they should be voting for.[20]

Some fear a backlash against the integrity of religion if partisanship continues. Others would have the church resist the temptation to remain silent, a criticism of some of the German clergy in the time of Nazism. Seeking to put the controversy to rest, Bishop James W. Malone of Youngstown, Ohio, president of the United States Catholic Conference, proclaimed in a clarifying statement for the Catholic bishops that clergy should speak out on public policy issues but not "take positions for or against political candidates." The bishop's statement of 9 August brought Catholic thinking back into line with the tradition of separation of church and state. It also brought the church back to positions it had taken in the 1960s.

A month later, on 5 September, the issue was raised again by a group of Protestant, Roman Catholic, and Jewish leaders. Here the issue was President Reagan, who, speaking to fundamentalists at a prayer breakfast in Dallas, declared there was an inseparable link between religion and morality. Those who disagreed, he explained, were "intolerant of religion."

In response to Reagan, the Reverend Dr. James M. Dunn, executive director of the Baptist Joint Committee on Public Affairs, warned, "We are seeing in this political campaign a deliberate attempt to collapse the distinction between mixing politics and religion."[21] The group called on the leaders of both parties to reject the "notion that only one brand of politics or religion meets with God's approval and the others are necessarily evil."[22] Rabbi Mordecai Waxman, head of an umbrella group for Reform, Conservative, and Orthodox

18. *New York Times,* 6 Aug. 1984.
19. *Washington Post,* 14 Aug. 1984.
20. Ibid.

21. "Interfaith Group Sees Church-State Peril," *Richmond Times-Dispatch,* 6 Sept. 1984.
22. Ibid.

movements in Judaism, declared that "the question of whether Americans are a religious people is not an issue; of course we are. But we are not one religion but many religions."[23] Howard I. Freedman, president of the American Jewish Committee, further warned that "the state has a duty not to intrude itself in religious terms."[24] The statement of the multireligious group added, "The state should not behave as if it were a church or a synagogue. The state should not do for citizens what, in their rightful free exercise of religion, they are perfectly capable of doing for themselves."[25] The First Amendment of the Constitution, after all, protects the freedom of religious conscience.

Reagan's challenge

In these latter-day criticisms, it is the state, not the Roman Catholic Church or the Moral Majority, that is viewed as the source of the challenge to historic church-state relations. The object of criticism has shifted to President Reagan's efforts to legislate various moral positions of particular religious groups, including tuition tax credits, school prayer, the outlawing of abortion, and the establishment of formal diplomatic relations between the United States and the Vatican. Columnist James R. Dickenson, in appraising the main themes of the 1984 Republican National Convention, wrote, "Religion was as powerful an issue in the Republican National Convention . . . as the traditional secular themes of tax cuts and a strong national defense." Dickenson explained, "The Republican platform all but made religion a Republican virtue. The Demo-

crats, it says, 'tried to build their brave new world by assaulting our basic values. . . . They attacked the integrity of the family and parental rights. They ignored traditional morality. And they still do.'"[26]

Thus Ronald Reagan stands at the center of the debate about the challenge to church-state relations. The controversy over religion and politics swirls around the person and practice of President Reagan. It may be no exaggeration to say that other controversies might have disappeared if the president were less central to the debate. For one thing, his own religion came to occupy the attention of columnists and the media. What is the average newspaper reader to make of reports that President Reagan seldom goes to church? Is he a deeply religious president who is prevented from going to church by security considerations? Or does habit play a part, as the Reverend Billy Graham, a friend of presidents since Dwight D. Eisenhower, explained when he said, "He has been hindered by the security situation and the fact he didn't always attend church regularly."[27] The Reverend Graham has acknowledged that he probably gave the president bad advice in 1981 when he was recuperating from an assassin's attempt on his life. As Graham remembers it, he told Reagan that "worship of God is disrupted if it becomes a media event." It might have been better, Graham now says, to suggest that the president hold church services in the White House. He is forgiving of the president and says he is sure that he misses not going to church.

Less forgiving are those who accuse Reagan for failing to practice what he

<hr>

23. Ibid.
24. Ibid.
25. Ibid.

26. *Washington Post*, 24 Aug. 1984.
27. Lou Cannon, "Reagan & Company," *Washington Post*, 16 Apr. 1984.

preaches. Reagan's long-time observer and friend Lou Cannon explains, "He extols religious and family values while rarely going to church or seeing his grandchildren."[28] Increasingly his piety seemed directed more at political ends than at radiating an inner faith. However, his former minister, Donn Moomaw, declares, "His faith is very pious and very personal."[29] When Graham called on Reagan in Sacramento, the then-governor asked Graham if he thought the Second Coming was imminent. How could anyone pose such a question, Graham asked, if he had any doubts about God or his own faith?

Nonetheless, it is difficult not to take notice of a shift in Reagan's public use of religion as a political weapon. Lou Cannon writes:

Most biographers, including this one [Cannon], have played down the importance of religion in Reagan's life. This may reflect our lack of understanding. But another reason is that Reagan, before yielding to temptations of the political season, treated religion as a private matter. His campaign vow that he would not "wear religion on my sleeve" reflected his basic attitude.[30]

To point the finger at the shift in the president's attitude, Cannon argues, does not deny that Reagan is religious. Reagan's intimates say that he prays before making decisions and that he offers spiritual consolation to those who have lost loved ones. He appears to be a compassionate and caring person, particularly in traditional areas. The Reverend Graham supports this version, recalling that "by your fruits shall you know them, not by their church attendance. In

his life, we have seen that he bears these fruits."[31]

The change that is being questioned, however, involves not Reagan's church attendance but his mixing of religion and politics. Cannon found that Reagan, in campaigning for reelection, violated an unstated understanding he had with the electorate. Throughout most of his political career he had "conveyed the impression of being a religious man who understood the difference between government and religion. He seemed to recognize he was President of Jews, Roman Catholics, Protestants, secularists, and unbelievers. Now he presumed to speak as an adviser on faith and morals."[32] He joined with fundamentalists and the right wing of his party in pressing the cause of school prayer. He championed the views of Catholics on abortion and on granting diplomatic recognition to the Vatican. He spoke to a Jewish leader about the coming of Armageddon, linking it with the Soviet-American conflict. He intensified the use of religion in an election year. Such actions cause consternation among those who do not share his religious views while they trivialize religious truths for those who do. In short, Reagan's admixture of piety and politics disturbs any number of religious groups, and irreligious groups as well.

Looking back on the president's most recent use of religion in politics, Mr. Cannon concludes,

When Reagan cites public opinion polls as a basis for a school prayer amendment and portrays his opponents as less religious than he, he gives the impression that he puts reelection ahead of his faith. What it suggests is not hypocrisy but opportunism. It is a ques-

28. Ibid.
29. Ibid.
30. Ibid.

31. Ibid.
32. Ibid.

tion more bothersome and of greater consequence than any computation of his church attendance.[33]

Historically, most churches and politicians have exercised a measure of self-restraint in the moral and religious claims they make for their policies. The need to build electoral coalitions among peoples and groups who do not share a leader's religious beliefs contributes to that restraint. When Senator Paul Laxalt sent his "Dear Christian Leader" letter to 45,000 fundamentalist ministers in 16 states, challenging them "to organize a voter registration drive in your church," his critics say he abandoned self-restraint.[34] As a rule, the churches have not endorsed a particular party or candidate, even when rallying public support for such issues as abolition of slavery, civil rights, or ending the war in Vietnam. The black churches are an exception because the church has been the one social institution available to blacks for promoting political concerns.

The challenge by President Reagan and his political associates in 1984 led Walter Mondale to accuse the president of "moral McCarthyism." In saying that "most Americans would be surprised to learn that God is a Republican," Mondale himself did a certain amount of mixing of religion and politics. In an address on 6 September to B'nai B'rith, he spoke, albeit uneasily, as the son of a Methodist minister, confessing, "What I am doing here today is something that, in 25 years of public life, I never thought I would do. I have never before had to defend my faith in a political campaign." But he did defend his faith and his stands on racism and anti-Semitism and concluded, "A determined band is raising doubts about people's faith. They

are reaching for government power to impose their own beliefs on other people. And the Reagan administration has opened its arms to them."[35]

A POSSIBLE RESOLUTION

Invoking religion in 1984 was good politics, and it is unlikely that politicians will forget the lesson of that success. It would be heartening if the result were a profound and socially relevant religious reawakening, but the data do not support so profound an event. Therefore, we must seek the more long-term lessons elsewhere. One lesson may be the truth that religion often serves selfish as well as exalted purposes. What Jefferson and Lincoln said about religion has echoed through the ages. Lincoln spoke often of religion and social problems, but one of his most memorable passages dealt with religion and slavery:

Certainly there is no contending against the Will of God; but still there is some difficulty in ascertaining and applying it, to particular cases. For instance we will suppose the Rev. Dr. Ross has a slave named Sambo, and the question is "Is it the Will of God that Sambo shall remain a slave, or be set free?" The Almighty gives no audible answer to the question, and his revelation—the Bible—gives none—or, at most, none but such as admits of a squabble, as to its meaning. No one thinks of asking Sambo's opinion on it. So, at last, it comes to this, that Dr. Ross is to decide the question. And while he consider[s] it, he sits in the shade, with gloves on his hands, and subsists on the bread that Sambo is earning in the burning sun. If he decides that God wills Sambo to continue a slave, he thereby retains his own comfortable position; but if he decides that God wills Sambo to be free, he thereby has to walk out of the shade, throw off his gloves, and delve for his

33. Ibid.
34. *Washington Post,* 3 Sept. 1984.

35. *Daily Progress* (Charlottesville, VA), 6 Sept. 1984.

own bread. Will Dr. Ross be activated by that perfect impartiality, which has ever been considered most favorable to correct decisions? But slavery is good for some people!!! As a good thing, slavery is strikingly peculiar in this, that it is the only good thing which no man ever seeks the good of, for *himself*.

Nonsense! wolves [devour] lambs not because it is good for their own greedy maws, but because it [is] good for the lambs!!![36]

Whatever Lincoln's skepticism that men were able to know the will of God, he could not believe that God willed either slavery or the destruction of the Union. American slavery, he felt, was "one of those offences which in the providence of God . . . He now wills to remove." Yet Lincoln also believed that God's will as to the time and place of the ending of slavery was unknown and unknowable. God's purpose might be different from the purposes of either party. If God willed that the war continue "until every drop of blood drawn with the lash, shall be paid by another drawn with the sword . . . the judgments of the Lord are true and righteous altogether." God knows best. With a fatalism about God's purposes that matched his skepticism about knowing God's mind, Lincoln, as the Civil War continued, told the Baltimore Presbyterian Synod that he reposed "reliance in God, knowing . . . that He would decide for the right."[37] Somewhere in the universe there was a script, and while Lincoln never claimed to know its content, he firmly believed it existed.

Religion towers above narrow and selfish human purposes. It speaks for a spiritual order that stands outside and beyond politics. Reinhold Niebuhr wrote during the presidential election of 1952,

Nothing that is worth doing can be achieved in our lifetime. Therefore, we must be saved by hope. Nothing which is true or beautiful or good makes complete sense in any immediate context of history. Therefore, we must be saved by faith. Nothing we do, however virtuous, can be accomplished alone. Therefore we are saved by love. No virtuous act is quite as virtuous from the standpoint of our friend or foe as it is from our own standpoint. Therefore, we must be saved by the final form of love, which is forgiveness."[38]

If those who relate religion to politics could capture some of the serenity in Niebuhr's words, they might help restore the balance between church and state.

Another lesson to be drawn is that any too-simple version of the relation between religion and politics can prompt in reaction more thoughtful and considered judgments. One such response was that of Cardinal Joseph L. Bernardin. On 26 October 1984, in an address at Georgetown University, he warned that there was no place for single-issue politics in the church's quest for a consistent moral vision. He reasoned that "the civil law must be rooted in the moral law, but it may not at times incorporate the full range of moral law." The "question is not whether the deepest personal convictions of politicians should influence their public choices, but how the two should be related." He added that "the development of public policy requires a wider consensus than the personal conviction of any individual—even a public figure." Without condemning fellow bishops, the Chicago prelate explained that the present world situation "resists a 'one-issue' focus by the church, even

---

36. Quoted in Hans J. Morgenthau and David Hein, *Essays on Lincoln's Faith and Politics* (Lanham, MD: University Press of America, 1983), p. 9.

37. Ibid.

38. Niebuhr, *Justice and Mercy*.

when the urgent issue is abortion or nuclear arms."[39]

Another reconsideration of the challenge to church-state relations came from the political side of the spectrum, from Governor Cuomo, speaking on 14 September 1984 at the University of Notre Dame. He found some of the challenges to traditional thought about church and state simplistic, most of them fragmentary, and "a few spoken with purely political intent, demagogic." He relayed a lesson in practical politics, saying, in language reminiscent of Reinhold Niebuhr and Walter Lippmann, "There is no church teaching that mandates the best political course for making our belief everyone's rule, for spreading this part of our Catholicism. There is neither an encyclical nor a catechism that spells out a political strategy for achieving legislative goals." Cuomo reminded church politicians that "most of us are offended when we see religion being trivialized by its appearance in political throwaway pamphlets. The American people need no course in philosophy of political science or church history to know that God should not be made into a celestial party chairman."[40]

Finally, those who seek the proper role for religion in politics must learn to discriminate between shallow propaganda and carefully thought-out positions. The pastoral letter on war and peace of the National Conference of Catholic Bishops

is a stunning achievement. It represents the labor of hundreds of able leaders grappling for more than two years under collective discipline "to develop and perfect" a theology of peace suited to a civilization poised on the brink of self-destruction. The letter was revised through a succession of drafts. Consultations were held with past and present government officials. The Vatican sponsored several international ecclesiastical sessions especially for European leaders. Looking back on the process and product, Ambassador George Kennan, a non-Catholic, could say, "This paper . . . may fairly be described as the most profound and searching inquiry yet conducted by any responsible collective body into the relations of nuclear weaponry, and indeed of modern war in general, to moral philosophy, to politics and to the conscience of the national state."[41] As a Protestant, I wish the denominations I know had made a comparable effort. To compare such an effort with off-the-cuff statements by politically ambitious, sometimes church-related politicians is little short of blasphemy.

If the present conflict over church-state relations is to be resolved, a return to the American tradition of constitutionalism and an even more respected 2000-year tradition of studying morality and politics is needed. Church-state relations are too important to leave to the politicians, whether they presume to speak for church or state.

39. "Cardinal Bernardin Urges Rejection of Single-Issue Politics," *Washington Post,* 26 Oct. 1984.

40. Quoted in the *New York Times,* 15 Sept. 1984.

41. George F. Kennan, "The Bishop's Letter," *New York Times,* 1 May 1983.

Revolution, Counterrevolution, and the Catholic Church in Chile

By PAUL E. SIGMUND

ABSTRACT: This article traces the moral and political role of the Catholic Church in Chile from the colonial period, through the nineteenth and early twentieth centuries, to the upheavals of the last 25 years. During the last period, conservative, reformist, revolutionary, and counterrevolutionary governments succeeded one another in power, and each sought legitimation—or at least cooperation—from the church. A pattern of increasing pluralism is traced from a nearly complete identification with the Conservative Party until the 1930s; to a choice, from the 1930s to the 1970s, between Conservatives and Christian Democrats in a state in which church and state were separated; to the movement to the left by some Catholics in the Allende period, 1970-73; to the effort by the Pinochet government after 1973 to use religion to support authoritarian government. It is argued that under the same leadership—especially that of Cardinal Raúl Silva—the church has successfully maintained its defense of moral values while avoiding too close an identification with existing regimes. In the Pinochet case, the church also emerged as an active defender of human rights and the poor and provided a political space for critics of the military government.

Paul E. Sigmund is professor of politics and director of the Latin American Studies Program at Princeton University. He has taught in Chile and written or edited 13 books and 100 articles on political theory and Latin American politics. Those most relevant to this article include The Overthrow of Allende and the Politics of Chile, 1964-1976 *(1977);* Natural Law in Political Thought *(1971); and* St. Thomas Aquinas: On Ethics and Politics *(1985). His next book will be on liberation theology in Latin America.*

MOST Americans believe that church and state should be separated. The grounds for this belief are not only the First Amendment to the Constitution, but also a recognition that the United States is a religiously pluralistic country. Any attempt to give a privileged position to any one church—or, according to more recent Supreme Court rulings, to religion in general over nonreligion—prefers one group of the citizenry over another and thus denies the equal protection of the laws. But what about countries in which the overwhelming majority of the citizens profess a single religious faith? Here, Americans would reply that religious leaders do not possess any special insight into what is politically useful or appropriate and that too close a link between a religious group and those who hold power both gives special privilege to a group that does not have democratic legitimacy and corrupts its religious character through exploitation for partisan advantage.

Yet, at the same time, most Americans accept that religious leaders have a role in speaking out in a pluralistic society on behalf of what they see to be fundamental moral values. While religious leaders may not be experts on politics, many citizens give special attention to their views on moral questions, because these leaders have special training in this area and because they are interpreters of one or another of the great religious traditions. Most political issues are moral issues. Does this not restore to the religious leader a political power that can be dangerous and corrupting?

The question of the proper role and limits of the religious leadership in the political process is a continual problem; finding the appropriate balance between moral leadership and political interference is a task for each society and religious group. Chile provides a particularly interesting example of this problem. It is a society that, at least nominally, is predominantly Catholic. The Catholic Church has had a special position both socially and politically throughout most of its history. For most of this century, church and state have been separated, but the struggles that have convulsed Chile have often caused the church to feel it must speak out.

How to avoid direct political involvement and yet maintain a moral influence has been a continuing challenge faced by the Chilean church. This article attempts to trace how it has faced the challenge and argues that, on the whole, the delicate balance we have mentioned has been maintained, despite the deep political divisions and violent governmental oscillations of the last 25 years.

LINKS BETWEEN CHURCH AND STATE

A direct link between church and state was built into the institutional structure in the Spanish colonial period. The Spanish monarch had the right of *patronato,* of suggesting or at least reviewing the names of those the Vatican selected to be bishops and of controlling the publication of Vatican communications within his realm. In addition, "the union of throne and altar" meant that the clergy were paid by the state and that the church had a central role in marriage, education, and burial. Following Chile's independence from Spain, all of these relationships were the subject of political controversy, as they were elsewhere in Latin America. The question of the relation between the church and the state became one of the issues dividing the Conservative Party and the Liberal Party—as did the issues of centralized versus federal government and of Hispanic versus French-oriented cultural models.

When, after a period of post-independence instability, Diego Portales established a centralized, authoritarian presidential system in the constitution of 1833, he also ensured the dominance of Conservative—in contemporary terms, *pelucón*, or "bigwig"—views on the role of the church. In 1861, what Chilean historians call the Aristocratic Republic gave way to the Liberal Republic period. At that time, the church's privileges were challenged by a coalition of the Liberals and the newly formed Radical Party that opposed the church's judicial independence, its monopoly over cemeteries and marriages, and its close ties to the state. Compromises were eventually reached on these issues, but a lasting alliance had been forged between the Catholic Church and its political defender, the Conservative Party, and a tradition of anticlericalism had been fostered among the Radicals that has only recently declined. The church's formal links with the state—and its less formal but still important tie with the Conservatives—remained until a separation of church and state was negotiated and carried out at the time of the adoption of the 1925 constitution.

In the twentieth century, tension arose within the Conservative Party due to the fact that although actual control of the party was in the hands of landowners and old families, it officially endorsed the social doctrine of the church as expressed in the labor encyclicals of Leo XIII, in 1891, and Pius XI, in 1931. This tension finally led to the departure from the party of a group of Conservative youth leaders who in 1938 formed the Falange—the ancestor of the present Christian Democratic Party. Despite its name, the Falange took socially advanced positions that favored cooperation with the Left on social legislation and, from the 1940s, that were critical of the Franco government. The Falange did not become a major party until 1957, when another breakaway group of the Conservatives—led by one of those who had expelled the Falangists twenty years earlier—joined with the Falange to form the Christian Democratic Party. From that time, the Conservatives could no longer claim the exclusive allegiance of devout Catholics, and, indeed, the Christian Democrats could argue that they better represented the social teaching of the church.

It is often assumed that in a Catholic country religious justifications are a major source of government legitimacy and party support. Indicators of religious belief and practice in Chile seem to indicate that this is not so—at least not to the degree one might expect. Various surveys carried out in Chile since 1940 indicate that only 12-15 percent of the Chilean population are regular churchgoers, and that figure conceals sharp differences between men and women, and between the upper classes—20-25 percent of whom attend regularly—and the working classes—4-8 percent of whom do.[1] It is true that surveys have shown that larger percentages consider themselves somewhat religious, but when 40 percent or more of the population has voted consistently for parties that are traditionally anticlerical—the Radicals,

1. Brian H. Smith, *The Church and Politics in Chile* (Princeton, NJ: Princeton University Press, 1982), p. 51; Kenneth P. Langton and Ronald Rapoport, "Religion and Leftist Mobilization in Chile," *Comparative Political Studies,* 9:277-308 (Oct. 1976).

the Socialists, and the Communists—it is clear that the church is not an overwhelmingly important source of legitimation. In addition, by the 1950s there was a division among practicing Catholics or those influenced by the church between those who viewed the Conservative Party as closer to traditional church teachings about hierarchy, authority, and state support for religion, and those—especially young people and intellectuals—who saw the Christian Democratic Party's emphasis on pluralism, religious freedom, communitarian approaches to social problems, and the promotion of the rights of workers and peasants as more in keeping with the Christian message. In addition, attempts had been made for many years to promote the organization of Christian trade unions as another application of church teachings, partly as a result of earlier Vatican concern that the Marxist Left would control the labor movement. Although Christian trade unions did not dominate labor, which was largely controlled by the Communists and Socialists, they formed a significant minority within it.

By the 1960s, when Chile was convulsed by rising demands for social and economic reform, the church had inspired, or at least influenced, two and perhaps three—if some of the more extreme leftist trade union leaders are included—sets of responses to the Latin American crisis. The Conservatives called for a paternalistic concern for the peasantry, association of workers and management in joint corporatist-style groupings, and the promotion of moral values. In fact, however, the Conservatives had become so close to their nineteenth-century Liberal opponents that they were able to join with them to form the National Party in 1966.

The Christian Democrats began to move to the left. They picked up agrarian reform as a central issue, called for partial nationalization—what they termed Chileanization—of the American-owned copper industry, and promoted the creation of groups of so-called marginalized slum dwellers, neighborhood committees, and mothers' centers that would give organizational expression to what they vaguely defined as communitarianism.

Many of these ideas and programs were developed at institutions sponsored by the church. A particularly influential research center was created by a Belgian Jesuit, Roger Vekemans, who was sent to Chile by his order to help to develop alternatives to the Marxist proposals for "revolutionary" change in Chile. The program inspired by Vekemans for a "revolution in liberty" brought Eduardo Frei, the Christian Democratic candidate, to a victory by an absolute majority—relatively rare in Chile—in the 1964 presidential elections.

The 1964 elections were watched by the whole world since they pitted Frei against Salvador Allende, the Marxist candidate, who had come very close to winning the elections six years earlier, in 1958. Frei's landslide victory seemed to promise the enactment of Catholic-influenced reforms that were "the last best hope" for reformist democracy in Latin America—or so one writer, Leonard Gross, believed.[2] However, the very fact that Frei's party was Catholic in

---

2. Leonard Gross, *The Last Best Hope: Eduardo Frei and Chilean Democracy* (New York: Random House, 1967). On this period, see Paul E. Sigmund, *The Overthrow of Allende and the Politics of Chile (1964-1976)* (Pittsburgh, PA: University of Pittsburgh Press, 1977), chaps. 3-5; George Grayson, "Chile's Christian Democratic Party: Power, Factions, and Ideology," *Review of Politics,* 31:147-71 (1969); and Michael Fleet, *The*

inspiration, although not in a formal institutional way, made it suspect to the Radicals and impeded the realization of his proposals for reform. While both Chileanization and agrarian reform were ultimately adopted, they were long delayed by the opposition-controlled Senate, and a process of polarization began to take place. The bulk of the Radicals moved closer to the Socialists and Communists, ultimately producing the Popular Unity coalition that elected Allende in 1970, while a minority of the Radicals moved closer to the National Party, which had become increasingly opposed to the Frei government as the agrarian reform was implemented. The religious inspiration of the Christian Democratic program was thus a two-edged sword. On the one hand, it was a source of innovative programs needed to meet the demand for reform, but on the other, it alienated an important sector of the middle classes that supported the Radical Party. That split was to have fateful consequences for the future of the country.

The official church—that is, the Bishops Conference—was not formally involved in this process. In fact, however, through appointments of progressive bishops like Raúl Silva Henríquez, who was named archbishop of Santiago in 1958, through statements by the bishops on the need for social reform, and through innovative experiments with the redistribution of church lands,[3] the Bishops Conference played a role in encouraging social reform. Its educational institutions, both formal and informal, also prepared those who would take the lead in social change.

However, there was disagreement concerning the pace and modalities of these experiments, and the church began to experience internal tensions that reflected the polarization that was occurring in the country as a whole. The Second Vatican Council, in the mid-1960s, had made cooperation with those of differing philosophical and religious beliefs permissible; and the 1968 meeting of all the bishops of Latin America in Medellín, Colombia, had been highly critical of the system of so-called institutionalized violence that was dominant, in the bishops' view, in Latin America. The Jesuit magazine *Mensaje*, widely read as much for its political and economic articles as for those of a religious character, seemed to take a more radically leftist position during the late 1960s. At the same time, an internal division within the Christian Democratic Party finally led to the departure, in early 1969, of several of its leaders. They formed the Movimiento de Acción Popular (MAPU) Party, which subsequently became a member of the Allende coalition. On the right, the Chilean Society for Tradition, Family, and Property began to attack liberal tendencies within the church, and at the Catholic University, the *gremialista* movement opposed the attempts of Catholic leftists to enlist the university in the service of the so-called revolution.

Now there were three political groups, conservative, reformist, and what was described as revolutionary, and each believed it was best in applying the principles of Christianity to Chilean politics. The revolutionaries argued, for example, that the Frei revolution in liberty had stalled and that more radical measures were required, measures that could

Rise and Fall of Chilean Christian Democracy (Princeton, NJ: Princeton University Press, 1985), chaps. 2-3.

3. See William C. Thiesenhusen, *Chile's Experiments in Agrarian Reform* (Madison: University of Wisconsin Press, 1966).

only be achieved by an alliance of Christians with the Marxist and anticlerical parties. Having successfully weathered the transition from a traditionalist, hierarchical, and paternalist church closely tied to the state, to a democratic, socially oriented reformism, could the church survive a further opening to the Left?[4]

A MARXIST GOVERNMENT

The test came with the election of an avowed Marxist, Salvador Allende, to the presidency of Chile on 4 September 1970. Polling data indicate that in the three-way race between Allende on the left, Radomiro Tomic for the Christian Democrats, and Jorge Alessandri on the right, Catholics were as divided as the country as a whole when it gave Allende 36.2 percent of the vote to Alessandri's 34.9 percent and Tomic's 27.9 percent. However, when these results are disaggregated by religious practice, respondents who described themselves as "regularly practicing" Catholics seem to have been more likely to vote for Alessandri, the conservative candidate of the National Party.[5] In the 1964 election, the bishops had expressed themselves clearly on the dangers of Marxism, but in 1970, they insisted that the church did not favor one political candidate and that Catholics could support any of the candidates. When, despite U.S. covert efforts to prevent it, Allende won the congressional runoff against Alessandri

in late October, a delegation of bishops led by Cardinal Raúl Silva went to his home to congratulate him, and after his swearing-in on 3 November, the traditional Te Deum, now organized ecumenically, was held in the cathedral.

Both the church and the Allende government sought to avoid church-state confrontation. The Allende government, although it was Marxist dominated, included several former Christian Democrats. Initially there was little tension between the two institutions; Cardinal Silva seems to have developed a friendly personal relationship with Allende.

Within the church, however, problems developed when a group of 80 priests organized a movement to support the Allende reforms. The group, which finally took the name of "Christians for Socialism," quoted a statement Cardinal Silva made shortly after Allende took office to the effect that socialism, in its goals, is closer to Christianity than is capitalism. Yet, this movement wished to go much further and formally identify Chilean socialism as the only option for Christians.

The arguments of Christians for Socialism and the genuine concern of Chilean Catholics as to the position that they should take toward a Marxist-dominated government led to the publication of an important document by the bishops entitled "The Gospel, Politics, and Socialisms" ("Evangelio, politica, y socialismos"). This was issued in May 1971, a month after the first public meeting of the 80 priests calling for ecclesiastical support of the Allende reforms. The bishops' letter argued that although the church could not endorse a specific political point of view, support for socialism was not incompatible with Christian beliefs and, indeed, might be seen as a direct application of its princi-

4. Paul E. Sigmund, "Latin American Catholicism's Opening to the Left," *Review of Politics,* 35:61-76 (Jan. 1973). For a biased, but useful—because based on original documentation—description of the divisions in the Chilean church, see David Mutchler, *The Church as a Political Factor in Latin America* (New York: Praeger, 1971).

5. Smith, *Church and Politics in Chile,* pp. 129-37.

ples. However, it warned that the Marxist variety of socialism was based on atheism, doctrines of class hatred, and a materialistic view of history—elements not compatible with Christian teaching. Christians were not prohibited from working with those who endorsed such views on specific political programs, but they could not embrace such doctrines themselves. The bishops were, therefore, both allowing for leftist Catholics—now organized as a result of a new split from the Christian Democrats into the Christian Left Party, or Izquierda Cristiana—to cooperate with Marxists and secularists such as the Radicals, and reiterating their earlier warning about Marxist philosophy. That their warnings were justified was demonstrated by the rapid leftward movement of the MAPU Party, as well as of much of the Radical Party, during the Allende period. In both cases, party documents now began to reflect an uncritical Marxist ideology, with particular emphasis on the class struggle and the inevitability of violence.[6]

The bishops took a stronger position after an international meeting of Christians for Socialism was held in Santiago, in April 1972. In May, the Conference of Latin American Bishops' Department of Social Action criticized the meeting as the political exploitation of the church by Marxists seeking to promote the revolution within the church. The Chilean hierarchy delayed taking action against the group, but finally decided to do so in April 1973, and subsequently prepared a statement on the subject that was not approved until 13 September, two days after Augusto Pinochet's coup.

The bishops criticized the Christians for Socialism movement on two grounds: the equation of a partisan political position with Christianity, and the direct participation of the clergy in politics. They also formally prohibited the clergy from participating in that or any other political movement.[7]

Apart from the formal statements of the hierarchy, lively polemics over the relation of Catholicism to Marxist movements were carried on in Chilean newspapers and magazines, but the only public disagreement between the church and the Allende government took place over the sensitive issue of education. Ever since the 1950s, private—mostly Catholic—schools had received substantial state aid, and by 1970, the Catholic University was receiving about half of its operating funds from the government. However, no attempt was made to use the financial link to influence the content of teaching until the tense political period immediately following the March 1973 congressional elections. At that time, the Allende government published plans for the establishment of a Unified National School system that would include instruction in "socialist humanism." The opposition seized on the plan as proof of the Marxist, totalitarian intentions of the Allende government, and demonstrations—some of them violent—were held against it. Cardinal Silva diplomatically argued that the proposal needed further study. Allende withdrew the plan, but not before a stormy meeting of 150 military men had discussed it with the minister of education—and the military defenders of the government had found themselves

6. For the relevant documents, see Carlos Oviedo, ed., *Documents del episcopado: Chile, 1970-1973* (Santiago: Ediciones Mundo, 1974), pp. 55-100; and Smith, *Church and Politics in Chile,* chap. 8.

7. See Oviedo, *Documentos,* pp. 178-212; and John Eagleson, ed., *Christians and Socialism: Documentation of the Christians for Socialism Movement in Latin America* (Maryknoll, NY: Orbis Books, 1975).

overwhelmingly outnumbered at a subsequent meeting of generals.[8]

Although the hierarchy, and especially Cardinal Silva, attempted to keep the church out of the controversy, arguments in favor of a natural-law right of revolution began to appear in right-wing Catholic journals, and a prominent clergyman from the Catholic University television station emerged as a leading critic of the government. In July, the bishops declared a national day of prayer for reconciliation among Chileans on the feast of the patroness of Chile, Our Lady of Mount Carmel, but the polarization and rising violence in the country seemed to be leading up to civil war. In August, Cardinal Silva arranged two meetings in his residence between the government and the opposition Christian Democrats, but neither meeting produced any results. On 11 September 1973, a violent military coup, which included the bombing of the presidential palace and the death of Allende, ended democracy in Chile.

PINOCHET AND THE CHURCH

Two days after the coup, the cardinal and the Permanent Committee of the Bishops issued a public statement deploring "the blood which has reddened our streets," calling for respect for those who had fallen—"first of all for the one who was until Tuesday, September 11, the President of the Republic"—and asking for "moderation towards the vanquished" and a "prompt return to institutional normality."[9] There was, of course, no such return, but rather massive repression of the Left; the Congress

was shut down; the universities, including the two belonging to the Church, were put under military control; political parties of the Left were banned and the other parties were declared "in recess"; and censorship of the media and a strictly enforced curfew were imposed.

The reaction of the bishops was mixed, with the more conservative prelates issuing statements in support of Chile's deliverance from Marxism and the others, including Cardinal Silva, being more guarded in their words and actions. The cardinal replaced the traditional Te Deum in the cathedral on 18 September, the national holiday, with a service of reconciliation. When reports began to come in of kidnappings, murder, and torture of the opposition, he set up an interdenominational Committee for Peace "to aid all families and persons affected by the current situation." Besides giving material assistance to the families of political prisoners, the committee kept track of instances of torture and murder reported by individuals and pastors. The churches also established a committee to aid refugees that worked with the United Nations to relocate the thousands of foreigners and leftist activists that were fleeing the country or taking refuge in foreign embassies.

The church was in a special position after the coup; since the Pinochet-led junta argued that it had acted to defend what it called Western Christian values against the threat of Marxism, the regime could hardly persecute the representative of those values, the church, in the same way that it had those in the universities and the media. The cardinal and the bishops pledged to work with the new government "since the church is not called upon to make or overthrow governments, to recognize or not to rec-

8. For details, see Sigmund, *Overthrow of Allende*, pp. 202-12.

9. Oviedo, *Documentos*, p. 174.

ognize them."[10] They also provided a sanctuary for those who were persecuted by the regime and used the church's international assistance networks to establish legal aid and employment programs and to open up soup kitchens in the lower-class settlements. These settlements were most adversely affected by both the political repression and the searing unemployment that resulted from the adoption of an economic shock treatment to end Chile's chronic inflation and to reorient its economy along laissez faire lines.

In March 1974, the junta published a Declaration of Principles, most of which had been written by a right-wing, Catholic former student leader, Jaime Guzmán. It drew on Catholic political thought both to justify the coup and to argue that the regime's attempts to privatize and decentralize the economy were applications of papal social principles, particularly the principle of subsidiarity enunciated by Pope Pius XI in 1931. However, the official statements of the Bishops Conference did not endorse these theories, and, beginning in April 1974, they began to criticize the abuses of the regime and to urge the restoration of democracy. In 1975, there were several public incidents involving opposition churchmen and by the following year, the bishops had issued much stronger statements criticizing the expulsion of several leading Christian Democrats and a recent, government-inspired airport demonstration against several bishops. Members of the Pinochet government in turn criticized the bishops for acting as "vehicles for Marxism." At the end of 1975, the Committee for Peace was dissolved at Pinochet's insistence, but its functions were taken over by a Catholic aid program, the Vicariate of Solidarity.

In 1976, the Chilean Society for Tradition, Family, and Property published a book, *La iglesia del silencio en Chile,* that attacked Cardinal Silva's links to Allende. The cover showed the cardinal joking with him at a public ceremony. Frictions with the government increased as the church expanded its human rights program and its support for the poor and the persecuted. Among the latter group were leftist intellectuals for whom the cardinal was instrumental in founding a kind of university in internal exile, the Academy of Christian Humanism. The academy, in turn, cosponsored with the United Nations Educational, Scientific, and Cultural Organization (UNESCO) a critical journal, *Analisis,* that, within limits, was vigorously critical of Pinochet, even publishing cartoons lampooning him. The Jesuit magazine *Mensaje* was also able to take advantage of its church sponsorship to publish articles that attacked the regime's human rights and economic policies. The bishops themselves kept calling for a return to constitutionalism and, in their most directly political statement, they advised a negative vote in the regime-manipulated plebiscite on the 1980 constitution. They criticized the lack of debate on the constitutional draft and the provisions added by Pinochet to keep himself in power until 1989 and possibly until 1997. Despite their criticisms, Pinochet won a two-thirds majority in the plebiscite.

By the early 1980s, it was clear that Cardinal Silva was a strong opponent of the regime. He had made many statements, especially to the foreign press, criticizing the regime for its human rights violations, for its economic policy, and especially for its failure to return to civilian rule. When he reached

10. Sigmund, *Overthrow of Allende,* p. 252.

the canonical retirement age of 75 he announced that he was stepping down; after the Vatican named as his successor Juan Francisco Fresno, one of the bishops who had spoken in favor of the coup in 1973, Mrs. Pinochet is supposed to have exclaimed, "God has answered our prayers."

Even under a much more moderate church leader, however, the church-state frictions continued. In late 1984, for instance, the government refused to allow the head of the Vicariate of Solidarity, who was a Spanish citizen, to return to the country. In addition, it would not permit Archbishop—later Cardinal—Fresno's statements on this and related subjects to be carried in the media; they were read from the pulpit. During the monthly demonstrations against Pinochet that rocked Chile from May 1983 until November 1984, when martial law was reimposed, Catholic trade unionists and politicians from the newly revived—although still technically illegal—Christian Democratic Party attempted to develop a centrist alternative to the polarized politics of Pinochet-or-Communism that the government was promoting. The bishops did not formally support this effort, but the new archbishop organized a dialogue between the minister of the interior and the opposition leaders.

A return to civilian rule is promised in the 1980 constitution, but only in a gradual fashion and under conditions that maintain a strong military influence over public life. While there is supposed to be a presidential election in 1989, the constitution permits the junta—made up of representatives of the armed services—to propose a candidate to be elected by plebiscite; Pinochet has already expressed interest in running again under those conditions. The con-stitution also calls for congressional elections in 1990, but the Pinochet government is in no hurry to permit the opening of active political competition and argues that this must await the adoption of a party law, an electoral law, and the preparation of electoral registries. In the absence of open, competitive democracy the church will no doubt remain an important and active political force in Chile during the coming years.

CONCLUSION

In colonial times, the church in Chile seems to have had vast power because of its close relationship with political authorities. In fact, it often found itself in a subservient position as little more than a branch of the state devoted to ministering to religious needs and justifying the monarchy. What power it had was threatened by the divisions that followed independence. When those divisions were expressed in party terms, the church became closely associated with a single political party, the Conservatives, and vigorously opposed by another, the Radicals. While its power seemed to have been diminished by the separation of church and state in 1925, the period since that time has paradoxically been marked by a renewal of moral and, ultimately, political influence, even as church authorities maintain that they are not politically involved. In Chile's democratic politics, the church's influence has been felt in education—Catholic secondary schools and universities are among the most lively and influential of the country's educational institutions—and among trade unions. The church has been especially influential through the political parties. The Christian Democratic Party, which was the government party from 1964 until 1970, has been the most important opposition party under both the Allende government and the Pinochet dictatorship.

However, internal disagreement within the church, particularly the division of Catholic political opinion between Conservatives and Christian Democrats, has limited its political influence. Its power to influence opinion was further diluted with the rise of the Catholic Left in the late 1960s and early 1970s. The presence of the Catholic Left made it all the more necessary for the church to refrain from specific political involvement; yet, this did not mean that the church leadership was passive. As we have seen, the bishops have continued to issue important statements, many with strong political implications, on a regular basis. The church considers its teaching mission to include statements on moral issues, and the changes that have taken place in Chile in recent years have had strong moral implications.

In the 1950s, the church saw its mission mainly as requiring condemnations of Communism. Then, in the early 1960s, social justice, particularly in the area of agrarian reform, received the church's attention. The two concerns came into conflict in the Allende period when a Marxist-dominated coalition, claiming to work for social justice, created both tension in the consciences of Christians and specific organizational problems including the development of the Christians for Socialism movement, made up principally of activist, leftist clergy. The bishops opposed the specific involvement of the clergy in politics, but them-

selves became central political actors in the period after the coup because (1) the new regime used Christian symbols to give itself legitimacy; (2) many, if not most, other organizations that could freely debate government policy were suppressed; and (3) above all, the church was able to act effectively for the protection of human rights at a time when these rights were seriously violated. The result has been that, despite extraordinarily difficult political circumstances, the church has increased its moral standing, has transcended the divisions of the past, and has extended its presence to lower-class areas where it had been almost absent in the earlier part of this century.

What about the future? Precedents can be found elsewhere in Latin America for the church's active role as an intermediary in a negotiated transition to civilian rule—and the new cardinal, unlike Cardinal Silva, has a sufficiently neutral reputation to make this possible. If such a transition takes place, and if there is a return to the constitutional democracy and civilian rule that Chile has known throughout most of its history, the importance of the church is likely to be diminished, as other actors, such as the political parties, the unions, the media, and others, become more salient. However, the way the church, as an institution, has dealt with very different governments and has maintained its moral position without being politicized is a case study in effective church leadership that will remain as an example to other countries and churches in similar circumstances.

The Politics of Religion in Revolutionary Nicaragua

By MICHAEL DODSON

ABSTRACT: The Popular Insurrection in Nicaragua is examined against the backdrop of the grass-roots mobilization and protest that built up between 1968 and 1978. Particular attention is given to the linkages between grass-roots religious change and political mobilization. It is argued that the democratization of religious experience in the decade following the 1968 meeting of the Conference of Latin American Bishops in Medellín greatly facilitated the participation of the poor in the Nicaraguan Revolution, but that it also sowed the seeds of intrachurch conflict after the Triumph of the Revolution. Post-Triumph conflict between church and state and between the church hierarchy and the so-called popular church are then examined, with a view to showing that the major religious issue in revolutionary Nicaragua is not Marxism versus the church, but democratization in the church and in the political order.

Michael Dodson is associate professor of political science at Texas Christian University. He has published numerous articles on the topic of religion and social change in Latin America. Most recently his research articles have appeared in Polity, *the* Journal of Latin American Studies, *and the* Journal of Interamerican Studies and World Affairs. *He was a member of the Latin American Studies Association observer delegation for the 1984 Nicaraguan election, and in the spring of 1985 he was a senior Fulbright lecturer in Great Britain.*

RELIGION and politics became dynamically intermingled in Central America during the past decade. Each sphere confronted revolutionary challenges the inner logic of which has brought them into conflict with each other on new bases. The result has been moments of intense conflict, as well as mutual support, between church and state. The maturing revolutionary challenge to existing regimes also reawakened the dormant interest of such external actors as the United States. The event that most compellingly triggered interest in Central America was the Popular Insurrection, which broke out in Nicaragua in late 1978 and finally led, in July 1979, to the overthrow of General Anastasio Somoza's dictatorship. The Insurrection brought to power a revolutionary government led by the Sandinista Front of National Liberation (FSLN). Just months after the Triumph in Nicaragua, armed opposition groups seemed poised to overthrow the regime in El Salvador, too, and the entire region appeared ripe for revolution.[1]

Whether viewed from the political or religious vantage point, this wave of revolutionary change surprised most observers, particularly those in government and churches outside Central America, who had been accustomed to paying scant attention to the area. Government leaders in the United States, for example, viewed Central America as of little strategic importance while religious leaders looked upon it as a mission field that lacked significant religious energy of its own. Neither group would have predicted that the revitalization of religious life that followed the 1968 meeting of the Conference of Latin American Bishops (CELAM) in Medellín, Colombia, would stimulate and facilitate political revolution. Today U.S. policymakers describe Central America as a region of vital strategic importance, and in 1983 Pope John Paul II saw it as important enough to world Catholicism to make an extended journey through the region, speaking in every country.[2] The interest of such external political and religious actors as these derives from the far-reaching changes in religion and politics that are afoot throughout Central America. Nowhere is such change more vivid than in Nicaragua, where a complex new pattern of church-state relations has evolved since the Triumph.

In the United States the coming to power of the FSLN was viewed with alarm by the Carter administration, which sought to prevent it by negotiating Somoza's resignation and preserving the National Guard. Failing in this aim, Carter tried to gain influence with the Sandinistas by offering economic aid.[3] However, the Reagan administration came into office convinced that Nicaragua had been lost to the Communist bloc, arguing that the Sandinistas posed a serious threat to democracy in the hemisphere. This administration characterized Sandinismo as a "political

1. Nicaraguans refer to the overthrow of the Somoza regime as the "Triumph"; therefore that term will be used throughout this article.

2. A forceful statement of the view of U.S. policymakers is Henry Kissinger et al., *Report of the Bipartisan Commission on Central America* (Washington, DC: Government Printing Office, 1984); and Andrés Opazo et al., *El papa en Centroamérica* (San José, Costa Rica: EDUCA, 1983), provides an illuminating account of the pope's visit to Central America.

3. The tortuous process of providing aid to the Sandinistas is described vividly in William M. LeoGrande, "The United States and the Nicaraguan Revolution," in *Nicaragua in Revolution*, ed. Thomas W. Walker (New York: Praeger, 1982), pp. 63-77.

extremism" that depended on aggressive external support from Cuba and the Soviet Union, and it described Nicaragua as a "Cuban-style regime," building totalitarianism at home and fostering subversion among its neighbors. These attacks have made frequent use of religious issues, charging that the Sandinistas have "harassed, persecuted and defamed legitimate church leaders" and that they seek to turn the church into an arm of the government by creating a "popular church."[4] In this way religion has been further politicized in Nicaragua by external actors. But the church was already an important force for political change during the Triumph due to initiatives of its own.

PATTERNS OF CHANGE
SINCE THE
SECOND VATICAN COUNCIL

Prior to the wave of serious political unrest that broke out in Central America in the late 1970s, politics had been the exclusive domain of a tiny minority. Under Somoza most people were simply outside the operation of the political system in Nicaragua. Political parties never developed a mass base, only making brief appeals to the masses immediately before elections, which were invariably fraudulent, and therefore cynicism pervaded the society. Dominated by the coercive power of the National Guard, and lacking political institutions responsive to themselves, the poor were mired in political apathy. Widespread illiteracy compounded the situation. In short, Nicaragua lacked the essential infrastructure of democratic politics.[5]

In September 1978, the country seemed to plunge into revolution without warning. The poor were mobilized rapidly as apathy gave way to intense participation, and the political landscape began to alter. What few outside observers realized was that the pathway leading many of the poor into the revolutionary movement had its origin in a religious awakening. Thousands of Christians, acting through grass-roots Christian organizations and communities, participated in all phases of the Popular Insurrection.[6] Leaders of the FSLN have acknowledged this participation and its importance to the Insurrection's success. A brief review of post-Medellín religious change in Nicaragua, and the mechanisms by which it facilitated the political participation of the poor, is essential to understanding church involvement in the Nicaraguan Revolution and the conflict it has generated.

In 1965, the final year of the Second Vatican Council, the church throughout Central America was deeply traditional in outlook, weak in resources, closely identified with existing social inequality, and dependent on extant political systems, and it had little meaningful contact with the mass of ordinary people. After 1968 this profile changed, at first slowly, then at an accelerated rate as pastoral roles were redefined, new conceptions of faith were developed, and the church was established among the poor on new terms. The initiatives that led to these changes were adopted by CELAM in its historic 1968 meeting in Medellín. In specific, obligating lan-

---

4. "Persecution of Christian Groups in Nicaragua," *White House Digest,* 29 Feb. 1984, pp. 1-2.

5. See the excellent discussion of this issue in

John A. Booth, *Nicaragua: The End and the Beginning* (Boulder, CO: Westview Press, 1982), esp. chap. 6.

6. Michael Dodson and T. S. Montgomery, "The Churches in the Nicaraguan Revolution," in *Nicaragua in Revolution,* ed. Walker, pp. 161-80.

guage, the bishops pledged to put the weight of the church on the side of the poor in their struggle for liberation. It is doubtful that many bishops understood at the time where these changes might lead, particularly in Central America, where they produced a new conception of the church itself by precipitating a momentous shift in theology and pastoral practice.

The key to the influence of the church in political change was the new pastoral method by which the preferential option for the poor was implemented. Given the severe shortage of clergy, particularly diocesan priests, it was necessary to shift responsibility for pastoral work to lower levels of the institution, to involve foreign priests, women religious, and the laity extensively and to give them a relatively free hand. Although Nicaragua was superficially a religious country, the institutional church in fact had little contact with the masses, except through popular festivals, due to its lack of resources and its traditional attitudes. The reorientation of pastoral work led to the formation of Christian base communities (CEBs), which incorporated the laity more actively into the church and acknowledged the laity's importance in the pastoral mission. Religious participation at the grass roots increased as a direct result, bringing new vitality to the church.

In political terms, peasants and the urban poor were traditionally prevented from organizing, or their organizations were controlled by the regime. Although religious in their aims, CEBs provided a politically relevant alternative by serving as vehicles through which poor people could organize and meet to discuss common problems. Being under the umbrella of the church, the CEBs were initially left alone. Within the CEBs, local leaders could be trained as catechists and as Delegates of the Word— lay pastors serving rural areas where priests were seldom available. By the mid-1970s a loose infrastructure of religious communities had been established through which people themselves held Bible study, worshiped together, and carried out projects of self-help. Such activity encouraged a new ethos of shared responsibility and capacity for self-direction. The relative autonomy of the CEBs stimulated their spiritual vitality and contributed to their efficacy as actors in society. After the Triumph, however, their autonomy became a severe tension within the church.

Innovative methods of organization were complemented by new methods of worship. Perhaps the most decisive innovation was putting the Bible directly into the hands of peasants and working-class people. The Bible was translated into the vernacular and the Mass offered in Spanish, giving the poor direct access to them for the first time. Encouraged by Delegates and activist priests to interpret the gospel in the light of their own experiences, the Bible became for the poor a resource for critical reflection on faith and politics. During religious services the priest faced the people and invited them to express their views. In due course people whose opinions had never been taken into account came to believe that their views were important.[7] Moreover, they made direct connections between the Bible and the problems faced in their daily lives. This was a crucial step toward the sense of personal efficacy that is essential to active political participation. What this reformulated faith may have lacked in theologi-

7. Daniel H. Levine, "Religion and Politics: Dimensions of Renewal," *Thought*, 59(233):117-35 (June 1984).

cal sophistication, it made up in the coherence it gave to a critical or prophetic attitude toward society, and the catalytic energy it gave to organization and action. In the disintegrating political atmosphere that overtook Nicaragua after the 1972 earthquake, this religious renewal generated radical demands for democratization.

The formation and growth of grass-roots Christian communities in Nicaragua mirrored and encouraged the emergence of the secular popular organizations that played a critical role in the Popular Insurrection and that have been so prominent in the Revolution. Delegates of the Word became political leaders in a setting that denied peasants a political role, while CEBs became models of popular participation that pointed toward the democratization of society. It was this democratizing impulse, rather than the adoption of a coherent Marxist ideology or a theology of liberation, that gave religion its revolutionary character. This point can be appreciated by recalling that, from the standpoint of popular participation, the traditional church and the bizarre form of Nicaraguan oligarchy known as Somocismo were also reflections of each other. Under Somocismo, the surface forms of democracy only thinly concealed a deliberate stifling of popular participation. The church, itself rigidly hierarchical and inegalitarian, acquiesced in this political reality, so that church and political system were at least tacitly supportive of each other.

The church had functioned in Nicaragua according to the idea that its mission of salvation transcended the class differences that so sharply marked the society, but its institutional roots were firmly fixed in the more privileged classes. This inconsistency was rationalized by adopting an official posture of nonpartisanship with regard to political issues; the church was above politics. The emergence of popular religion after Medellín seriously challenged this view, not only ideologically but in the most practical terms. Those at the grass roots, who had been only superficially attended by the church in earlier generations, and whose Catholicism had been taken for granted, now had their own religious communities, were developing their own theology, and thought themselves entitled to contribute their share to the nation's religious and political agendas. In the two or three years preceding the Insurrection, the FSLN mobilized these grass-roots Christians into the uprising against Somoza, but it did not create their organizations any more than it created their demand for participation. On their own initiative they brought the church into opposition to the political order; from there they moved, albeit hesitantly and sometimes painfully, into the mainstream of revolutionary struggle.

INITIAL RESPONSES TO THE REVOLUTION

Nearly all Nicaraguans would agree that 19 July 1979 began a new era in the nation's history, but not all agree that Sandinista rule is fulfilling that promise. At the time of the Triumph the country's most immediate task was the reconstruction of a devastated land, both materially and morally. In the final two months of the Insurrection, Somoza's struggle to retain power had become indiscriminate. He authorized heavy bombing of key cities, and even churches became targets of attack.[8] The Sandinistas came to power intent upon effecting

8. I personally visited churches that had been attacked in the cities of Managua, Masaya, Matagalpa, Jinotega, and Estelí.

a social revolution and asserting Nicaraguan sovereignty in foreign affairs. The political system they inherited was totally discredited and had effectively collapsed, leaving little functioning administrative apparatus and no viable political institutions. Thus, the task the FSLN set for the new Government of National Reconstruction was that of nation building. This task united the two aims of creating new political institutions responsive to the needs of the poor majority and pursuing a nonaligned foreign policy.[9]

As it set out on a revolutionary course in 1979, Nicaragua could be contrasted with Mexico in 1910 or Cuba in 1959. Unlike the two earlier revolutions of these countries, Nicaragua was distinguished by the large number of Christians who offered active support and accepted the leadership of the revolutionary movement. Their loyalty stemmed from earlier participation in change at the grass roots. At the same time, there were some people in the churches who approached the Revolution apprehensively. In the course of five years of struggle and change, these different levels of expectation and commitment regarding the Revolution have generated three types of conflict over the church's role in society.

By far the most publicized conflicts have been those between church and state, especially between certain members of the Catholic hierarchy and Sandinista leaders. This type of conflict represents only one level of church involvement in the Revolution, however, and not always the most important, either for the church's future or the Revolution's integrity. A second kind of

9. For a description of the original Sandinista program, see George Black, *Triumph of the People* (London: Zed Press, 1981), pp. 121-22.

conflict lies within the church itself, involving deep discord between elements of the hierarchy and the base over matters of theology, ecclesiology, and pastoral strategies. This conflict may be of greater long-term importance to the church and the Revolution than the first. A third tension lies at the grassroots level of the church, where Christians are trying to stay active in both the church and the Revolution, integrating these important aspects of their lives in an atmosphere that discourages that integration. The difficulty arises from the great demands made on them by the Revolution, which are exacerbated by the protracted war in which Nicaragua now finds itself, and is compounded by resistance on the part of some bishops to such an integration.

Both among clergy and laity, Nicaraguans who feared the Revolution frequently focused their criticism on the emergence of what they called a popular church as opposed to the true church. They believed the FSLN was exalting the former and trying to isolate the latter. These fears are genuine insofar as they have an objective basis in a polarization between different groups in the church. But the simple cause-and-effect explanation adduced—namely, that the atheistic, totalitarian ideology of the FSLN produces the polarization—is less apparent. A common response to the fear has been to reassert hierarchical control and to demand obedience to authority exercised in the traditional manner. In this way tradition has been pitted against innovation, hierarchy against base, elite control against the democratizing trends unleashed by Medellín and by the Insurrection. As if these internal stresses were not enough, external actors have taken a keen interest in the church's role in the Revolution and indeed have gone to considerable lengths to influence it.

In the setting of frenzied destruction that marked the final days of Somoza, the Nicaraguan bishops issued a pastoral letter upholding the right of an oppressed people to defend itself against tyranny. Even in those extreme circumstances the letter was a bold step for an episcopal conference and it was celebrated by Christians throughout the country as a sign of the bishops' solidarity with their struggle.

The letter did not, however, imply identification with the coming revolution, for the bishops were not pastorally identified with the physical struggle in the way that, for example, Archbishop Romero was in El Salvador; nor did they have links with the popular organizations or the FSLN. On the very day the Sandinistas entered Managua, Archbishop Obando y Bravo was in Venezuela taking part in negotiations aimed at creating a moderate transition government that would prevent them from assuming power. It was not surprising, therefore, that the bishops issued another text just two weeks after the Triumph that, while acknowledging that "a new era in our history has begun," also talked at length of "anxieties and fears" over the ideology and goals of the Sandinistas. Fully half the text was devoted to the future of religion in Nicaragua and warned the government against trying to "impose something foreign."[10] While Christians at the base welcomed the Revolution and sought involvement in it, the hierarchy approached it skeptically and from a greater distance.

Even so, the first year of the Revolution was marked by a general mood of euphoria. Most Nicaraguans who stayed in the country shared in the sense of liberation that accompanied the defeat of Somocismo. Presented with the fact of the Revolution, the Carter administration pledged economic aid, as did other countries. The immediate tasks of reconstruction absorbed the great energies that had been released by the Triumph. The initial governing junta included members of the middle class and private sector organizations that had joined the opposition to Somoza after the January 1978 assassination of Pedro Joaquin Chamorro, publisher of *La prensa*.[11] It was the honeymoon year of the Revolution; external opposition was low, and internal, multiclass cooperation was relatively high. A number of priests held important positions in the government.

During this period, on 17 November 1979, the bishops issued their remarkable pastoral letter, "Christian Commitment for a New Nicaragua." This letter, issued just four months after the Triumph, marked the apogee of church-state relations and internal church solidarity. In it the bishops acknowledged the authentic Christian and pastoral character of the CEBs and seemed to invite active dialogue between themselves and the base. They acknowledged the depth of Christian participation in the revolutionary process and recognized the FSLN as the new nation's political leadership. The letter even embraced "the dramatic conversion of our church" and "the dynamic fact of class struggle that should lead to a just transformation of structures."[12] But accepting such changes in the euphoria

10. "Nicaraguan Bishops Speak to Catholics and All Nicaraguans," *LADOC*, 10(2):20-23 (Nov.-Dec. 1979).

11. Black, *Triumph*, pp. 107-18.

12. Phillip Berryman, *The Religious Roots of Rebellion* (Maryknoll, NY: Orbis Books, 1984), p. 235.

of the moment, before divisive ideological struggle had broken out and before external actors had begun to exert pressure on Nicaragua, proved much easier than accepting them in the actual carrying out of the Revolution.

This pastoral letter, too, expressed reservations about the future and referred to the concerns and fears the bishops thought many Nicaraguans held regarding the possible course of the Revolution. The bishops mentioned in the letter their worry that some groups that "contributed generously" to making the Revolution possible would be excluded from shaping the nation's future, although there was no specific mention of whom the bishops had in mind.[13] The letter only hinted at an issue that later became a source of protracted conflict when it suggested that the base must be in communion with the hierarchy. Apparently even at this positive stage some bishops were skeptical about whether the revolution was in the interests of the church and were ill disposed toward active popular participation in its programs.

These misgivings may well have been reinforced by the speed with which the FSLN consolidated its position as the nation's leading political force. Within the first six months it organized a government, created an army that it controlled, and launched major programs of land reform and literacy training. Widespread support of these programs among the popular sectors was obvious, and their participation was mobilized through grass-roots organizations either controlled by, or loyal to, the FSLN.

Theological and pastoral support for the Revolution was organized quickly as well. Only one month after the Triumph an ecumenical center, called the Antonio Valdivieso Center, was set up in Managua by Catholic clergy and Protestant pastors who were closely identified with the popular sectors and sympathetic to the Revolution. Their purpose was to promote dialogue between church and government and to encourage the participation of Christians in the Revolution. Through such measures as the sponsorship of conferences and workshops, the publication of a wide assortment of theological and pastoral materials, and the training of pastoral leaders for the local level, the Antonio Valdivieso Center rapidly acquired a high profile as a pro-revolutionary Christian entity.[14] Its work was complemented by that of the Central American Historical Institute, based in the Jesuit university, and by the Center for Rural Education and Development, which had been set up by the Jesuits a decade earlier to train peasant leaders, providing skills for agriculture, community development, and worship.[15] Seen in their entirety, these organizations linked together a pro-revolutionary intellectual leadership within the church and the mass-based Christian organizations, rendering mutual support and encouragement. They also gave these elements of the church strong contacts with Christians outside Nicaragua.

The hierarchy pursued a similar but divergent path. In January 1980, the bishops met with leaders of CELAM in San José, Costa Rica. At this meeting the latter offered "fraternal assistance" to the Nicaraguan church, pledging to distribute Bibles and CELAM publica-

13. "Hablan los obispos de Nicaragua," *Cuadernos de capitación* (Lima: CELADEC, 1979), no. 5, p. 21.

14. Interview with James Goff, Managua, 13 Apr. 1983.

15. Berryman, *Religious Roots,* pp. 71, 231.

tions, to help develop courses in catechesis, and to devise an overall pastoral plan for the country. Note was taken of the serious problem of illiteracy in Nicaragua and more than $300,000 in support was offered. While some bishops seemed enthusiastic, Christians at the local level were upset by this initiative. The core of their disagreement marked a major fault line of conflict in the ensuing years. They pointed out that Christians such as themselves, who were closest to the reality of poor Nicaraguans, were not consulted about the church's pastoral needs. Nor had mention been made of the Literacy Crusade then being mobilized by the government and directed by a Nicaraguan Jesuit. Instead, both CELAM leaders and their own bishops approached the matter with a missionary mentality, a mentality that did not fit a revolutionary society wherein pastoral work could, and should, reflect the people's own historical experience.[16]

DEEPENING CONFLICTS OVER RELIGION

Latent conflict involving the church broke out openly toward the end of the first year. Two of the three non-Sandinista members of the five-person governing junta resigned in April 1980. In a matter of weeks the episcopal conference, without prior consultation, called upon priests serving in the government to resign. Rather than obeying, the priests sought dialogue, while grass-roots Christian groups closed ranks in their support and the Antonio Valdivieso Center publicly questioned the bishops' motives. In the short run the matter was left unresolved, with the priests remaining in

their positions and the hierarchy seeking support for their demands in Rome. At this same time the Literacy Campaign was under way with widespread church support. All of Nicaragua's 52 congregations of Catholic women religious took part, Catholic schools were used extensively, and thousands of Catholic students, known as *brigadistas*, served as teachers. Yet, in the atmosphere of rising tension within the church, no bishop participated in the campaign's closing ceremony in Managua, and subsequently some bishops criticized the campaign as Sandinista propaganda. Archbishop Obando pointedly refused to take part in a ceremony prepared by his own Youth Pastoral Team to welcome the *brigadistas*, reportedly because he was not scheduled to preside over it.[17]

Perceiving that rising criticism of the Revolution was being expressed through religion, the FSLN, on 7 October 1980, published the "Official Communiqué Concerning Religion," which applauded the vital role played by Christians in the Insurrection, praising both the hierarchy and the grass roots for their varied contributions. It guaranteed religious freedom and held that religion and politics were separate spheres. The communique seemed to aim at reassuring the church hierarchy that the Revolution would not undercut religion, but the bishops responded coldly to the initiative. They argued that both liberal and totalitarian governments deny the church a valid participation in society. Totalitarian regimes do so by rendering the church merely "an appendage of the state."[18] In

16. José Revelas, "Lopez Trujillo envía conquistadores: El clero local firme en el gobierno," *Proceso*, 26 May 1980, pp. 2-3.

17. "The Catholic Church in Nicaragua and the Revolution: A Chronology," *Envío,* 1 Dec. 1983, p. 86.

18. "Documento de la conferencia episcopal de Nicaragua," in *Nicaragua: La hora de los desafíos* (Lima: CEP, 1981), pp. 113-24.

that context they again raised the issue of priests in the government, charging that they were merely being "instrumentalized" by the Sandinistas. To the bishops, the criteria of religious freedom and church-state coexistence outlined by the FSLN were an "open door" to "political abuse, above all by those who want to eliminate religion from human life."[19]

Clearly, at least some of the bishops had deep-seated fears of the Revolution, even at this early stage. They saw it as latently totalitarian and were convinced of its hostility to religion. This conviction took the form of a premise rather than a conclusion based on experience. No actions had been taken against the church—neither confiscations of church property, nor restrictions on religious freedom. Church schools continued to operate and indeed received a generous subsidy from the government. The minister of education was one of the most prominent lay Catholics in the country.[20] But an experiential and theological divide now separated Christians. Some bishops were prepared to resist attacks on the church that they were sure would come, even if it meant conflict with those in the church who supported the Revolution. The original fluidity of religion and politics gave way to increasing polarization.

During the year 1981 roving bands of ex-Somocista guardsmen began to attack isolated settlements in Nicaragua from camps in Honduras. By the end of the year they were relatively well organized, the attacks had become more systematic, and Nicaragua was feeling the impact. Many of the attacks occurred in Miskito lands of Northern Zelaya, near the Honduran border. Counterrevolutionary bands headed by Miskito leader Steadman Fagoth disrupted the government's health campaign. A serious incident in late 1981 led to the decision to relocate a large number of Miskito Indians further south, both for their protection and so the Sandinista Army could secure the Rio Coco area. This was done in early 1982.

On 18 February, without having visited the area to see for themselves, the bishops issued a statement condemning the transfer of the Miskitos and charging that there had been grave violations of the Indians' rights. The charges did not originate with Bishop Schleafer, in whose diocese the Miskitos lived, but in the archdiocese of Managua. In their statement, the bishops referred to the *contras* as "political adversaries" of the FSLN and did not condemn their actions. This event precipitated a serious confrontation between church and state and also sharply increased tensions within the church. Christian groups that visited the new settlements disputed the bishops' accusations, while the government responded with a vigorous refutation and asked the Vatican to send a delegation to Nicaragua to mediate the problems of church-state relations.[21]

The next three years were marked by a series of conflicts that reflected the

---

19. Ibid.

20. At that time the minister of education was Carlos Tunnerman, who was confirmed as ambassador to the United States in July 1984. His successor was Father Fernando Cardenal, who was subsequently required to leave the Jesuit order to accept this post. From the beginning of the Revolution, education in Nicaragua has been overseen by Catholic individuals, albeit ones who support the Revolution.

21. Interview with Leana Nuñez of the National Directorate of the FSLN, in Managua, 18 Aug. 1984. The government had already sent delegations to the Vatican to discuss religious questions on three previous occasions, and others were sent after February 1982.

pattern of the Miskito controversy, two of them over particularly sensitive political issues. The first involved the military draft law, passed by the Council of State in September 1983. The second concerned the letter on reconciliation issued by the hierarchy at Easter, 1984.

By mid-1983 the *contra* war was making great material and human demands on Nicaragua. The FSLN determined that the rapid increase in the size of the *contra* forces required a larger military mobilization. Much of the fighting at the front was being carried by militia rather than regular army. Consequently, a bill on patriotic military service was introduced into the Council of State. On 29 August, while it was still being debated, the church hierarchy issued a letter entitled "General Considerations on Military Service," which was signed only by the secretary of the episcopal conference and was printed in *La prensa* on 1 September.

In a general section on military service, the pastoral letter alluded to the pattern of "all countries with totalitarian governments" wherein the army is used to impose an alien ideology. Such countries seek to establish the "absolute dictatorship of a political party." Arguing from this viewpoint, the letter cited a passage in the bill that said military service would "promote in our young people a sense of revolutionary ethics and discipline." This statement was interpreted to mean that "the army will become an obligatory center for political indoctrination in favor of the Sandinista Party." To forestall such manipulation, the hierarchy urged those who did not share the Sandinista ideology to refuse military service on grounds of "conscientious objection."[22]

A range of Christian groups in sympathy with the Revolution responded in *El nuevo diario* two weeks later. They argued that in the atmosphere of constant *contra* attacks and the escalation of threats from the United States, the hierarchy's message looked like a "call to desertion." They pointed out that the letter was not based on any biblical texts or church documents, and argued that it was the first time in contemporary church history that an episcopal conference had declared obligatory military service illegitimate. Asserting their support for the law, they asked, "What totalitarian state would tolerate . . . the hierarchy publicly proclaiming its illegitimacy and publicly calling on the people to desert it at a time of threat and danger?"[23] In fact, the hierarchy was not unified in taking this approach to the draft. One bishop was out of the country when the letter was published and two others subsequently made statements defending the draft.

The pastoral letter on reconciliation, like that on compulsory military service, addressed the most explosive issue in Nicaraguan politics, the *contra* war. The letter generated not a move toward reconciliation, but intense, divisive controversy. This can be attributed in part to its accusatory tone and content, and in part to what the letter did not say. Commencing at a general, abstract level, the letter urged that Nicaraguans be open to conversion, live according to Christian standards and values, and "end . . . participation in injustice and violence." It then proceeded to indict the government and its supporters in the church, attacking them for sponsoring "materialist and atheistic education,"

22. "Conferencia episcopal sugiere 'objeción de conciencia': Nadie puede ser obligado a tomar armas por un partido," *La prensa*, 1 Sept. 1983, p. 1.

23. "Al pueblo de Nicaragua y al mundo," *El nuevo diario*, 13 Sept. 1983, p. 2.

and for exploiting the Mothers of Heroes and Martyrs[24] to "incite hatred." Christians who support the Revolution were described as having "abandoned ecclesiastical unity and surrendered to tenets of a materialistic ideology." The roots of this situation were traced to "individual sin" and to "political ambition and abuse of power."[25]

The path leading to reconciliation was seen to lie in self-criticism that revealed "our faults," faults that "affront the church." Since only the Sandinistas were criticized explicitly in the letter, it was their conversion to which attention was drawn. This was made explicit in the basis for dialogue laid out by the bishops. The letter characterized the war as a "civil war" and asserted that the Sandinistas were "dishonest to blame internal aggression and violence on foreign aggression." It then called for the incorporation of those "Nicaraguans who have taken up arms against the government" in any dialogue for peace. Indeed, the government was urged to "welcome them with an open heart." The only reference to foreign involvement in the war was as follows: "The great powers, which are involved in this problem for ideological or economic reasons, must leave the Nicaraguans free from coercion."[26]

The letter on reconciliation bore a strong similarity to the homily delivered by Pope John Paul II in March 1983, during his visit to Nicaragua. In each case the posture and tone adopted by church leaders was peremptory and confrontational, contrasting sharply with their professed aim. In each case church leaders addressed an audience of common people without coming to grips with their religious and political reality as they themselves experienced it. The pope accused Christians at the grassroots level of seeking to live apart from the true church and demanded their obedience to the bishops. He made no mention of the war, of the poor who had given their lives in it, and ignored the Mothers of Heroes and Martyrs who stood before him. The letter on reconciliation was even more aggressive, explicitly attacking both grass-roots Christians and the FSLN and offering an interpretation of the war that made no mention of the U.S. role or previous government offers of amnesty. It was an interpretation that only a small minority of Nicaraguans would accept.

The repercussions of episcopal hostility to the Revolution have been felt most keenly among Christians at the grass roots, particularly in Managua and among those in CEBs who are identified as supportive of the Revolution. After 1981, as conflict intensified and divergent attitudes toward the Revolution became more evident in the church, CEBs located in the archdiocese of Managua experienced demoralization and some loss of vitality. Their relative autonomy of the pre-Triumph period, and their loose identification with a growing popular movement, gave way to the competing demands of loyalty to the institutional church and their own desire to participate in the programs of the Revolution. The most active leaders of CEBs were in great demand for the skills they could bring to tasks of reconstruction. The advance of the war and the state of military mobilization added to the demands made upon them. Some of the clergy upon whom the CEBs

24. The name given to mothers whose sons and daughters have died in *contra* attacks. Such mothers now number in the thousands.

25. "Pastoral Letter on Reconciliation from the Nicaraguan Bishops," trans. U.S. Department of State, pp. 3, 6, 7 (22 Apr. 1984).

26. Ibid., pp. 9-12.

depended for linkage to the institutional church were either moved to other parishes by Archbishop Obando or were so intent upon nurturing support for building the new nation that they gave insufficient attention to the traditional religious acitivities that were still important to CEB members.[27]

CEBs in rural areas have been less directly affected. They retain more of their earlier autonomy and are loosely coordinated by the Center for Rural Education and Development, which, although it has been disavowed by the bishops, continues to be an active and vigorous organization. The most vital areas for rural CEBs are in Leon, Chinandega, and Estelí, in the north of the country.

To cope with the pressures from the church and the Revolution, CEBs have undertaken a serious, critical self-examination. In early 1983 they set up a school to train new lay leaders, offering instruction in theology, social science, and methods of organization. The curriculum is geared to cultivating religious identity within an active participation in a revolutionary society. It is informed by an orientation that sees Christianity and revolution as compatible, but avoids identifying the two. In the final analysis, this seems to be the point of greatest disagreement between the base and hierarchy, for some bishops seem convinced that religion and the Revolution are irretrievably incompatible.

CONCLUSION

Those accounts of church-state relations in the Nicaraguan Revolution that portray the Sandinistas as hostile to religion and bent upon its destruction are tendentious and misleading. Nicaragua is not Poland and there is no official orthodoxy that religion is a vestige of the class society that must be rooted out to facilitate the liberation of the people. There have been intense strain and periodic outbursts of hostility between some Sandinista leaders and some members of the Catholic hierarchy. The fears of the hierarchy have been documented briefly in these pages. In their opposition to the Revolution, the bishops are sometimes portrayed as defenders of democratic freedoms. At the same time, priests in the government and Christians at the local level who support the Revolution are seen to represent an antidemocratic politicization of the church, and it is suggested that they are merely being manipulated by the FSLN.[28]

This article has sought to show that such a view, whether it comes from the Nicaraguan bishops, from CELAM, from the Vatican, or from the White House, ignores the indigenous process of democratization that took place in both church and society before the Triumph. The view also ignores the catalytic effect that religious change had in the political arena. The real issue in Nicaragua is not Marxism versus religion, but democratization in church and polity. Ironically, such democratization may be jeopardized by the deepening *contra* war that is being waged against Nicaragua in the name of democracy.

Finally, the most important conflict over religion in Nicaragua today is going on within the church. The government and the bishops maintain a dialogue through official representatives. Bishop Vega, president of the episcopal confer-

27. Interview with Father Antonio Castro, Managua, 16 Apr. 1983.

28. See *White House Digest*, 29 Feb. 1984; see also Humberto Belli, *Christians under Fire* (Grand Rapids, MI: John Paul II Institute, 1983).

ence, attended the swearing-in ceremony for president-elect Daniel Ortega in January 1985. There is less dialogue between hierarchy and base. They face the future with different histories, different conceptions of the church, and different aspirations. The challenge of the years to come is whether church unity must be purchased at the price of obedience and uniformity, or whether the post-Vatican church can continue to accept pluralism in its own midst and grant a measure of status and authority to the laity, including the poor.

Religion, Legitimacy, and Conflict in Nigeria

By HENRY BIENEN

ABSTRACT: Nigeria has not evolved political formulas that explicitly allow religion or religious authorities to define legitimacy. There have, however, been struggles carried out in religious terms over constitutional mechanisms for adjudicating conflict. Religion also has been an element in the conflict between ethnic-language groups. Finally, religion provides a language, a set of values, and institutions through which groups struggle and over which groups contend, both within and between religious communities. It has been necessary for northern leaders to stress Islam in order to maintain northern unity. However, Islam itself has worked to intensify fissures opened up by social and economic change in Nigeria. Islam in Nigeria continues to be contentious in both domestic and foreign policy.

Henry Bienen is James S. McDonnell Distinguished University Professor at Princeton University. He is director of Princeton's Center of International Studies and editor of World Politics. *Professor Bienen has taught at Makerere University, Uganda; University of Nairobi; and University of Ibadan, Nigeria. His latest book is* Political Conflict and Economic Change in Nigeria.

NOTE: I wish to thank the Institute for Advanced Study in Princeton, New Jersey, for its support.

NIGERIA does not have a state religion. The secular nature of the Nigerian state was established at independence in 1960 and has been reaffirmed under successive military and civilian governments. Nigeria has not had official membership in international Islamic organizations in order to avoid giving Islam an official status. Nonetheless, the role and place of religion— especially of Islam—in domestic and foreign affairs has been contentious in recent Nigerian history. The nature of Nigeria's secularity has been fiercely debated.

When the military regime headed by General Olusegun Obasanjo determined to return Nigeria to civilian rule in 1979, after 13 years of military government, it convened first a Constitutional Drafting Committee and then an elected Constitutional Assembly. The most contentious and divisive debates in these forums occurred over the place of *sharia,* or Islamic law, in the Second Republic. Disputes over Islamic law were important in determining principles of legitimacy. However, the debate over whether the new constitution should recognize Islamic law at the federal or state levels through the creation of state or federal *sharia* courts was also a struggle between elites with different regional and religious bases in Nigeria. Arguments over Islamic law replayed, sometimes implicitly, many of the old themes about the nature of Nigerian federalism and the nature of the power of the central government, the relationships between north and south, and the relationships between dominant and minority ethnic communities.[1]

In the debate over whether an Islamic court should have constitutional status in Nigeria, some members of the northern intelligentsia argued that for a Muslim to live in a secular state would be an "abomination." Northern delegates to the Constitutional Drafting Committee argued that Muslims must have their cases adjudicated under Islamic personal law and that this meant giving *sharia* a federal status by appointing Muslims to the Supreme Court and stipulating that only such judges should preside over cases involving *sharia.*

Northern delegates remained unified on this issue. Their demands implied recognition of Islam as a state religion, an idea southerners never have accepted and would not accept. If the issue could not have been resolved, the military would not have been able to turn power back to civilians in 1979.[2] Thus a compromise was reached in the Constitutional Drafting Committee via a proposal for a federal *sharia* Court of Appeal, but the compromise was rejected by southerners when debate moved to the Constituent Assembly. After a walkout by northern delegates, another compromise was eventually reached through a formula for establishing a *sharia* Court of Appeal at the state, but not the federal, level.[3]

The debate over the *sharia* court turned on whether Nigeria would remain

---

1. For analyses of the constitutional debates, I have relied on Billy Dudley, *An Introduction to Nigerian Government and Politics* (Bloomington: Indiana University Press, 1982), pp. 150-62; Alaba Ogunsanwo, *The Public Debate on Nigeria's Constitution: October 1976-September 1977* (Princeton, NJ: Center of International Studies, 1980); David Laitin, "The Shari'a Debate and the Origins of Nigeria's Second Republic," *Journal of Modern African Studies*, 20(3):411-30 (1982). The debates have been published in *Proceedings of the Constituent Assembly, Official Report* (Lagos: Government Printer, 1977).

2. Dudley, *Introduction to Nigerian Government and Politics*, pp. 163-64.

3. Ibid., p. 164.

a secular state. It also reflected the deep splits between northerners and southerners, and, with the exception of the Yorubas—an ethnic-language group that contains both Muslims and Christians—it reflected divisions between ethnic-religious communities. In order to understand the full impact of the split over the *sharia* court, the ethnic and religious arithmetic of Nigeria must be sketched.

ENUMERATION OF
THE POPULATION

There has been no accepted census in Nigeria since the colonial period. Indeed, every attempt at a new census has been controversial, and a number have been canceled after the fact. The government continues to make extrapolations from a 1963 census base. The 1963 census, however, was itself widely questioned within Nigeria. The failure of various censuses to be accepted broadly within Nigeria reflects problems not only with census data collection and enumeration, but also with the numerical breakdown in terms of religion, ethnicity, language, and place of residence. These numbers, in turn, are crucial for revenue allocation,[4] for the distribution of seats in elected legislative bodies, and generally for the distribution of valued goods and services in Nigeria's religiously and ethnically heterogenous federal system.

In the 1979 federal elections, 200 seats in the House of Representatives were allocated on a population basis to

the 9 southern states and 249 seats were allocated to the 10 northern states. Some southern states are overwhelmingly Christian. Ibo-speaking Imo and Anambra, for example, are largely Catholic; 0.1 percent and 0.6 percent of their respective populations are Muslim. But the populations in the Yoruba-speaking states of western Nigeria run from as little as 12 percent Muslim in Ondo State to 62 percent Muslim in Oyo State, where the largest city, Ibadan, is predominantly Muslim.[5] Some of the states of the former Northern Region— such as Sokoto, Kano, and Borno—are above 93 percent Muslim. Proportions of this nature reflect the Hausa-Fulani composition for Sokoto and Kano and the Kanuri ethnic dominance in Borno. But the states of what has been called the Middle Belt of the Northern Region are very mixed with respect to the Muslim proportion of their populations, running from 12 percent in Benue to 25 percent and 34 percent for Plateau and Gongola to 75 percent for Kwara. Some of the northern heartland states, such as Niger and Kaduna, are less than 60 percent Muslim, although the latter contains Muslim political and civil service elites that are among the most powerful in Nigeria.

Observers put the Muslim population of Nigeria between approximately 50 and 55 percent and the Christian population at about 35 percent or more, with the rest not belonging to a world religion. As noted, Christians are mostly in the southern and Middle Belt states. Muslims may make up half of all Yoruba speakers and are also found in significant numbers in the Middle Belt. About

---

4. On revenue allocation, see Douglas Rimmer, "Development in Nigeria, An Overview," in *The Political Economy of Income Distribution in Nigeria* ed. Henry Bienen and V. P. Diejomaoh (New York: Holmes & Meier, 1981), pp. 29-88; Lawrence A. Rupley, "Revenue Sharing in the Nigerian Federation," *Journal of Modern African Studies*, 19(2):257-78 (1981).

5. Let me reiterate that giving percentages here should not lull the reader into thinking that we are dealing with hard figures.

TABLE 1
NIGERIA: RELIGIOUS AFFILIATIONS BY REGION, 1952 AND 1963
(Percentage of the Population)

Region	Muslim		Christian		Other	
	1952	1963	1952	1963	1952	1963
North	73.0	71.7	2.7	9.7	24.3	18.6
West	32.8	43.4	36.9	48.8	30.3	7.9
East	0.6	0.3	46.2	77.2	50.2	22.5
Lagos	41.0	44.3	53.0	54.6	6.0	1.1
Mid-West	—	4.2	—	54.9	—	40.9
Total	44.4	49.0	22.0	34.0	33.6	17.0

SOURCES: *Nigerian Census, 1952: Nigeria Yearbook, 1969* (Lagos: Times Press, 1970), p. 193. As found in J. N. Paden, *Religion and Political Culture in Kano* (Berkeley: University of California Press, 1973), p. 44. Reprinted by permission.

half of Nigeria's population is either Hausa-Fulani, Yoruba, or Ibo, and the rest consists of so-called minorities people.

ISLAM: A FORCE FOR UNITY OR DIVISION?

If we try to get beyond numbers and percentages to look at the ways that Islam cuts across ethnic-language groups to forge a wider community of believers, or reinforces ethnic differences by superimposing religion on them, we must be careful in the absence of large-scale survey data or many in-depth small-scale analyses.

There is some evidence to suggest that in the large cities of the north of Nigeria, workers from different ethnic groups share feelings of commonality based on membership in the Islamic community. Hausa speakers express more tolerance for non-Hausas who are Muslim than for non-Hausas who are not Muslim, but Yoruba Muslims are an exception to this tolerance.[6] Yorubas

have been very competitive with Hausas for national power, and Yoruba Muslims themselves have objected to the Hausa Muslims' religious and economic separatism in Ibadan.[7] Ethnicity, not religion, has been critical for the social and economic networks through which business has been carried out among the Yoruba.

In the 1979 elections, the Yoruba leader of the Unity Party of Nigeria, Chief Awolowo, swept all the Yoruba-speaking states, from the dominantly Christian Ondo State to the majority-Muslim Oyo State. In the 1983 elections, while the Unity Party of Nigeria lost ground to the National Party of Nigeria (NPN), led by a northern Muslim, Shehu Shagari, and even lost a gu-

Nigeria," in *The Development of an African Working Class*, ed. R. Sandbrook and R. Cohen (London: Longman, 1975); "Contrasts and Continuity in a Dependent City: The Case of Kano, Nigeria," in *Third World Urbanization*, ed. J. Abu-Lughod and C. Hay (Chicago: Maaroufa Press, 1977). A forthcoming book of Lubeck's gives details from the surveys.

6. I have very much benefited from reading the work of Paul Lubeck, who carried out surveys among Hausa workers in Kano in the early 1970s. Among the published articles by Lubeck are "Unions, Workers and Consciousness in Kano,

7. Abner Cohen, "The Politics of the Kola Trade," in *Readings in the Applied Economics of Africa*, vol. 1, *Microeconomics*, ed. Edith Whetham and Jean Currie (London: Cambridge University Press, 1967).

TABLE 2
MUSLIM PORTION OF STATE POPULATIONS AND
PARTY VOTES IN NIGERIA, 1979 (Percentage)

State	Muslim	National Party of Nigeria*	Great Nigeria People's Party*	People's Redemption Party	Unity Party of Nigeria	Nigerian People's Party
Sokoto	97.6	66.5	26.1	3.3	2.5	0.9
Kano	97.4	19.9	1.5	76.4	1.2	0.9
Borno	93.1	34.7	54.0	6.5	3.4	1.4
Bauchi	80.6	62.5	15.4	14.3	3.0	4.7
Kwara	75.2	53.6	5.7	0.7	39.5	0.5
Oyo	62.4	12.8	0.6	0.3	85.8	0.6
Niger	59.7	74.9	16.5	4.0	3.7	1.1
Kaduna	56.4	53.1	13.8	31.7	6.7	4.7
Ogun	54.3	6.2	0.5	6.2	92.1	0.3
Lagos	44.3	7.2	0.5	0.5	82.3	9.6
Gongola	34.1	35.5	34.1	4.3	21.7	4.4
Plateau	25.7	34.7	6.8	4.0	5.3	49.2
Ondo	12.3	4.2	0.3	0.2	94.5	0.9
Benue	11.3	76.4	7.9	1.4	2.6	11.7
Bendel	7.4	36.2	1.2	0.7	53.2	8.6
Rivers	0.2	72.7	2.2	0.5	10.3	14.4
Cross Rivers	0.1	64.4	15.1	1.0	11.8	7.7
Imo	0.1	8.8	3.0	0.9	0.6	86.7
Anambra	0.6	13.5	1.7	1.2	0.8	82.9

*Presidential candidate was Muslim. Candidates for the National Party of Nigeria, the Great Nigerian People's Party, and the People's Redemption Party were, respectively, Alhaji Shehu Shagari, Alhaji Waziri Ibrahim, and Alhaji Aminu Kano.

bernatorial race in the west amid cries of fraud, Chief Awolowo once again carried Yorubaland (see Table 2).

Factional splits among the Yoruba cannot be correlated with Christian-Muslim divisions. When the ruling Action Group in the Yoruba Western Region was split in 1962, the leader of the faction that broke with Awolowo and wanted to take the Yorubas into an alliance with the north was Chief Samuel Akintola, who was Christian. The man who became premier of the Western Region when Awolowo moved to the federal arena was his ally, Alhaji Adegbenro. The splits within the Action Group appeared largely factional although they had ideological and ethnic components. The ethnic component was based on historical distinctions between areas of Yorubaland, such as Ijebu or Oyo, and not on a Muslim-Christian

division, although it is also true that Ijebu Yoruba are more heavily Christian than are Oyo Yoruba.

Among the delegates to the Constituent Assembly who debated the *sharia* issue, Yorubas were the most given to compromising. They took moderate positions: some Yoruba Muslims were against the *sharia* court while some Yoruba Christians were in favor of it.[8] Even during a period of Islamic resurgence in the Middle East and in northern Nigeria, religion did not become the basis for cleavage within Yorubaland.[9]

8. Laitin, "Shari'a Debate."

9. This position is argued with persuasiveness and sophistication in David Laitin, *Hegemony and Culture: The Politics of Religious Change among the Yoruba* (forthcoming). Laitin argues that in Yorubaland religious symbols were constrained while another cultural division, based on membership of different city kingdoms, informed practical life.

Organizing politically as Muslims and aligning with the NPN was not within the calculus of Yorubas.[10]

In the northern part of Nigeria, especially in the far north, most people are Muslim. But in the cities, social interaction and intermarriage between Muslims of different ethnic groups are not all that widespread. Moreover, distinctions exist between brotherhoods. People may be members of the Tijaniyya or Qadiriyya Brotherhoods, for example. There are further distinctions between traditional and reformed movements among the brotherhoods. Individual emirs have had strong links to Muslim brotherhoods and brotherhood movements. For example, the Kano emirate became the base for the extension of the Reformed Tijaniyya movement, whereas the Sokoto emirate has been tied to the Qadiriyyas.[11] Membership in different brotherhood movements is not always the basis for conflict, although membership in the Tijaniyya has been associated sometimes with political party affiliations to the Northern Elements' Progressive Union in the First Republic and to the People's Redemption Party (PRP) in the Second Republic. Members of the Mahdiyya have had limited strength in the post-independence period,[12] although this movement may be growing around Kano.

The northern areas of Nigeria, which were relatively quiescent politically in the mid-twentieth century after British rule had been consolidated, have been politically the most roiled in recent years. Some observers of Nigeria have argued that class divisions are emerging rapidly in the north both in the cities and in rural areas and that historical splits between commoners and officeholders have exacerbated divisions based on new economic formations. The role of religion in this situation has different facets and effects. For example, Islam served as a nationalist ideology for northern groups who opposed British power, and it continues to serve as a cohesive element for Nigerians who oppose Western economic and political influence in their country and want to differentiate themselves culturally from the West.

There have been assertions that any Muslim born in the north was born into the community of the Usmaniyya, which emerged as a transbrotherhood religious community in the independence era.[13] Paden notes that this movement was to some extent pushed forward by the northern regional civil service.[14] But since the early independence period, there have been many attempts to assert northern unity on the basis of Islamic membership and on the basis of the relationship between traditional authority and community. As traditional authorities have faced pressures from new elites, they have had recourse to the symbols and content of Islam to bolster themselves. But modern elites, too—civil servants, military men, businessmen—have had recourse to Islam to try to maintain their place at the top of political and economic hierarchies.

10. This is argued in ibid.; and in David Laitin, "Hegemony and Religious Conflict" (Paper delivered at the Annual Meeting of the American Political Science Association, Denver, CO, Aug. 1982), p. 18.

11. An extensive discussion of brotherhoods can be found in John Paden, *Religion and Political Culture in Kano* (Berkeley: University of California Press, 1973).

12. Ibid., p. 179. There are sizable numbers of the Mahdiyya, sometimes called Ahmadiyya, among the Yorubas.

13. Ibid., pp. 179-80. The Usmaniyya saw themselves as heirs to the legacy of the northern leader Usman dab Fodio.

14. Ibid., p. 180.

Egalitarianism

It would be misleading, however, to see Islam merely as a religion of status and hierarchy in northern Nigeria. We can find highly egalitarian strands in Islam as we can in Christianity. Depending on the social and historical milieus in which we look at the propagation and organization of these religions, we can find the religions acting as vehicles for egalitarian demands or as justifications for the status quo.

Laitin argues that Muslims have a rigid sense of social equality and that this ideal is not just a doctrinal matter but observable in behavior. All members of the mosque have a moral responsibility to enforce community standards.[15] As many have pointed out, Islam demands of the rich that they give *zakat,* or "alms," to the poor. It also requires that inheritance be spread among heirs. This said, we should not overstate the link between Islam and equity. There are many varieties of land tenure and inheritance patterns among Muslims in Nigeria.

In the west, Yorubas—Christian as well as Muslim—are hardly bent on income redistribution or on abolishing status and the hierarchy of traditional authorities. The Yoruba-based Unity Party of Nigeria campaigned in the 1979 and 1983 elections on a populist platform that stressed the delivery of services. It did not campaign for redistribution of income.

In the north, Islam cuts different ways with regard to equality. True, Muslim northern Nigeria is the most hierarchical part of the country. This is expressed in terms of relations between the sexes. Fewer women attend school in the Islamic north than in the south, despite Nigeria's commitment to universal primary education. Women are channeled into a narrower range of occupations. Religion provides a rationale for the existing social order while providing an institutional framework through which women fulfill the economic and social roles assigned to them.[16]

The gulf between commoners and royalty seems large in the northern emirates, and Islam is used to justify status inequalities in both the political and economic realms. Class-based deprivation and criteria for leadership are likely to be mediated through an Islamic ideology, "less because of a deep religiosity, but more because, for uneducated workers, it is the only known and accepted standard of legitimacy."[17]

We must be careful, however, not to see Islam simply as a component of an ideology that justifies inequality, for Islam in the north has acted powerfully as an integrative mechanism through which demands for equality are made. A common language and set of symbols links managers and owners to workers. Workers in Kano see themselves as Hausa and as Muslims, like the owners of the industries in which they work or the managers with whom they have contact. When economically squeezed, they see a violation of Islamic norms and a repudiation of ethnic brotherhood. These intensify ill feelings if redress is not

15. David Laitin, "Conversion and Political Change: A Study of (Anglican) Christianity and Islam among the Yorubas of the Ile-Ife" (Paper delivered at the Annual Meeting of the American Political Science Association, Washington, DC, 28-31 Aug. 1980).

16. Dorothy Remy, "Underdevelopment and the Experience of Women: A Nigerian Case Study," in *Nigeria: Economy and Society*, ed. Gavin Williams (London: Collings, 1976), p. 24.

17. Lubeck, "Unions, Workers and Consciousness," p. 169.

made. Islam has provided a language and values through which to express egalitarian demands. But more than this, participation in Islamic institutions in the north has enhanced workers' self-esteem. Workers who have been to Koranic schools and are members of Islamic groups make more economic and political demands.[18]

Furthermore, the most radical demands in periods of electoral politics by substantial organized parties were those made by a splinter faction of the PRP that controlled the governorships of two Muslim states, Kano and Kaduna, between 1979 and 1983. Before the PRP split in 1979, it was led by Aminu Kano, a Muslim *mallam,* who earlier had been the leader of the Northern Elements' Progressive Union in the First Republic. The PRP's manifesto called for the state to take command of the economy and was more socialist in orientation than the other parties' platforms, although many PRP ideas remained highly general. When two PRP governors were elected—although in Kaduna State the legislature remained in the hands of the NPN—they embarked on a radical program. They abolished head and cattle taxes and pushed to democratize local government procedures and to reform land-tenure systems. They made common cause with governors from parties other than the NPN and were expelled from their own PRP. Eventually the governor of Kaduna State, Alhaji Balarabe Musa, was impeached by the state assembly in 1981.

The point of retelling these stories is to show that it has been in the Muslim north, especially in Kaduna City and Kano City, the largest urban concentrations in northern Nigeria, that radical and conservative forces have faced each other directly. The expelled PRP governors and their supporters saw both the NPN and the established PRP as oligarchic and reactionary. The governors and their supporters were viewed in turn as dangerous radicals.

Very different economic and social interests and programs are developed in the context of struggle between traditional emirate authority and secular leaders. Different religious and traditional authorities with bases in the states of Kano and Sokoto also contend with each other; and different Muslim movements and sects operate in the fluid political and religious milieu of Nigeria's north. Parts of northern Nigeria continue to be roiled by movements of Islamic sects calling for reform and purification, and by conflict between secular and religious or traditional authorities.

In July 1981, riots broke out in Kano City as the governor of Kano State, Alhaji Abubakar Rimi, sent to the traditional ruler, the emir of Kano, a letter in which he charged the emir with disrespect to the secular authority. The emir's supporters were outraged by the letter. State government offices were sacked and the governor's political advisor was killed.

The armed forces' takeover at the very end of 1983 suspended for a time the direct confrontation between populist forces represented by elements of the trade union movement and splinter wings of the PRP that regrouped in other parties for the 1983 election. These populist forces had challenged traditional authorities through electoral and trade union politics, with all the contenders trying to use Islam to legitimate their demands and struggles.

---

18. This is argued in a forthcoming manuscript by Paul Lubeck, based on his surveys in Kano.

The Yan Tatsine

The military takeover did not end the challenges to local and national authorities posed by the Islamic sect variously called the Yan Tatsine, Maitatsine, or Yan Izala. In December 1980, large-scale rioting in Kano City led to the death of 1000 to 10,000 people as the sect led by Muhammudu Marwa Maitatsine fought pitched battles with Nigerian police and army. Marwa was to have been a leader of the Yan Tatsine sect, whose stated aims are to contend against materialism and privilege and to purify Islamic practice. The sect has been supported by refugees from Chad and Niger, as well as by recent rural migrants to Kano City. The police and army put down the rioting with great violence, and it may have been that the perception of the sect as heretical led to the lack of restraint by the army and police.

Marwa was killed in the 1980 fighting in Kano City. Further outbreaks of violence in which the sect was involved occurred in Maiduguri—in Borno State—and Kaduna City in 1982 and then in Yola, the administrative capital of Gongola State, in early 1984. Explanations abound for the rise of the sect, its violence, and its challenge to the legitimacy of secular and established Islamic authorities. Some observers call attention to the general Islamic revival expressed through a variety of institutional and social movements that, although they are diverse in terms of origins, recruitment, and ideology, share a common commitment to moral and political reforms and express outrage against corruption in state and society.[19]

Michael Watts sees the Yan Tatsine as a movement that attacks the materialism and inequality that accompanied the petroleum boom in Nigeria.[20] Marwa, however, had been preaching against all materialism and modernity well before Nigeria's oil boom. But it is likely that the number of Marwa's recruits was increased by the large dislocations that took place in and around the great cities of the north. Migration to Kano and Kaduna swelled in the 1970s, and inequality intensified. The numbers of displaced and wandering Koranic students (*gardi*) grew, and these wanderers, once accorded status in the society, now were perceived by better-off elements as a threatening *lumpenproletariat*.

It may be that the Yan Tatsine should be thought of as specifically anticapitalist, as some would argue. It may be that the movement is more in the tradition of a protest against all authority. We do not yet know enough about it to tell. It does appear that the social dislocations attendant on inflation and economic change in the north increased the Yan Tatsine's following. It appears also that for this movement, as for earlier Islamic-based protests and political movements, Islamic norms and culture do provide mechanisms and values for the popular classes assessing society, wealth, government performance, and legitimacy. Thus Watts argues, "Islamic populism . . . generates enormous possibilities for resisting cooptation, particularly where the state, as in Nigeria, is seen to be only

---

19. See Michael Watts, "State, Oil and Accumulation: From Boom to Crisis," *Environment and Planning: Society and Space,* 2:20 (1984). I am grateful to Professor Watts for sending me this essay in advance of publication. See also Michael Watts and Paul Lubeck, "The Oil Boom and the Popular Classes," in *The Political Economy of Nigeria,* ed. I. W. Zartman (New York: Praeger, 1984), pp. 105-45.

20. Ibid., p. 22.

partially legitimate in relation to the Muslim community as a whole."[21]

CONCLUSION

Nigeria does not have a religion to which the overwhelming majority of its citizens adhere. Muslims may be a majority, but if so they are barely that. Islam has functioned in cultural and political terms to create unity in northern Nigeria. Indeed, as Nigeria moved to a 12-state system in 1967 from one of four regions and then to a federal republic with 19 states in 1976, it became necessary to stress Islamic unity in the 10 northern states where two-thirds of the population was Muslim. In order to maintain the dominance of the north in national politics, Islam had to provide the glue that had disappeared with the demise of the old Native Administration, the regional bureaucracy, and the party that had ruled the north in the First Republic—the Northern Peoples' Congress.[22]

When the military left power in 1979, the NPN tried to appeal beyond the north. Under constitutional provisions, in order to elect a president, it had to win at least a quarter of the votes in two-thirds of the states.[23] The NPN could not campaign as a Muslim party and it had lost the administrative grid that had supported the old ruling Northern Peoples' Congress. But it retained the support of Islamic elites in the north and it also had the support of many high-ranking officers, some but not all of whom were Muslims.[24] The NPN was seen as a Muslim party in the north. With the chairman of the NPN coming from the west, the president of the republic from the north, the vice president from the east—an alignment sustained in the second election of 1983—NPN's commitment to zone party leaders would have been under pressure if the civilian regime had continued and the posts had to be rotated by place of origin in 1988.

At the same time, as it became necessary to stress Islam in order to maintain northern unity that was under pressure from the creation of more states, Islam itself often worked to intensify fissures opened up by social and economic changes. Appeals for social justice were made in Islamic terms. Thus, as reform and purification movements continued to proliferate, Islam as a religion and a set of cultural symbols was not solely a force for unity in the northern states. It was interpreted variably by different social groups. Elites tried to maintain their dominance by manipulating modern and traditional institutions in the name of Islam while businessmen built mosques and workers made demands through Islamic terminology. At the same time, Muhammadu Marwa appealed to fringe groups to follow him to an Islamic revival.[25] Furthermore, the

21. Ibid., p. 23.

22. Dudley, *Introduction to Nigerian Government and Politics*, p. 163.

23. In fact, Shehu Shagari did not win quite 25 percent of the vote in 12 states but in a series of contested court actions he was declared president in the 1979 elections by virtue of having won 20 percent of the vote in the twelfth state.

24. The Buhari regime, which came in at the end of 1983, actually has had the most Muslims among its leadership of all the five military regimes since 1966—the other four being Ironsi's, Gowon's, Mohammed's, Obasanjo's. Ironsi and Gowon were Christians, as was Obasanjo. Not only is Buhari a Muslim but high-ranking Yoruba officers in the government, including the regime's second highest, and other officers are largely Muslims.

25. I am indebted to Paul Lubeck for this formulation of Islam's appeals, but he is not responsible for my use of his formulation, of course.

place of Islam in Nigeria continued to be contentious, as was made only too clear in the debate on the judiciary in the late 1970s.

I have focused much more on the impact of Islam than of Christianity on political legitimacy and the role of the state in Nigeria because Islam has been, in the north, an unofficial state religion. Moreover, the struggle to define the relationship of religion to the state has been a struggle around the role of Islamic law in Nigeria. The overt manipulation of religious symbols both to justify the rule of elites and to challenge that rule has been a manipulation of Islamic values and symbols more than Christian ones.

There is reason to believe, however, that some Christian sects provide for their followers a measure of autonomy from established authority, both religious and secular. The development of Aladura Christianity—the praying churches such as the Christ Apostolic Church and the Cherubim and Seraphim in Yorubaland—seems to go hand in glove with the development of values and attitudes of industriousness and business. That is, the adherents of the Aladura churches do not appear as economic radicals, although they may insist on a measure of political independence from established authorities.[26] So far, though, the impact of Christianity in Nigeria has been less directly consequential for the struggle for political legitimacy and control of authoritative roles at central and state levels than has been the impact of Islam.

Nigeria has not evolved political formulas that explicitly allow religion or religious authorities to define legitimacy. But there have been struggles carried out in religious terms over constitutional mechanisms for adjudicating conflict. Religion has been an element in the conflict between ethnic-language groups. And religion provides a language, a set of values, and institutions through which groups struggle and over which groups contend, both within and between religious communities.

26. For a major study of the adoption of Aladura Christianity, see J.D.Y. Peel, *Aladura: A Religious Movement among the Yoruba* (London: Oxford University Press, 1968). Peel is concerned to explain the fundamental character of a religion of industrialization in the Yoruba context as a new morality of obeying rules. Ibid., p. 299.

Religion and State in Libya:
The Politics of Identity

By LISA ANDERSON

ABSTRACT: Striking as the role of religion has been in the modern political history of Libya, it illustrates ambiguities in political identity that are, in fact, common throughout the Muslim Arab world. The tensions between the concepts of political legitimacy bequeathed by the historical Islamic empires and Western-inspired notions of ethnic nationalism and state patriotism have created dilemmas for rulers and the ruled in the Muslim Arab world since the beginning of the twentieth century. The Libyan governments' reliance on Islamic formulas to inspire political loyalty reflects the weakness of both Arab and Libyan nationalist traditions in the country. Qadhdhafi's revolutionary ideology constitutes an effort to transcend the dilemmas of Libyan national identity, but it has not proved persuasive to most of his compatriots.

Lisa Anderson, who received her Ph.D. from Columbia University, is assistant professor of government and director of the Moroccan Studies Program at the Center for Middle Eastern Studies at Harvard University. She is author of the forthcoming State and Social Transformation in Tunisia and Libya, 1830-1980.

THE role of religion in modern politics in Libya is unusual among the countries of the Muslim Arab world. Unlike the rest of the Arab successor states of the Ottoman Empire, whose twentieth-century monarchs and military leaders have usually professed various shades of secular nationalism, Libya has been ruled since independence by governments attached to an often idiosyncratic but nonetheless explicit interpretation of Islamic imperatives.[1] The individual tapestry of Libyan politics and history is woven of threads common throughout the region, however, and the Libyan case provides both an illustration and, in its individuality, a counterpoint to the dilemmas of identity and loyalty that confront leaders and peoples throughout the Arab world. The historical legacies of the Islamic empires and of the modern encounter with European imperialism provide the context for appreciation of the questions raised today about the role of the state and of religion in requiring and providing legitimacy in Muslim Arab society. A brief examination of the modern experience of Islamic and European rule in the Arab world thus serves as appropriate background for exploration of Libya's specific experience of the roles of religion and statehood in shaping political identity.

RELIGION AND THE STATE
IN THE OTTOMAN AND
EUROPEAN EMPIRES

Until the nineteenth century, the rationale of the state in the Middle East was its role in the administration of the affairs of the Islamic community of the faithful. The demands made upon the people by their rulers were provided with religious sanction, if they did not originate in religious imperatives directly. Thus, for example, tax obligations were defined by religion. Muslims—members of the community—paid taxes understood to constitute religious obligations, such as *zakat*, "alms," while non-Muslims were subject to special levies reflecting their nonadherence to the community of the faithful. Similarly, military service was cast as a religious duty, as participation in a holy struggle, or *jihad*, and non-Muslims were ordinarily exempted from military conscription.

Naturally, the complexity and extension of the bureaucracies of the Islamic empires, particularly that of the Ottomans, fostered practices and institutions that were a far cry from those of the Prophet's original community of the faithful. Customary law and practice often served as the rule when the law based on the Koran and the Prophet's traditions provided no precedent, and secular institutions bulked large in the imperial administrations. Nonetheless, the ruler of the Ottoman Empire resolved what tensions existed between the secular and religious realms by combining in his person the office of the secular power, the sultan, with that of the leader of the community of the faithful, the caliph. Until the nineteenth century, the question of whether any given policy or practice had its origins in Islamic law or in local custom was of little practical import except to those reformists who decried the government's falling away from the path of righteousness; the community's essential definition as a religious one was unchallenged.

---

1. The other major exception, Saudi Arabia, did not have strong ties with the Ottoman Empire. See James P. Piscatori, "Ideological Politics in Sa'udi Arabia," in *Islamic in the Political Process,* ed. James P. Piscatori (Cambridge: Cambridge University Press, 1983), pp. 56-72.

The coming of Europeans in the age of imperialism brought new notions of political identity and loyalty. Flush with the excitement of the American and French Revolutions and their challenge to kings who had ruled by divine right, with new notions of the rights of citizens and the emancipation of religious minorities, and with new nationalisms based on common language and culture, the Europeans disdained religious community as the principal rationale for political legitimacy or political loyalty. The apparent decay of the Ottoman Empire and its Muslim counterparts in India, Persia, and northern Africa in the face of Europe's vitality led to painful soul-searching among many in the intelligentsia of the Middle East. Europe's overwhelming political and economic power lent these new secular political philosophies a credence they had never before had; and so, during the nineteenth century, European political forms were adopted and adapted throughout the Middle East and North Africa. Standing armies were created, novel taxes imposed to pay for them, and new justifications borrowed to provide the rationale for innovation. By the middle decades of the century, written constitutions were promulgated in the Ottoman Empire and in several of its autonomous provinces, such as Tunisia, and secular legal tribunals were introduced in Egypt, Tunisia, and elsewhere in the Ottoman realms.

Many of these reforms were heartily resisted by rulers and subjects alike, who viewed them as unnecessary and foolish concessions to precisely those secular values that endangered Islam and Islamic faith, and the constitutional period in both Tunisia and the Ottoman Empire was brief indeed. The ideological contest that these innovations symbolized, however, was not so easily won, and the political ferment that marked the last days of the Ottoman Empire and the era of direct European rule between the world wars reverberates still.

Among the first rationales for political innovation in the Ottoman Empire had been the defense and reform of what was newly defined as an imperial or dynastic state.[2] The populations of the empire were no longer simply members of the community of the faithful but subjects of the sultan, or perhaps even citizens of the Ottoman Empire. While this perspective provided a justification for the abolition of legal discrimination between Muslims and non-Muslims, much decried by the Europeans of the day, it was a notion of identity that was patently ridiculous to the average Muslim subject of the empire, whose loyalty to the sultan reflected the ruler's religious role as caliph rather than his secular powers, and who saw emancipation of non-Muslims as the very denial of the prophecy of Muhammad. Moreover, and more important in the short run, this notion of legitimacy gave primacy to a political system—that of the Ottoman sick man of Europe—which was obviously failing.

The triumph of the Ottoman loyalists was to be short-lived, and by the turn of the century the sultan and his advisors were advocating instead a politicized pan-Islamic rationale for fealty to the empire. The Ottoman state was por-

2. On the ideological developments of the nineteenth and early twentieth centuries, see C. Ernest Dawn, *From Ottomanism to Arabism: Essays on the Origins of Arab Nationalism* (Urbana: University of Illinois Press, 1973); Bernard Lewis, *The Emergence of Modern Turkey* (London: Oxford University Press, 1961); Albert Hourani, *The Emergence of the Modern Middle East* (Berkeley: University of California Press, 1981).

trayed as the last best hope for the defense of the community of the faithful against Christian Europe's encroachment. This was a much more plausible rationale for political action at the popular level, and it permitted and even encouraged continued economic and social reform. Perhaps unfortunately for its longevity, however, it did not address the political question of popular participation posed by the democratic movements in Europe, and it soon came to be synonymous with the alleged despotism of the sultan.

Those who advocated political reform rather than simply defensive modernization turned to yet another notion of political identity: cultural or linguistic nationalism. Such ideas were, of course, well known at the time in Europe, and cultural revival had been advocated in early literacy movements among both Turkish and Arabic speakers in the Ottoman Empire well before the turn of the century. The political expression of nationalism based on ethnicity moved to the center of the Middle Eastern stage with the Young Turk Revolution of 1908.

The Turkish-speaking leaders of the Revolution of 1908 associated the revival of the empire and of the Muslim community with what proved to be ethnic Turkish hegemony. They advocated, and during their brief reign imposed, educational and administrative policies that required the use of the Turkish language. These were understandably unpopular in what had always been a polyglot empire, particularly since Islam had always reserved a special place for the language of the Koran and the Prophet, Arabic. The new rulers' Turkification policies prompted a reaction among the Arab intelligentsia and contributed to the political awakening of Arab nationalism.[3]

During World War I, the European combatants, notably the British, fostered the development of Arab nationalism in hopes of sparking revolts against the Ottoman rulers that would aid in the defeat of the empire. In this the Europeans were successful, as the Arab Revolt of 1916 demonstrated; but with the demise of the empire at the close of the war, the Europeans abandoned their erstwhile nationalist allies to carve the former Ottoman territories of the Arab world into European-ruled mandates and protectorates.

During the interwar period, the nationalists of the region faced European interlocutors who would not recognize political demands based on religious or ethnic identities that extended beyond the boundaries they had drawn within the formerly Ottoman lands. Moreover, the histories of each of the successor states diverged, and Egyptians, Syrians, Palestinians, Iraqis, and Lebanese each had distinctive experiences of European rule. Thus regional identities developed political significance and created the context for local nationalisms.

By World War II, numerous definitions of political identity and loyalty competed for primacy in the Middle East and no single formula for legitimacy had triumphed. "Nationalist" had

3. For two particularly interesting case studies of the role of the Young Turk Revolution in contributing to the political awakening of Arab nationalism, see Philip Khoury, *Urban Notables and Arab Nationalism: The Politics of Damascus, 1880-1920* (Cambridge: Cambridge University Press, 1983); Muhammad Y. Muslih, "Urban Notables, Ottomanism, Arabism, and the Rise of Palestinian Nationalism, 1864-1920" (Ph.D. diss., Columbia University, 1984).

come to be a term of elegant ambiguity, denoting opposition to European rule and connoting loyalties as various as the Muslim community of the faithful, the Arab cultural world, and the local state. While the nationalists were contesting European rule, these ambiguous connotations mattered little, but as the countries of the Middle East reached independence, the bases on which governments would claim legitimacy became a major preoccupation.

In the immediate postindependence period, Arab nationalism appeared to have won the hearts of many of the rulers of the region. The inter-Arab contests of the 1950s and 1960s were cast in its idiom, and the unification of the Arab world was the standard by which political figures like Egypt's Gamal Abdel Nasser measured political success and defeat. Nasser's own failure to achieve the goal he had set for himself, however, led eventually to a reassessment of the goal itself. The unresolved dilemmas of identity and loyalty revived in the 1970s with the reappearance of local nationalisms, like that of Nasser's successor in Egypt, Anwar el-Sadat, for whom Egypt itself was the focus of political loyalty. What might now be called Muslim nationalism also reappeared among, for example, the Egyptians responsible for Sadat's demise after he was seen to have sacrificed the cause of Muslim righteousness and solidarity to Egyptian localism.[4]

Thus, the Islamic and European empires in the Middle East left among their legacies a still unresolved contest among three principal sources of political identity and political loyalty: Islam, Arabism, and the local state. Each government of the countries of the Arab world drew upon these loyalties in different combinations and proportions; Libya's experience, however singular, suggests some of the historical factors that have influenced how the choices among the available sources of political legitimacy have been made.

HISTORICAL LEGACIES:
THE LIBYAN EXPERIENCE

For Libya, the identity provided by Islam has been inestimably more important than it has been for the Ottoman successor states of the Arab East, whereas the traditions of both Arab and Libyan nationalism have been considerably weaker. This reflects the special character and timing of the modern Libyan encounter with Europe.[5]

At the turn of the twentieth century, Libya was in the midst of a period of relative prosperity. The nineteenth-century Ottoman reforms had contributed to social and economic development in the province, but unlike its counterparts in the Arab East, Libya had not experienced significant direct European influence and few of the intellectuals in the province sympathized with Western pretensions to political and cultural superiority. Moreover, since there was no counterpart to the Christian community of the Arab East, there was little of the local impetus to development of secular nationalist ideologies that characterized the early appearance of Arab

<hr>

4. On the Arab nationalism of the 1950s and 1960s, see Malcolm Kerr, *The Arab Cold War: Gamal 'Abd al-Nasir and His Rivals, 1958-1970* (Oxford: Oxford University Press, 1971); on Sadat, see his own aptly titled *In Search of Identity: An Autobiography* (New York: Harper & Row, 1978).

5. Modern Libyan history is accessibly treated in John Wright, *Libya: A Modern History* (Baltimore, MD: Johns Hopkins University Press, 1982).

nationalism in Egypt and the Levant. The Young Turk Revolution of 1908 nonetheless precipitated the same upheaval in Libya as it did throughout the Arab lands of the Ottoman Empire, as administrators were turned out of office in favor of sympathizers with the Young Turk goals.

The disaffection from the new leaders of the empire that marked the reaction of the Arab elites elsewhere was suspended in Libya, however, by the Italian invasion of the province in 1911. The Young Turk rulers responded to the simultaneous Italian declaration of war on the empire by sending military reinforcements to Libya—including the officer Mustafa Kemal, who would later be better known as Atatürk, the founder of the Turkish Republic—to organize resistance against the invasion. This experience of Ottoman support against the European invader—support that would become informal but no less real after the Ottoman-Italian peace treaty of 1912—reinforced the popular attachment to pan-Islamic sentiments that was elsewhere eroded by the disputes between Turkish and Arab nationalists.

By the middle of World War I, when it became clear that the Ottoman Empire could no longer provide a genuine alternative to the Italian regime in Libya, the Libyan elite attempted to establish local governments. These constituted the only genuine attempts to forge national sentiment on a local level before independence after World War II, and both the efforts themselves and their ultimate failure illustrated the ambiguities of local Libyan nationalism.

In the eastern part of the country, known as Cyrenaica, a religious brotherhood or order, the Sanusiyyah, began styling itself a government. The order, which was founded in Cyrenaica in the mid nineteenth century, had cooperated with the forward Ottoman policy in Africa and it both reflected and fostered the pan-Islamic sentiments with which the Ottomans had attempted to rally support. No less dismayed by the Young Turks than their Arab compatriots elsewhere, the Sanusi leaders had nonetheless welcomed Young Turk support in defense of the province against the Italians.[6] After World War I broke out, the imperial military officers in Libya persuaded the Sanusi leadership to launch an attack on British positions in Egypt, hoping to spark a revolt that would weaken the British war effort. This reverse Arab revolt eventually failed, but what was most striking was that this had been not an Arab revolt per se, but an Islamic one: at precisely the same time that the British capitalized on Arab resentment of Turkish rule in the Arab East, the Ottomans persuaded a Muslim religious brotherhood to cooperate against the Christian occupiers of Egypt. Once again, Libyans experienced anti-imperialism as a Muslim, not an Arab or local, cause.

The only secular effort to create a local government came in western Libya, or Tripolitania, where a group of former Ottoman officials and local notables established the first formally republican government in the Arab world, the Tripoli Republic, in 1918.[7] Although the Italians, in straitened circumstances after the war, briefly negotiated with the republic's leadership in hopes of winning with words what they were too

6. See E. E. Evans-Pritchard, *The Sanusi of Cyrenaica* (Oxford: Oxford University Press, 1949).

7. Lisa Anderson, "The Tripoli Republic, 1918-1922," in *Social and Economic Development of Libya,* ed. E.G.H. Joffe and K. S. MacLachlan (London: MENAS Press, 1982).

exhausted to win by arms, they did not seriously entertain the claims of independence forwarded by the republic's promoters. Among the guiding lights of the Tripoli Republic was Azzam Pasha, an Egyptian who would later become the first secretary-general of the Arab League. He probably constituted one of the very few genuine pan-Arab nationalists in Libya at the time, but the failure of the Tripoli Republic to win concessions from the Italians led eventually to the republic's collapse and Azzam Pasha's return to Egypt. This experience not only weakened fidelity to the cause of pan-Arab nationalism in Libya but undermined national Libyan identity by contributing to the divergent paths of Tripolitania and Cyrenaica in the resistance.

In 1922, and as the Fascists consolidated their power at home, the Italians began what they would call their *riconquista* of Libya. In the decade-long and exceptionally devastating military campaigns by which the Italians pacified their colony, over half the entire population and virtually all the educated elite of the province died or fled into exile. During the interwar period, when Egyptian, Tunisian, Palestinian, and other local nationalist movements were gathering steam, the Libyans were fighting for their lives, less concerned with their definition of identity than with their survival.

By the end of World War II, Italy had lost its colony in the North African campaigns of the war, and Libya was administered as occupied enemy territory by the British and French. The Italians had done nothing to improve the lot of their Libyan subjects—the country would come to independence in 1951 with a college-educated population said to be between 7 and 14 people—and there was no nationwide elite or admin-istration. The few leaders who returned to Tripolitania and Cyrenaica from exile were more often loyal to their provincial identities than to the notion of a Libyan state.

The Great Powers were unanimous in their estimation that, with a per capita income of $25 a year, Libya was too poor for self-rule. They could not agree on a suitable disposition of the territory, however, and after considerable wrangling, the decision was finally reached to grant Libya independence under the head of the Sanusi order, Idris, as king. Idris, who had become leader of the order after the fruitless attack on British positions during World War I, had fled Cyrenaica in 1922 and spent the interwar years in Cairo, where he enjoyed cordial relations with the British. The British and the United States agreed to provide subventions to the government budget in return for rights to military installations on Libyan territory.

AFTER INDEPENDENCE:
THE AMBIGUITIES
OF IDENTITY

Libya at independence was as much a strategic convenience for the Great Powers as it was a genuine state. Illiteracy approached 90 percent, the country's major export was scrap metal from the debris of the World War II military campaigns, and the government's operating budget was provided by its foreign supporters. There were few competent bureaucrats, and there was no genuine nationwide elite and little to inspire patriotism.

By necessity, government administration was informal.[8] An elaborate

8. On politics under the monarchy, see particularly Majid Khadduri, *Modern Libya: A Study in Political Development* (Baltimore, MD: Johns Hopkins University Press, 1963); Ruth First,

structure had been devised during the years that preceded independence, designed to give the country a unified national government while simultaneously permitting considerable autonomy to the three provinces: Tripolitania, the most populous; Cyrenaica, the home of the Sanusi king; and Fazzan, in the south. The provincial administrations each disposed of larger budgets and staffs than did the national government. Local autonomy both reflected and exacerbated the simple truth of Libyan politics at the time: administrative authority was delegated to locally powerful families. The distinction between the public treasury and the privy purse was ambiguous at the top, as the king's royal household openly and repeatedly intervened in national politics, and was virtually nonexistent at the local level, where locally prominent notables viewed administrative posts as vehicles to further their private interests.

What legitimacy the king enjoyed was based on neither Libyan patriotism nor Arab nationalism. He made no secret of his primary loyalty to Cyrenaica and of his distrust of political ideologies of all sorts, outlawing political parties soon after independence. Domestic politics was a game of family alliances, while foreign policy was a reflection of Great Power interests. Gamal Abdel Nasser, who overthrew the Egyptian monarch the year after Libya became independent, had nothing but contempt for monarchies in general, and monarchies with close ties to Britain and the United States in particular; and his activist stance did nothing to assuage the king's fears of Arab nationalism.

The king's principal source of political legitimacy was religious, a function

of his leadership of the Sanusiyyah. He was widely reputed to be personally pious and his neglect of the day-to-day politics of his realm seemed to suggest, at least to the well-disposed, that he was attending to the less mundane concerns of the community of the faithful. Although the secular legal codes introduced during the Ottoman and Italian periods were retained, and alcohol publicly sold and consumed, the king was nonetheless accepted, if not always enthusiastically, as a Muslim leader of the faithful.

Had Libya remained as poor as it had been at independence, such a political system might have proved adequate. As it was, of course, oil was discovered in 1959, and exports began in earnest in the early 1960s; by 1969, per capita income had risen to $1500 a year. When the country had been poor, the confusion of public funds and private earnings had served to attract people to administrative positions that otherwise would have gone unfilled. As the country became wealthy, the same confusion led to massive corruption that the king and his associates, many of whom were not blameless in the scandals, proved unable to stem.

Thus the era of the monarchy did little to resolve the dilemmas of identity and loyalty that Libya faced at independence. Arab nationalism was made the more attractive to young Libyans by Nasser's genuinely charismatic advocacy and the king's inflexible opposition, but it had no recognized Libyan spokesman and it had had little role in recent Libyan history. Loyalty to the Libyan state itself was hindered by the national government's preferential treatment of Cyrenaica and by the corruption that wracked the administration. Even Islam seemed devalued by the ill-gotten gains

<hr>

Libya: The Elusive Revolution (Baltimore, MD: Penguin Books, 1974).

of the king's entourage and by the favoritism shown the Sanusi religious establishment to the detriment of the orthodox religious leaders, or *ulama*. By the end of the 1960s it was apparent to all that the monarchy was soon to see its last days, and on 1 September 1969, a military coup brought Muammar el-Qadhdhafi to power.[9]

Under the circumstances it is hardly surprising that the new government cast its appeals for support and legitimacy widely. The military conspiracy in which it originated had had little contact with the civilian opposition to the monarchy, and there was, in any event, little agreement among the opponents of the old regime on a positive program for reform. The religious establishment, particularly those who were not affiliated with the Sanusiyyah, had had reason to be dismayed with the widespread corruption, the maintenance of secular legal codes, and the favored treatment of the Sanusiyyah itself. The Arab nationalists had been unhappy with the monarchy's continued close ties with Britain and the United States that, particularly after the coming of oil-related wealth, had become associated with government corruption. Finally, Libyan patriots viewed the monarchy's corruption as detrimental to the political and economic development of the country, and they saw the government's regional bias as damaging to national unity.

The early policies of the new regime were designed to appeal to all these constituencies. For the Arab nationalists, the regime was openly committed from the outset to the goals of nonalignment and anti-imperialism. The British and

Americans were asked to evacuate their military bases, and they did so; Qadhdhafi early made known his admiration of Egypt's Nasser and of Nasser's attachment to the Palestinian cause; and the regime's statements reflected the common Arab nationalist themes of international neutrality and domestic populism. Indeed, Qadhdhafi insisted that it was the military officers' humble origins that gave them knowledge of the needs and desires of the people, and he explicitly rejected the notion that his own origin in a saintly, or *murabit,* tribe said to be descended, like the Sanusi family, from the Prophet, gave him any special right to rule.

If the principal focus of the new regime was an Arab nationalist one, however, the concerns of the other constituencies were not neglected. The regionalism that had characterized the old regime was promptly repudiated, and the various regional backgrounds of the new leaders—Qadhdhafi himself came from the border area between the major provinces—reassured the Libyan nationalists that this would not be a regime devoted to internal provincialisms. Moreover, a concerted, and reasonably successful, campaign to rid the government of corruption and to distribute the oil revenues more equitably also seemed to indicate a commitment to Libyan national development.

These were not unusual stances among the military regimes of the Arab world. What was novel was the new regime's simultaneous appeals to religious sentiment. Although the Sanusi properties were promptly seized, the regime made much of its devotion to Islamic precepts. Religious criminal codes were reinstated; orthodox *ulama* were given positions of prominence in the legal administration; the sale and consumption of alcohol

---

9. On Qadhdhafi's domestic policies, see Wright, *A Modern History*; First, *Elusive Revolution*; Marius K. Deeb and Mary Jane Deeb, *Libya since the Revolution* (New York: Praeger, 1982).

were banned; churches, cathedrals, night-clubs, and cafes were closed; and Qadhdhafi let it be known that although he felt no special calling because of his family's saintly origins, he did draw inspiration from his daily reading of the Koran.

For many, this renewed attachment to Islam seemed to herald the beginning of an Islamic revolution; and until the Iranian revolution, Qadhdhafi held pride of place as the principal ruling spokesman of Islam as a political force. In fact, however, as his subsequent policies were to demonstrate, Qadhdhafi's use of Islamic formulas was as much forced upon him by Libyan history and society as it was a reflection of his political beliefs. On the eve of his seizure of power, Libya had known a relationship between religion and politics so intimate that even the most fervent secularist would have been required to confront it. Moreover, the alternatives—Libyan national identity or pan-Arab loyalty—had historically been so feeble that they were slender reeds on which to hang anything so important as a government's legitimacy.

As he grew more secure in power, Qadhdhafi eventually developed his own, avowedly revolutionary, ideology, which he would call the Third International Theory and publish in the three slim volumes of *The Green Book*. Here he revealed his dissatisfaction and disappointment with all of the prevailing notions of legitimacy and loyalty in the Muslim Arab world. Although he continued to give lip service to Islamic and Arab nationalist causes, as he himself insisted, "the Third International Theory is based on religion and nationalism—any religion and any nationalism." Similarly, he rejected Libyan state patriotism; as he put it, his revolution was grounded in "an international ideology, not a

national movement"; and true to his word, his support of opponents of the world status quo—whom he viewed as supporters of revolutionary causes—ranged far beyond not only the Libyan state but beyond the Arab world and the Islamic community as well.[10]

By the end of his first decade in power, and despite his egalitarian distribution of what grew to be a per capita income of $8000 a year, Qadhdhafi's revolution had profoundly alienated not only many of the leaders of the rest of the Arab world but many of the Libyan patriots, who felt that the government's high spending on foreign involvements was detrimental to Libyan national development. Also unhappy was the Libyan religious establishment, for by that time Qadhdhafi had begun to abandon religious orthodoxy.[11] He argued that the *ulama* were a superfluous and late accretion to true Islam, a religion that was based, or so he said, on the individual's direct and unmediated communication with God. As the *ulama* began to protest his domestic policies, including economic reforms that left them without their traditional sources of income, Qadhdhafi went on the offensive, instructing the masses to "seize the mosques" and decreeing a change in the Muslim calendar. For almost 1400 years the Muslim calendar had been

10. These quotes are from interviews published in *Thus Spoke Colonel Moammar Kazzafi* (Beirut, 1974) and *Time,* 9 Apr. 1979.

11. On the unhappiness of the Libyan nationalists and technocrats, which precipitated a split in the regime and a failed coup attempt in 1975, see Raymond Hinnebusch, "Libya: Personalistic Leadership of a Populist Revolution," in *Political Elites in Arab North Africa,* I. W. Zartman et al. (New York: Longman, 1982); on the disputes with the religious leadership, see Lisa Anderson, "Qaddafi's Islam," in *Voices of Resurgent Islam,* ed. John L. Esposito (Oxford: Oxford University Press, 1983).

dated from the Prophet's emigration from Mecca to Medina; Qadhdhafi argued that it should begin 10 years later, with the Prophet's death. In 1979, official Libyan stationery began carrying dates that were 10 years out of step with orthodox Muslim conventions, and the country's principal religious leader, the grand mufti of Tripoli, whom Qadhdhafi had appointed soon after he came to power, resigned.

Qadhdhafi's rejection of conventional Islam was born in part of his distrust of the tradition of religious leadership exemplified in Libya by the Sanusiyyah. Not only had the Sanusi king been too willing to collaborate with Western powers, but his government had been neither egalitarian nor responsive at home, and Qadhdhafi equated political corruption with moral degeneracy. Nonetheless, because of the domestic weakness of alternative identities—of both Libyan patriotism and Arab nationalism—it was not until he was confident of his own ideological position that he felt free to abandon orthodox Islam as a source of legitimacy. By the time the Third International Theory had been published, he felt free to announce that "the Green Book is the gospel. The new gospel. The gospel of the new era, the era of the masses. . . ."[12]

His terminology was revealing. Despite his unorthodox Islam, Qadhdhafi's politics were still inextricably linked with religion. He wished for his ideology, which might as easily have been described as a philosophy, a manifesto, or a call to arms, the extrapolitical legitimacy conferred by religious referents. In this he reflected the continued dilem-

mas of political loyalty and legitimacy in the Muslim Arab world. Although Qadhdhafi's eclectic combination of religion, nationalism, and populism was very much his own, his desire to find a synthesis of the competing norms of politics that confront the peoples of his country and region was widely shared.

In this respect, however, Qadhdhafi's legacy was likely to be little different from the king's. Although he himself may have been satisfied that his revolution transcended and resolved the dilemmas of religion and nationalism in providing a new revolutionary identity, by the mid-1980s it was clear that many Libyans remained unpersuaded. His revolutionary policies had sown disaffection well beyond the religious establishment, and the growing unhappiness with the regime among Arab nationalists and Libyan patriots alike left the questions of identity and legitimacy in Libya unanswered, for political action coalesced around support of or opposition to the regime itself.[13] Having alienated all the potential constituencies to whom he originally directed his appeal and having come to rely increasingly on simple repression, Qadhdhafi once again postponed resolution of the debates about the bases on which the Libyan government would be held accountable.

Religion and religious sentiment have been unusually significant in modern Libyan politics from the early resistance to European imperialism, through the years of abject poverty and undreamed wealth, to the eras of conservative monarchy and radical revolution. In-

12. Oriana Fallaci, "The Iranians Are Our Brothers: An Interview with Col. Muammar el-Qaddafi of Libya," *New York Times Magazine,* 16 Dec. 1979.

13. The Libyan opposition is articulate in its complaints, but, apart from plans for a transitional democratic government, somewhat vague about its vision of Libya's future. See, for example, the *Newsletter of the National Front for the Salvation of Libya* (London).

deed, the turmoil of the twentieth century in Libya cannot but have contributed to continued attachment to the solace and inspiration of religious devotion. The importance of Islam in Libya also reflects, however, the particular historical experience of the country and the absence of durable representatives of secular political philosophies. Most important, it mirrors in its individual way the larger questions of political identity in the Muslim Arab world, where the *raison d'être* of the state remains unresolved.

Iran's Religious Regime: What Makes It Tick? Will It Ever Run Down?

By WILLIAM O. BEEMAN

ABSTRACT: Clerical aspiration for governance in Iran is not a phenomenon that originated with the revolution of 1978-79. It has roots that go back at least three centuries and are well established in Iranian cultural tradition. The current regime is the only fully functioning theocracy in the world at present. It has managed to stabilize its rule and is likely to persist even after the death of Ayatollah Ruhollah Khomeini, its current leader. Internal decay is likely to be the only source of political change in Iran for the immediate future.

William O. Beeman is associate professor of anthropology at Brown University. He has conducted research in Iran since 1967. He is the author of Language, Power and Strategy in Iran; Language, Culture and Performance in Iran; *and numerous professional and popular articles on Iran. He has served as consultant to the U.S. State Department on Iranian affairs and is associate editor of Pacific News Service.*

SINCE the fall of the shah in 1978-79, Iran's Islamic Republic has proved to be a terrifyingly puzzling phenomenon for most of the rest of the world. Suddenly Tehran seemed filled with turbaned, bearded old men espousing a combination of religious and political philosophy that was strange to Westernized ears.

Almost from the beginning, political commentators predicted that the Islamic Republic could not survive—that it must fall as a result of its own anachronisms and lack of popular support. Nevertheless, as of May 1985, the clerics had managed to survive for over six years, despite crises that would have long since destroyed most European-style governments.

Clearly, then, there is much that the outside world does not understand about Iran's current regime, its historical background, its political philosophy, and its directions for the future. These are things that other governments cannot afford to ignore, for Iran remains as strategically important a nation today as ever it was in the past. It is the quintessential buffer state standing between the Soviet Union and the oil-producing states of the Persian Gulf; separating Europeanized Turkey and the nations of Asia; straddling the principal route for the world's principal energy resource, oil.

The Islamic Republic of Iran is the only modern example of a working theocracy in the world, with the possible technical exception of the Vatican. In this regard it is important to understand why its present government continually insists that the *mullah*s will never step down from power, and why their continued role in political life is seen as essential, even when they seem totally inept at governing their nation successfully.

A HISTORY OF SPIRITUAL LEADERSHIP

Shiite Islam, as opposed to the majority Sunni sect, has been the state religion in Iran since the seventeenth century. Even at the time of its establishment as the official creed, however, the clergy was counseling the population not to obey its secular rulers, who were characterized as impious and anti-Islamic in their conduct.[1] Shiite doctrine differs very little from that of Sunni Islam in most respects. The principal difference lies in determining the succession of the faith's leadership.

For Sunni Muslims, leadership was thought of as proceeding through a line of officials elected by the community of believers following the death of the Prophet Muhammad. Eventually leadership of Sunni Muslims was institutionalized in the caliphate, which passed into the hands of essentially secular rulers. The sultan of the Ottoman Empire was simultaneously caliph of Sunni Muslims until the elimination of the caliphate by Kemal Atatürk, in 1926.

Shiite Muslims adopted a doctrine of succession passing through the direct bloodline of the Prophet through a series of spiritual leaders, called *imam*s. Different readings of lines of blood succession have produced various sects and offshoots of Shiism, including the Alawites of Syria; the Druze of Lebanon, Israel, and Syria; and the Ismailis, whose head, the Aga Khan, rules a large worldwide community.

The largest community of Shiite believers is the Ithna Ashara, or twelver community of believers, so named because there are twelve *imam*s recognized by the community. In this community of

1. Nikki Keddie, *Roots of Revolution: An Interpretive History of Modern Iran* (New Haven, CT: Yale University Press, 1981), p. 18.

believers, three of the *imam*s hold special significance.

The first important *imam* is Ali, cousin and son-in-law of Muhammad; Muhammad had no male heirs. Ali was the only leader to be accepted by both Shiite and Sunni factions in the early days of Islam. Consequently, in the current Iranian political belief, Ali's rule was the most perfect in history. It was a unified rule of all Muslims, sanctioned by the Prophet, combining the functions of temporal and spiritual power in one leader.

The second important *imam* is Ali's second son, Hussein. Hussein's claim to leadership of the faith was challenged by the caliph of Damascus, Yazid. Rather than concede leadership to an illegitimate individual, Hussein chose martyrdom on the plains of Kerbala, near present-day Baghdad. There he and his followers were slaughtered by Yazid's troops in a particularly brutal fashion, having been held without food and water for 10 days.

Imam Hussein's death has been commemorated continually in Iran since at least the ninth century. Every religious occasion is a potential setting for the retelling of the story of his death. He is the prototype for all martyrs and for all those who struggle and sacrifice themselves for the legitimate faith. In this regard, Hussein occupies a place within Shiite religious and political life roughly equivalent to Jesus' in Christianity.[2]

The third of the great *imam*s is the twelfth *imam*, the Mahdi. Twelver Shias believe that the Mahdi went into hiding, or occultation; he is expected to return at the day of judgment. Following his disappearance, there were four interpreters of the will of the Mahdi. When the fourth died, there was no one left alive who had religious infallibility.[3]

The basic premise of governance in the Islamic Republic rests on the principle of restoration of the leadership of the *imam*s in human affairs. The current government is seen as ruling in place of the Mahdi and as continuing to do so until he returns to earth. Ayatollah[4] Ruhollah Khomeini is often called "Imam Khomeini" by the population, but his correct title is *nayyeb ol-imam*, literally "*imam*'s representative" or more colloquially "vice-*imam*." He bears another title: *faqih*, or "chief jurisprudent," indicating his superiority in religious and legal judgment.

The effort to establish a state ruled in principle by the *imam*s or their representatives is a movement with considerable historical background. In the seventeenth century the clerical leaders began to withdraw support from the secular rulers of the Safavid dynasty and urged the population to follow their guidance instead. Gradually the doctrine developed that urged that the Mahdi be considered as the only legitimate representative of God's law. This quickly led to the conclusion that no temporal ruler could have any authority over human beings. The only true authority was that of the Mahdi himself or, failing that, the best representatives that could be found. It was the Ayatollah Khomeini, how-

---

2. Material concerning celebration of Imam Hussein's martyrdom is very extensive. One excellent source is Peter Chelkowski, ed., *Ta'ziyeh: Ritual and Drama in Iran* (New York: New York University Press and Sorush Press, 1979). See also Michael Fischer, *Iran: From Religious Dispute to Revolution* (Cambridge, MA: Harvard University Press, 1980), pp. 10-13 on the "Karbala [*sic*] paradigm."

3. Keddie, *Roots of Revolution*, p. 8.

4. "Ayatollah" is a religious title meaning "image" or "reflection" of God.

ever, who first extended this doctrine to direct rule by the chief *faqih* as the only proper representation of the Mahdi on earth.[5]

This sort of preaching did not make the clergy popular with Iran's rulers, and many religious leaders throughout history were forced to exile themselves to the great Shiite shrine cities near Kerbala. These cities were always governed by Sunni rulers—first the Ottoman sultans, then Iraqi rulers—who were never much threatened by the presence of the Shiite clergy. Thus the Shiite religious leaders could, for fully three centuries, keep up the attack against secular rulers in Iran in comparative safety. They could also continue to press for establishment of a religious state. It may seem to some in the West that concern with *imams* and religious legitimacy is somewhat esoteric and unrelated to bombings, war, and internal executions in Iran today. In fact, Shiite history is fraught with violence, usually stemming from questions of legitimacy in the imamate.

Early Shiite struggles against the more powerful Sunni rulers gave the world the term "assassin." The term comes from *hashish*; the *hashishin* were a group of Shiite raiders who would use hashish to provide them with the courage to carry out their exploits. The martyrdom of Imam Hussein is another violent episode, very much alive in people's minds. The clergy has never shirked from exhorting the population to resist its temporal rulers in political struggle. Several violent clashes with the secular government took place in the twentieth century, the revolution against the shah

being only the most recent and spectacular example.

In a more important sense, however, the question of legitimacy of the government is one of the greatest sources of support for the current regime. Whatever excesses are carried out by the rulers of the Islamic Republic, whatever violence is perpetrated by unforgiving clergymen in mock trials leading to mass executions, still the public is presented with a government that claims to be sanctioned by God.

The population of Iran has been fed the doctrine of the legitimate rule of the Mahdi and his representatives for a long while and in a systematic fashion. Now that the establishment of Islamic rule has actually come to pass, the population has been extremely uncomfortable in opposing it. To move to eliminate Ayatollah Khomeini and the Islamic Republic raises the question of whether one might not be warring with God himself. In the case of the shah, no such question had to be asked. Because he was a temporal ruler, Mohammad Reza Shah Pahlavi was automatically illegitimate in the eyes of religious authority. The population had only to be convinced that he was corrupt as well and that he could be overthrown in order for their support to be enlisted in the revolution.[6]

THE MATERIALISTIC CLERGY

There is another face to the Iranian clergy, however, one that helps to explain why resistance to its rule has continued support even in the face of its superior

5. Cf. Hamid Algar, "The Oppositional Role of the Ulema in Twentieth Century Iran," in *Scholars, Saints and Sufis*, ed. Nikki Keddie (Berkeley: University of California Press, 1972).

6. Cf. William Beeman, "Images of the Great Satan: Symbolic Conceptions of the United States in the Iranian Revolution," in *Religion and Politics in Iran,* ed. Nikki Keddie (New Haven, CT: Yale University Press, 1983).

claims to legitimacy in establishing the Islamic Republic.

Before the advent, in 1926, of the Pahlavi regime with Reza Shah, father of the recently deposed shah, the clergy as a body enjoyed enormous wealth and power within Iran itself. Many clerics were wealthy landholders in their own right. Additionally, the clergy was charged with the administration of religious bequests, much of which was in the form of property. Other moneys in the form of charitable giving and tithing, considered to be cardinal religious duties in Islam, were paid directly to the clergy for distribution to worthy institutions.

This enormous access to capital made it possible for some of the clergy to build virtual empires of their own. They were also able to command what amounted to private armies, made up particularly of religious students, who could cause disturbances and terrorize the government, especially if they were joined by urban crowds. More important, before 1926 the entire court system—as well as the educational system—was in the hands of the clergy. When added to the control exercised over the economic system through the control of bequests, tithing, and charitable giving, it can be seen that the clergy was an extremely powerful force in every way.

Reza Shah realized that if he were to consolidate his rule, he would have to break the back of the clergy, and he worked steadily at this task. He built up the secular Iranian army as a source of military control from the throne independent of other sectors in society. With that military force to back him up, he then proceeded to secularize the courts and the schools, building large new secular universities as a counter to theological schools. Eventually, under his son, the religious bequests were taken out of clerical hands for administration by the state. Finally, the large landholdings of some clergy were eliminated during land reform in 1963. Land reform hit clergymen particularly hard. Other large landowners could take their capital and establish industrial and business concerns. Members of the clergy would have to give up their profession to take advantage of the new industrial climate in the land. Absentee landholding was ideal for them, because it provided an income with little work on their part. Capital investment required real commitments of time and labor, which were not compatible with a full-time religious life.

Therefore, at least one aspect of the present Islamic regime in Iran involves a feeling on the part of the clergy that its takeover of power amounts to the legitimate regaining of right and privilege that had been illegitimately seized from its hands during the Pahlavi era. In reestablishing what they consider to be their proper place in society the clerics may have overreacted. Tales of clergymen who were somewhat poor before the revolution now living in luxurious houses and driving Mercedes Benz automobiles are told everywhere in Iran. Because almost nothing can be accomplished without the permission of a cleric, the possibilities for bribery are enormous. Not surprisingly, many young men who might have thought of engineering or medicine as a profession have now decided that theology is not such a bad line of work after all, and they have filled the theological schools in droves. This new educational movement has been aided by the fact that the nation's secular universities were closed for two years following the revolution. Another route for joining the clerical establishment is in attaching oneself to the new religious army, the Islamic Guard. This organization was clearly conceived as an alternative to the secular army of the Pahlavis. Indeed, if the war with Iraq had not continued to rage, the regular army might long since have been totally eliminated.

OPPOSITION TO THE CLERGY

It is this materialistic and overtly political aspect of the role of the clergy in Iranian life that has provided the strongest basis for opposition to them. The average person in Iran has long noted the tendency for dishonesty and hypocrisy to slip into the day-to-day practice of clergymen. The rural comic theater and puppet drama are full of stories structured around dishonest clerics.

Such humorous characterizations are probably unfair reflections of the actual practice of most members of the clergy, but the popular stereotype of the greedy, flea-ridden *mullah* still remains alive in the minds of many individuals. In the past, the influence of these men at the village level was doubly pernicious, for not only did they speak with legal authority, but also with the authority of God. From such judgment there was no appeal, for who would appeal the word of God? Parenthetically, postrevolutionary legal practice has tended to follow this line. In trying antistate elements, Ayatollah Khomeini specifically called for the elimination of any appeal process. A judgment once rendered under proper practice of religious law was to be considered inviolate, for it reflected divine authority.

This history of heavy-handed practice, combined with the enormous influence of the clergy on the thought of the Iranian masses, has led in the twentieth century to overt expressions of anticleri-cism by the newly emerging secular intelligentsia. Important intellectual figures such as literary and language scholar Ali Akbar Dehkhoda denounced the clerics as a body. The most outspoken of these writers was historian Ahmad Kasravi, the principal authority on the constitutional revolution of 1906. Kasravi was assassinated in 1946 by a Muslim activist because of his anticlerical writing, and his books were symbolically burned in public.

Far more serious a challenge to clerical authority has been mounted in recent years by persons working for reform within Islam itself. The most influential of these reformers is the late Ali Shariati, who died under mysterious circumstances in England in 1977. Shariati's writings have inspired a whole generation of young Iranians and are as intellectually forceful today as they were during his lifetime.

Shariati was trained as a sociologist at the Sorbonne in Paris. In his view, Islam is not merely a set of religious doctrines but a total social ideology. His philosophy envisions Shiism as a source for the betterment of all aspects of human life and a source for an all-encompassing revolution of thought, word, and deed—an Islamic protestant-ism with an emphasis on protest. Religion, he believes, should be a process that touches on all areas of knowledge. In this regard, he denounces the clerical establishment for restricting its focus to one narrow activity, the conduct of jurisprudence. By taking refuge in legalisms and judicial acts the clerics are seen by Shariati as neglecting their true duty as Islamic leaders to enlighten the public and lead it to a greater sense of its social responsibility in terms of Islam. Instead, they merely snare the people in an encircling web of legalisms and prohibitions.

Thus, he points out, under the traditional clergy, Islamic philosophy, which should serve to free a person's mind for meaningful humanitarian action, becomes reduced to a sterile code of rules applied in an automatic fashion.

Shariati's writings seem at times somewhat lightweight and oratorial. Nevertheless, their impact on young men and women has been tremendous. Indeed, Shariati has been described as the principal theoretician of the revolution of 1978-79. Significantly, Ayatollah Khomeini has never once acknowledged Shariati or his writings, despite their obvious importance in inspiring young revolutionaries.[7]

Shariati's influence is not limited exclusively to the young. Many of his principal ideas have been supported wholeheartedly by respected members of the clerical establishment itself. Not surprisingly, these clerics now stand in severe opposition to the present government of the Islamic Republic. Ayatollah Sayyid Mahmud Taleghani, a progressive theologian teaching at the University of Tehran, espoused Shariati's view of the need for Shiite Islam to provide the basis for revolutionary change. Indeed, this was the basis on which Taleghani himself supported the revolution to overthrow the shah. Nevertheless, Taleghani quickly became disenchanted with the leadership of Ayatollah Khomeini. When Khomeini moved to establish a new constitution of the Islamic Republic—a constitution that formalized the direct rule of the *faqih*, Taleghani turned in full revolt, publicly denouncing Khomeini's position. He was placed under virtual house arrest,

his family was molested, and he died a few months later, in 1979, under highly suspicious circumstances. Later his religious writings were banned by the Islamic courts.

A similar fate befell Ayatollah Sayyid Kazem Shariat-Madari. Ayatollah Shariat-Madari was acknowledged to be the chief clerical leader of the revolution residing within Iran during the events leading to the fall of the shah. His support was strongest among the Turkish population of Azerbaijan, which makes up perhaps 30 percent of the total Iranian population. Indeed, during the revolution, when the picture of Ayatollah Khomeini was hung in every store window throughout Iran, in Azerbaijan it was Shariat-Madari's picture that was seen. Shariat-Madari, like Taleghani, opposed Khomeini's doctrine of rule by the *faqih*, spoke out against the war being waged against the Kurds, and in general served to embarrass the new regime. He was falsely implicated in a plot to overthrow Ayatollah Khomeini and was stripped of his religious titles. He is at present under house arrest and has been effectively silenced.

Shiite Islam has four other grand ayatollahs besides Khomeini. These are men who by consensus are given the greatest authority to determine the interpretation of Islamic law. All four of these authorities have denounced Khomeini's view of Islamic government privately. One, Ayatollah Rabbani Shirazi, has made strong attacks in European publications. All of these religious figures have been silenced through threats to themselves or their families.

The one group that has not been silenced is the Mujaheddin-e Khalq, the People's Crusaders. This group has been in existence in one form or another for over 20 years, but it gained strength dur-

7. Cf. Mangol Bayat-Philip, "Shi'ism in Contemporary Iranian Politics: The Case of Ali Shari'-ati," in *Iran: Toward Modernity*, ed. Sylvia Haim and Elie Kedourie (London: Frank Cass, 1980).

ing the 1960s when it emerged as a major force confronting the shah's government. The Mujaheddin actually comprise smaller groups with slightly differing philosophies. All have been heavily influenced by the writings of Shariati and are deeply committed to Islam. They have also been influenced by leftist and Marxist philosophies, especially those that support the idea of revolutionary liberation movements. Shariati himself was deeply influenced by the writings of Franz Fanon, and that writer remains an important influence among the Mujaheddin.

There is now excellent evidence to show that the Mujaheddin were the actual effective forces in bringing down the last vestiges of the shah's government. Following the establishment of the Islamic Republic they demanded a role in the new government. Their request was flatly turned down by the leaders then in power, and their war with the clerical establishment began in earnest.

It has been primarily the Mujaheddin that have borne the brunt of the massive executions that have taken place in Iran since the ouster of President Bani-Sadr. Their principal leader, Massoud Rajavi, fled with Bani-Sadr to Paris, where he has been serving as a self-declared prime minister of a government in exile. Despite brave words and assertions that Khomeini's regime is about to fall and give way to a "new Islamic order" in which democracy will prevail, it seems that the efforts of the Mujaheddin and other opposition groups have not been able to succeed in weakening the existing political power structure. Indeed, bombings, assassinations, and other violent acts against the clerics seem to do little more than cement the political structure into an even tighter and more rigid structure than before. As one cleric is eliminated, others quickly move in to fill his place.

Thus it seems that, for the time being, assaults on the political order of the Islamic Republic from without will not be successful in eliminating the regime of Ayatollah Khomeini. The Iraqi assault on Iranian territory, which was designed to topple the Tehran regime, was a miserable failure; the urban guerrilla warfare of the Mujaheddin and other groups has not succeeded either. International censure of the extreme actions of the government have only served to strengthen government claims that it is under seige from corrupt external forces.

INTERNAL DECAY— THE ONLY LIKELY SOURCE FOR CHANGE

The only source for change in the immediate future, then, seems to lie within Iran itself. Several possibilities present themselves. The death of Ayatollah Khomeini, who is now 86 years old, will be an obvious turning point in Iranian affairs. Former Prime Minister Mehdi Bazargan, who was forced to resign because of his inability to control events surrounding the taking of the U.S. hostages in 1979, once warned Khomeini, "The Constitution of the Islamic Republic will not outlive you." This feeling must be shared by many in Iran who hope to replace the Islamic Republic with something more to their own liking upon Khomeini's death. For their part, the clerics are moving to groom Khomeini's handpicked successor, Ayatollah Hosein Ali Montazari, for his job. Ayatollah Montazari may himself be the source for change—because of his weakness and lack of public standing. Most observers acknowledge that he will never be able to fill Khomeini's shoes adequately. This will lead to an almost automatic downgrading of the entire clerical establishment in the eyes of the Iranian public.

Early signs show that other movements are beginning within the ranks of the Islamic Republican Party itself. The newly elected president, Hojatolislam—a title one degree lower than ayatollah—Ali Khameinei, had some difficulty in selecting a prime minister. Ayatollah Mohammed Reza Mahdavi-Kani, the provisional prime minister, had resigned to give the new president a free choice in selecting his new government, but he fully expected to be reappointed. For whatever reason, Khameinei chose his own candidate, Ali-Akbar Velayati, a Western-trained physician. Ayatollah Khomeini refused to endorse Velayati, and as a result he failed to gain parliamentary approval. Subsequently Mir-Hosein Moussavi, the former foreign minister, was selected.

In a copyrighted article for Pacific News Service of San Francisco, Mansur Farhang, the first Iranian ambassador to the United Nations appointed by the Khomeini regime, suggests that wrangling over selection of the prime minister showed the first factional cracks in the organization of the Islamic Republican Party. One faction is led by Khameinei, and another by Parliament Speaker Ayatollah Ali-Akbar Rafsanjani, claims Farhang. It is likely that as outside opposition to the Islamic Republican Party is driven further underground by its somewhat ruthless persecution by Tehran's rulers, the internal factions will make themselves felt to a much greater extent.

The principal danger to the current order, however, comes from another source all together. The clerics have succeeded in establishing themselves in power and defending themselves from usurpers. However, Ali Shariati's critique of the clergy as too narrow and solopsistic in its approach to religion and government is showing itself to be all too true. Iran is suffering mightily on the economic front, and the prognosis for recovery is not good at present.

The clerical attitude toward the economy seems to have been to attend to the implementation of Islamic law, leaving the economy to take care of itself. This may have been a reasonable philosophy in the day of Imam Ali, but in today's world Iran is intimately tied into an international economic network without which it will perish.

From 1974 through 1978 oil was in short supply, and Iranian revolutionary leaders felt that the world would continue to beat a path to Iran's door to buy petroleum products no matter what the internal conditions of the country. Now the world is swimming in oil. In such conditions, no one is interested in Iranian oil products at all, if purchase of them can be avoided. Indeed, Japanese oil contracts with Iran, the most reliable source of oil income for the Islamic Republic, have been renegotiated downward several times.

Internal political conditions in Iran seem so unstable to the outside world that no reasonable business concern wants to commit itself to long-term arrangements. Recently, Massoud Rajavi added an ominous note to this situation, warning international businesses that anyone dealing with the Khomeini regime would undergo sanctions by any government that would replace it in the future. Moreover, Iranians do not seem to be able to present any kind of climate for reasonable international investment at present.

One extended controversy over a

joint Iran-Japanese petrochemical plant being constructed in Bandar Khomeini in southern Iran is a case in point. When the project was 85 percent complete, the giant Mitsui Corporation, a partner in the venture, understandably refused to invest any more capital in an operation that would never provide it any profit. After all, Mitsui reasoned, once the Iranian plant begins operations, to whom will the product be sold? Iranian internal industry is at a complete standstill, so no market will exist within Iran. Moreover, the plant is not likely to be able to produce products of export quality at competitive international prices. In the shah's Iran, where even inefficient industry made money through protectionist tariffs, guaranteed purchase by government-controlled industry, and heavy subsidies, this investment seemed a good thing. Now it is a giant white elephant. The *Japan Times* recently printed a plaintive editorial urging Mitsui to find some way to continue the operation indirectly so as not to sever the last major commercial tie between Iran and Japan; but however inconvenient it may be politically for Japan and Iran, Mitsui's stand is a correct business decision. Either the new rulers of Iran must find some way to guarantee the investment climate of their country, or they must simply contract with outsiders—cash on the line—for construction of the facilities they feel they need.

This raises another question, Where is the cash going to come from? Ali Reza Nobari, head of Iran's Central Bank under former President Bani-Sadr, revealed in 1982 that the nation is virtually bankrupt. The reduced oil exports now only attract enough cash to continue the import of consumer goods and food; the imports are probably essential to avoid massive public protests. Most impor-

tant, the country is not able to get the sophisticated spare parts it needs to rebuild its oil industry. Aid promised from Eastern-bloc nations, such as Rumania, is unlikely to be much help in rebuilding the largely American-made facilities. Moreover, the Iranians are now totally crippled in their ability to borrow funds on the international market. "Their credibility for borrowing from banks is zero, even from the World Bank or the [International Monetary Fund]," claimed Nobari in an interview with Reuters.

These conditions present the clerics in Tehran with a difficult set of dilemmas that political solidarity, executions, and moral posturing will not solve. Declining living conditions may well overcome the religious support of the masses for the current regime, particularly after the death of Khomeini.

The possibility of Communist intervention cannot here be dismissed. As Iran loses access to the West either through lack of foreign exchange or through inability to provide an adequate business climate, the temptation will be greater and greater to turn to Eastern-bloc countries to fill industrial and consumer needs. The Soviet Union and its satellites will likely be willing to let Iran ride along for a few years on credit in hopes of cementing a more permanent relationship in the future, but such a relationship would not be an unmixed blessing for the Soviets. Iran has proved to be just as sticky in dealing with them as with the West—especially concerning Afghanistan. Iran's one big play for international respectability in recent years has been a small initiative in arranging a peace settlement for Afghanistan. Iran's plans were not unreasonable, and were likely workable, but they were rejected out of hand by the Afghan government. This rejection and a purge of the pro-Moscow Tudeh Party in 1982 and 1983 have soured Soviet-Iranian relations for the near future, and any closer dealings by the Soviet bloc with Iran are likely to involve uncomfortable dealings on the Afghanistan issue.

The war with Iraq is both the greatest asset and the greatest liability for Iran's government. This war, which has lasted longer than World War I, maintains the clerics in power while creating growing discontent on the part of families whose children have died in it. War casualties number over 100,000 at present.

The picture that emerges of the Iranian leadership is one of a group of men who are involved in the protection of their own power at almost any cost. To this end they have devoted almost all of their energy to fighting their enemies on the one hand and placating the population—with the Koran and imported food and consumer goods—on the other. To be sure, their mission is felt by many of them to be a sacred one—literally to establish a kingdom of God on earth. But this divine mission has served to blind them to the fact that Iran must learn to live with the world around it—and that the world is not likely to accept Iran on Iran's terms alone.

The Religious Right in the State of Israel

By ARTHUR HERTZBERG

ABSTRACT: The modern Jewish quest for a homeland arose in the nineteenth century in Europe. From the beginning there was tension between a secular nationalism and a more religiously based one. Religious fundamentalism is a political factor today in Israel, as elsewhere in the Middle East. Governments in this region would best avoid their overthrow at the hands of religious fundamentalists by working together.

Arthur Hertzberg is a professor of religion at Dartmouth College. He is also a senior research associate at the Middle East Institute and an adjunct professor of history at Columbia University. He is the author of Zionist Idea, *among other books.*

FOR 18 centuries after the destruction of the Second Temple in Jerusalem in the year A.D. 70, Jews prayed at least three times a day for their restoration to the Holy Land. This hope was part of their theology; it expressed the certainty that God himself would redeem his people from the exile that he had ordained as punishment for their sins. There were several attempts during this time to rebuild at least some Jewish presence in the Holy Land, but it was never imagined that human efforts would effect the redemption. On the contrary, the dominant religious view remained firmly wedded to passivity: any human attempt to restore Jewish sovereignty over the land prematurely—that is, in the absence of divine intervention—was regarded as heretical. It was forbidden to try to force God's hand.

These religious conceptions held firm until the dawn of the modern era, which for Jews began at least a century later than for the other inhabitants of western and central Europe. By the end of the eighteenth century, some Jews were beginning to unlearn the attitude of political passivity, particularly those Jews who were most closely in touch with Western culture and had become impatient for a share in this world. Even before the French Revolution, some advanced Jewish circles in France, England, and Germany were pressing for economic equality and for a role in society. During the French Revolution and for most of the following century, the battle in Europe became one for legal equality. By 1870, legal equality had been won everywhere except in Rumania and in the Russian Empire—but that was where the bulk of European Jews lived. Even in western and central Europe, anti-Semitic movements appeared almost immediately after the achievement of equality in law and, in some cases, before such decrees of emancipation had been passed. The question remained whether the emancipation of Jews as individuals by the modern state was sufficient to solve what was called the Jewish problem. Would legal equality be enough, as anti-Semitism persisted, to move the Jews in Europe from their former status as barely tolerated resident aliens to full participants in all segments of the existing social order?

Revolutionaries of various kinds arose, especially among the socialists, who maintained that true equality for all men, and especially for the Jews, required the building of a new social order.[1] As long as class inequality existed, Jews, as the most striking capitalists—according to Karl Marx—would continue to be disliked and treated as a breed apart. Only a complete social revolution could create the possibility of true equality for everyone, including the Jews.

JEWISH NATIONALISM

During the nineteenth century, a succession of small Jewish nationalist groups proposed another option. The Western world was now organizing itself into nation-states; peoples were increasingly governed by their own kind. Jewish nationalists argued from the very beginning that despite their dispersal in many lands, the Jews had remained one nation; it was, therefore, proper to call upon these dispersed coreligionists to come together in their own land. The Greeks were winning their independence from Turkey and the Italians were uniting to form a nation-state. Jews, it was proposed, should similarly recreate their ancient nation-state.

1. Karl Marx had argued this in 1843 in an early essay, "On the Jewish Question."

As a corollary to this self-definition of the Jews as a nation, a new explanation of anti-Semitism was put forward: Jews were persecuted because they were an anomaly. They alone among the nations were a minority everywhere. "We are guests everywhere and nowhere are we the host," exclaimed Leon Pinsker in a pamphlet entitled *Auto-emancipation*, written in response to the pogroms of 1881 in Russia. Anti-Semitism would disappear if only the Jews would move back to their own country—or at the very least to a territory of their own anywhere in the world, as some nationalists argued, including Theodor Herzl, at the beginning of his career. The Jewish question would be solved forever, because the Jews would have become a nation among the nations.

There were, indeed, some among the earliest Zionists who did imagine nationalist efforts in the here and now to be a preamble to the great redemption that would come through divine grace. They made it their business to establish, contrary to majority opinion, that such efforts were not a denial of God. Without exception they quoted the cabalah, which posited "stirring below" as a way of evoking "stirrings above." The main thrust of modern Zionism was, however, in the opposite direction. Zionism's greatest ideological figures—Moses Hess, Leon Pinsker, Ahad Ha-Am, Theodor Herzl, and Vladimir Jabotinsky—were all postreligious figures. Their followers, the people who actually created the seeds of the modern Jewish settlement in Palestine, were largely motivated by the desire to establish a new Jewish life in modern, secular style.

Yet, a substantial element of religious memory inhered even in these secularists. They insisted on creating a new Jewish life in the land of the Bible, refusing to settle elsewhere. The holy language, Hebrew, was remade into the everyday tongue of a contemporary community, but even at its most secular, modern Hebrew remained rooted in the Bible. Although the Sabbath and the Jewish holidays were not observed according to religious tradition by the majority, these days became days of rest for everyone in Israel's secular calendar.

There was a constant tension between willed secularism and a deep current of religious national mysticism. David Ben-Gurion, the first prime minister of Israel, was an announced agnostic, but he defended the claims of the Jews to the land of their ancestors and reinforced their self-image as a chosen people with the fierceness of a biblical prophet. The chief rabbi of Palestine in the 1920s and 1930s, Abraham Isaac Kook, asserted that the doctrinaire secularists who were building the new Zionist settlement in the Holy Land were unwitting instruments of the messianic redemption that he believed had already begun. The secular Zionists might see themselves as carrying out an important task in the realm of human politics and social engineering—normalizing and secularizing the Jewish people to assure its survival under contemporary conditions. But to Rabbi Kook, the most important religious philosopher and theologian of the first third of the twentieth century, this very enterprise had grandiose religious meanings, far beyond the understanding of the very makers of the new life.

From its earliest beginnings in the 1830s, the main theme of modern Zionism was devising a way for the Jews to enter the modern world, and the countertheme was religion. The earliest religious Zionists were defensive, on two fronts. Looking backward on life in the ghetto, they defended their activism for a new life. Some of them were socialists, without being Marxists. Especially after the appearance of Rabbi Kook, it became an article of faith for religious Zionists that the effort to create a Jewish state was "the first root of our redemption."[2] Nonetheless, the basic mood and outlook even of the religious Zionists until 1967 was sober. Yes, they believed that redemption was on the way, but the struggling state Palestine—which seemed destined to go on struggling for the forseeable future—was hardly to be defined as anything other than a human achievement that answered the needs of this era. One could pray for God's intervention, but the policy of a small and always endangered people could be conducted only with circumspection and absolute avoidance of adventurism.

The turning point came with the Six Day War in 1967. Israel suddenly extended to the Nile and to the river Jordan. The military victories seemed so heroic and unprecedented that even the secularists called them a miracle. There was a brief period immediately after the victory of June 1967 when permanent peace might have been made with the Arabs on the basis of almost total return of the territories. The prime minister, Levi Eshkol, favored this course of action, as did the aging David Ben-Gurion, who virtually shouted its merits from the housetops. There was, unfortunately, no vast groundswell of support; the thought of returning to the earlier borders simply became unthinkable to most Jews, both in Israel and in the Diaspora. The dominant view in Israel was that the Arabs, in their utter defeat, were no threat and that they would, in any case, eventually come and sue for peace.

In the fall of 1967, the Arab states made a declaration that effectively put an end to any serious talk of peace. In Khartoum, they pronounced a famous set of negatives: there would be no peace, no negotiation, and no recognition of the state of Israel. Eshkol died soon thereafter, Ben-Gurion came to be regarded evermore as simply an old man in his angry dotage, and Israel settled down to enjoy the ease and expansiveness that the valor of its arms had won.

In this environment two changes took place in the policy of the Jewish state. Both involved the question of Jewish settlement in the newly occupied territories, but the motivations behind each differed.

The relatively sober and secular Labor Zionist Party, which was to stay in power for the next decade, took the view that some Jewish settlements should indeed be established on the West Bank and on the old border with Egypt. By design, most of the newly won territory was thinly held and served a quasimilitary function. They were designed to make the defense of Israel easier by providing early warning of marauders and invaders and by providing strategic depth. It was quite clear to everyone, including the Arabs, that most if not all of these points were negotiable in some future political settlement, if Israel's security could be guaranteed by alternative means.

Jerusalem was the one area that was not to serve as a security stronghold. East Jerusalem was annexed almost immediately and the boundaries of the city were extended, to secure the inclusion of the Old City into Israel. The new territory was built up and densely settled very rapidly. There was very little oppo-

2. This role of a Jewish state is asserted in the standard prayer for the state of Israel as enjoined by Israel's Chief Rabbinate.

sition to this action in Israel. The memory of the devastation by the Jordanians of all the Jewish shrines in the Old City during the nearly two decades that it was sealed off from Jews was, and remains, too vivid. Whatever political settlement may ultimately be made for the status of Jerusalem, there is no Jewish support at all for ever returning the city to its former occupiers. Here the most coolheaded secularists stand with the most passionate believers in the national myth about the land of Israel's biblical boundaries.

The secular Zionists did not mind, in their growing majority, that some of the settlements established for security reasons on the West Bank tended to change the map of the land by becoming permanent and ever less negotiable. In theory, however, pragmatic concerns dominated their politics; their slogan became, and has remained, the notion that they would trade territories for peace.

RELIGIOUS AND MILITANT

The second major policy change regarding the question of settlements occurred with the appearance in 1967 of a much more revolutionary, dynamic, and troubling group of activists. These men and women believed that the victory in the Six Day War was quite literally a miracle. God himself had intervened, not merely to deliver the many into the hands of the few or the unrighteous into the hands of the righteous; the events of June 1967 were interpreted, with bold religious certainty, as the beginning of the messianic era. The Jewish people as a whole could no longer retain an attitude of waiting for the redemption. After June 1967, this small group of messianists asserted, all Jewish action had to be pointed toward hastening the coming of the Messiah.

The religious framework for this outlook had been quietly in place before the Six Day War. The gentle rabbi Abraham Isaac Kook had founded a unique *yeshiva*, a school for talmudic studies, in the 1920s in Jerusalem. The curriculum of this *yeshiva* was suffused with the idea that God's ultimate mercy might be shown very soon. After Rabbi Kook's death in 1935, this *yeshiva* continued in his path, but its students became more impatient and more militant. His son, Zvi Yehudah Kook, who inherited the central role in this academy, raised a generation on his activist reinterpretation of his father's ideas.

War was imminent when Zvi Yehudah Kook delivered an important speech to his disciples on Israeli Independence Day in May 1967. He announced that the redemption of the whole of the land of Israel was the divine command of the hour. When these lands were actually conquered a few weeks later, Zvi Yehudah Kook and his disciples had no doubt that this was a giant step in a process that had, in their view, begun with the appearance of modern Zionism: the coming of the messianic era. The Jewish state was now commanded by God himself to hold on to the whole of the land of Israel, which meant at the very least to all of the territory between the Mediterranean and the river Jordan. This was to be done not for security, nor for future bargaining with the Arabs. It was of no account whatsoever that the newly won territories—the biblical Judea and Samaria, and the Gaza Strip—contained at least a million Arabs and that Israel thus had an Arab population of very nearly 40 percent. Never mind that the international political community was unanimously opposed to annexation and pronounced it to be against international law. At the center of the faith of these religious activists was the certainty that they were on God's side— they were his partners in a climactic, transcendent drama, making all pragmatic, rational considerations irrelevant.

It cannot be emphasized enough that this group of religious messianists are radically different from any group that has emerged within modern Zionism. These men and women know how to use modern technology and many of them seem Westernized, but these characteristics are deceptive. They think in biblical categories. Unlike the secular founders of modern Zionism, these religious messianists are not at all interested in ending the tensions between Jews and the nations of the world. In biblical times, when Joshua led the Jewish invaders from the desert into the Promised Land, he knew that all the nations were against him. Joshua persevered and ultimately won because God was on his side. To the militant messianists of our day, what is said in Washington or even by the predominantly secular government in Jerusalem does not matter. International law or the law of the state of Israel are as nothing before the will of God.

By the same token, all of the pained discussions about finding some way of living with the Arabs are irrelevant. In the times of the biblical conquest some of the native population chose to remain in the land and work for the Jews, others ran away, and still others resisted and were destroyed. Among the contemporary messianists these options are repeated as the solution to the Arab question. Even the gentlest of these believers does not imagine equal rights for Arabs in the undivided land. A fierce minority among them is even prepared to say that the Arabs of the West Bank are the lineal descendants of the seven aboriginal nations whom Joshua and his successors found in the land and destroyed. In any event, the task of uniting Judea and Samaria with the rest of the Holy Land is a divinely appointed mission. One can, therefore, proceed to accomplish this task without regard for any immediate difficulties with the Arabs or with those political forces that insist on raising the Arab question. As the messianic era unfolds, the Arab question will find its solution in ways that God has not yet revealed.

THE WEST BANK

In the first years after the Six Day War, relatively few settlements were established on the West Bank, except those in the immediate neighborhood of Jerusalem. Even as late as 1982, despite five years of large, even feverish, activity under a very favoring right-wing government, there were no more than 40 Jewish settlements in Judea and Samaria. The Jewish population of the region as of June 1985 is most reliably estimated to be around 50,000. Although the settlements do not seem to be of great demographic importance, they have radically and probably irrevocably altered the political map. The essential factor is not that many hundreds of millions of dollars have been spent on these establishments and on the preemption of the public land in the region by the Israeli government. More important is that the messianists have succeeded in changing the inner tone of Israel's political life.

Immediately after the 1967 war the most single-minded of these messianists, Rabbi Moshe Levinger, insisted on reestablishing a Jewish presence in the city of Hebron. In 1929, the town had been the scene of the single bloodiest riot by

Arabs against Jews, and its ancient Jewish community had been forced to leave the city. Levinger and his few followers insisted that the Jewish installations that had been abandoned must be reclaimed; it was a religious and national duty for Jews to dwell again in the town where the tombs of the patriarchs were located. There were some halfhearted attempts to persuade Levinger to leave Hebron, because his presence was arousing the anger of the Arabs and was creating a security problem. But no great sentiment existed in Israel for the forceful removal of a patriot from a city that was holy to Jews. The students of Zvi Yehudah Kook, who increasingly dominated the National Religious Party, were particularly opposed to such a move.

Some of Kook's students had organized into a pressure group for settlements under the name Gush Emunim (the League of the Faithful) in the aftermath of the Israeli-Egyptian war of October 1973. This body had begun as a pressure group within the National Religious Party, but declared its independence in 1974. Its members soon made seven attempts to settle—without government permission—in the very heart of the Arab population on the West Bank, but the government ordered the army to dismantle these settlements. Their eighth attempt, in December 1975, succeeded; the coalition cabinet of the day could no longer find the will for another confrontation with Gush Emunim.

Four years later, in 1979, Menachem Begin had just signed a peace treaty with Egypt and was being accused of being willing to institute a moratorium on settlements when the leader of the young guard in the National Religious Party, Zevulun Hammer, issued a statement threatening to resign from the coalition government and thus bring it down:

The settlements are important to us. If the government decides that we will not continue to settle or decides to remove settlements from Judea and Samaria—we will regard this as crossing over the red line we have set for ourselves on this issue. . . . We are waiting for the actualization of the principle of settlements which is superficially accepted by the government. These decisions and their practical character will affect our attitude to the government.[3]

Since the inconclusive election of July 1984, and the subsequent creation of an unprecedented coalition government in Israel, new settlements have not been established. There are two reasons for their absence. First, the Labor half of the coalition government remains opposed to the messianistic ideology of Gush Emunim. Second and more immediately important, the economic crisis in Israel is of such magnitude that there is no money for such endeavors. The existing Jewish towns and villages in Judea and Samaria continue to increase their populations quite successfully, with newcomers who are not necessarily ideological believers. Judea and Samaria are areas in which housing, always expensive in Israel, can be bought on the most favorable terms.

Some observers—most notably, a former deputy mayor of Jerusalem, Meron Benvenisti—insist that the West Bank is now annexed de facto. This judgment seems too sweeping. An Israeli government could yet make some political arrangement for the West Bank in the form of power sharing with an Arab state or entity; and the Gush Emunim, and those sympathetic to it, would be

3. *Ha-aretz*, 5 Jan. 1979.

unable to veto a territorial redivision of the West Bank or some form of condominium between Israel and Jordan. Benvenisti is, however, right in asserting that present settlements could not be dismantled. Any Israeli government contemplating such action would face far greater difficulties than Begin faced when he finally, and grudgingly, evacuated the town of Yamit in 1981, as required by the peace treaty with Egypt.

SHARED FUNDAMENTALISM

A much more important change has occurred in Israel than can be expressed by simply asserting that, after Yamit, no place in which Jews live can ever be surrendered by the Israeli government, even for diplomatic advantage. A majority in Israel still supports the old politics of rational self-interest and the pursuit of international acceptance, but this majority is getting smaller. In recent elections the younger generation has voted more and more right wing. Meir Kahane, the most bellicose of Israel's politicians, was elected to the Knesset with the votes of the young, and pollsters predict that in a new election his party would gain four seats. Within Israel's right wing as a whole, the movement has been away from older doctrines of national maximalism. There are increasing outcries against the Western world that echo perceptions of continuous anti-Semitism currently and in the past. There are also repeated, and vehement, assertions that the Arabs understand only strength and that any willingness to compromise would be regarded as a sign of weakness. With very minor changes in language, this is the political doctrine of Islamic fundamentalism in Iran, or, for that matter, of born-again Christians of the American right wing. All three doctrines posit

enemies who are regarded as beyond compromise and who must be opposed in the name of divinely received values, whether they be those of the Hebrew Bible, the New Testament, or the Koran.

In the Middle East, rational politicians are still at the head of most of the governments: Shimon Peres in Israel, Hosni Mubarak in Egypt, King Hussein in Jordan, and even the far more ruthless Hafez al-Assad in Syria. Nonetheless, each of these governments is threatened by the rise of religious fundamentalism. Individual political leaders continue to attempt to live with their domestic tigers by repressing them or, occasionally, by riding them. Such temporizations work for a while, but in the long run none of these regimes is secure against its right wing. Even in Israel, which is by far the stablest democracy in the area, it has begun to be conceivable that General Ariel Sharon could come to power with the votes of some of Israel's proletariat and poorest shopkeepers. The overthrow of the Western-style regimes in Jordan, Egypt, and Syria by local versions of Ayatollah Ruhollah Khomeini is even more thinkable.

Historically, most decision makers in the Middle East have avoided the pain of large-scale political settlements with other countries in the region. Fundamentalism seems to be reversing that equation. The existing governments, both Jewish and Arab, have a stake in saving themselves, together, from the fundamentalist intransigents who would replace them. Pragmatic, rational political settlements in the region are the necessary preamble to solving the inner problems of these various countries. Otherwise, there will be turmoil—soon. Wise state officials still have the opportunity to use the pervading fear of messianic politics as reason for them to work together. They can have order and stability at home only by accommodating, and thus sustaining, one another.

India: Religion, Political Legitimacy, and the Secular State

By RALPH BUULTJENS

ABSTRACT: In no region of the world have so many political entities intermingled with so many religious traditions for so long as in India. The early Hindu experience established a legitimizing link between religion and the state. Later, non-Hindu faiths adopted similar legitimizing practices. British colonialism displaced local religions as political legitimizers of the state and replaced them with Anglicized Christianity. Indian religions then became legitimizers of anticolonial freedom movements. After independence and partition of the subcontinent in 1947, India had a predominantly Hindu population, but the new state was created as a secular entity. Although secularism has been endangered and pressured in the past four decades, it remains largely intact at the national level; however, there are inconsistencies in its application and threats to its integrity at the regional and state level. Religion has, however, ceased to be the key legitimizing instrument of the state; democratic voting has replaced it. Yet, religious issues remain a vital part of Indian politics. The future appears optimistic for the continuity of the secular state, although severe problems could erode the concept.

Ralph Buultjens is Presidential Professor at the Colorado School of Mines and professor at the Maryknoll Graduate School, the New School for Social Research, and New York University. In 1984 he was awarded the Toynbee Prize for the Social Sciences. He is the author of several books including Rebuilding the Temple—Tradition and Change in Modern Asia; The Decline of Democracy; *and* The Secret of Karl Marx. *Professor Buultjens is chairman of the International Development Forum, the New York Buddhist Council, and the Nehru Memorial Committee (North America). He is also senior fellow of the Institute of Fundamental Studies in Sri Lanka.*

ANY larger examination of the relationship between political power and religious authority leads eventually to India. There is no region of the world in which so many political entities have intermingled with so many religious traditions for so long.

India has a long history embracing two themes: political consolidation and religious realization. Over many centuries, a number of governmental centers have sought to establish themselves and then expand their control over part or all of India. At the same time, a variety of religious faiths have sought to root their beliefs in Indian soil and then to extend their spiritual mandate. These thrusts and the interaction between them have produced extraordinary experiences, finally resulting in modern efforts to separate church and state by establishing the principle of secularism in government.

LEGITIMIZING POLITICAL POWER

In most political arenas, the first impulse of governmental power has been to seek some rationale of legitimacy. In India, more than in most other societies, force alone has been unable to sustain government. By itself, crude muscular strength has not proven sufficiently effective in evoking the recognition that enables governments to govern for long periods of time. While there have been administrations dependent only on violent methods and instruments, these governments have traditionally had little success in obtaining the effective cooperation of their Indian subjects and have generally been short-lived. Both rulers and ruled have recognized the importance of a higher rationale. The quest for this legitimacy took government to religion.

From historic times, religion has been a powerful force in India. The early Aryans, as they moved into north India about 35 centuries or more ago, brought their hymns, the Vedas, with them. These prayers defined much of the social life of Hindu communities.[1] Other religious works gave sanction to the social order.[2] Intellectual efforts were often expressed in philosophic and spiritual terms. The imagination, the minds, and the hearts of the peoples of the subcontinent were profoundly shaped by religion. And so, it was natural that any traditional ruler in search of legitimizing credentials would turn to religion. Political consolidation was most effectively accomplished with religious reinforcement in ancient Hindu society. As Kautilya, author of the classical Hindu treatise on statecraft, declared, "Vedic lore is only a cloak for one conversant with the ways of the world."[3]

The use of religion as an agent of legitimacy was not always due to the venality of rulers. It is important to remember that alternate sources of legitimacy, ways to which we have become more accustomed in modern times, were then not much recognized or available. Secular ideologies had not developed. The concept of popular mandates was not fully understood. Constitutional succession was an idea still far in the future. Even primogeniture or heredi-

1. Ralph Griffith, trans., *The Hymns of the Rgveda*, new rev. ed. (Delhi: Motilal Banarsidass, 1973).

2. Arthur Coke Burnell, trans., *The Ordinances of Manu* (New Delhi: Oriental Books Reprint, 1971).

3. R. P. Kangle, trans., *The Kautilya Arthasastra* (Bombay: University of Bombay, 1972), p. 6. The Arthasastra was reportedly advice on governance given by Kautilya, a minister in the Maurya Empire in North India circa fourth century B.C.

tary succession did not always go unchallenged. Religious sanction was probably the only credential widely agreed upon by everyone in society.

Such validation of political claims did not, of course, come without a price. Historically, Hindu practice granted those of the Brahman caste a monopoly over ritual and mediation between gods and humans. The Brahmans, the most prestigious caste in the Hindu social hierarchy, acquired an advisory political role and a high level of patronage. Mythology and early histories tell us about the important role of the Brahman *purohitas*, the royal chaplains and counselors, who exercised considerable influence in the courts of Hindu kings. They accompanied rulers into battle, blessed royal enterprises, mediated for godly favors, often advised on statecraft, and received many benefits and much recognition.[4] And so, in early Hindu society, the link between church and state was effectively forged.

The effective nature of this relationship in establishing the legitimacy of Hindu rulers was not lost on political leaders of non-Hindu dynasties. As Buddhism developed into a major religion, kings like the Emperor Asoka, who ruled from 273 to 232 B.C., adopted its ideas as the official ideology of the state. When Islamic Mogul monarchs carved empires out of north India, they claimed that they ruled in the name of Allah. Later, the rise of the Sikh faith continued this trend. Sikh religious leaders were often warriors or endorsed them; these affirmations were witnessed by the weapons that their religion enjoined them to carry. Hindu and non-

Hindu governors had both accepted religion as a key legitimizing element and extended their patronage in return for religious sanction usually delivered by the clergy.

LEGITIMIZING EXPANSION

Legitimacy provided the rationale for the popular acceptance of governments. It also enabled governments to undertake another activity that infused political policy in traditional India—expansion. Ancient India consisted, for the most part, of many contending kingdoms. Expansion through war was an important way of political life in a society that evaluated prestige in terms of people and land. Often, political survival depended on extension of the kingdom or on its defense.

Mobilization for war was not an easy task. Armies had to be raised and trained; supplies had to be prepared. These activities required the support of essentially agrarian people, disruption of their regular ways of living, and frequent sequestration of their assets. It was necessary to have as much popular cooperation as possible. Religious endorsement of the government and general or specific endorsement of its policies helped to secure this support in a way that no other source could do.

Two religious constructs underwrote the wars of kings in historic India. The first was the idea that the ruler was assigned the protection of the people and that his judgment in these matters was absolute.[5] The second was the idea that certain castes had a duty to fight; it was their *dharma*—obligation to their caste and their faith.[6]

4. For example, see the discourse by the Brahman Kanika to King Dhritarashtra, in Potap Chandra Roy, trans., *The Mahabharata (Adi Parva)* (Calcutta: Bharata Press, 1884), pp. 416-24.

5. S. N. Joshi and R. C. Kinjvadekar, eds., *Mahabharata* (Poona, 1929-33), vol. 3, sec. 185.26, and vol. 1, sec. 42.27-31.

6. Burnell, trans., *Ordinances of Manu*.

In addition, the ruler was always able to refer to religious authority to claim that he was fighting for the return of the reign of righteousness. In the Bhagavad Gita, the Lord Krishna speaks to this:

Think thou also of thy duty and do not waver. There is no greater good for a warrior than to fight in a righteous war. . . . There is a war that opens the door of heaven. . . . Happy the warriors whose fate is to fight such a war . . . to forgo this fight for righteousness is to forgo thy duty and honor.[7]

In sum, then, the principal needs of traditional government in India were underwritten by the authority of religion. As part of an exchange, religion received its due from the traditional state.

RELIGION NEEDS
THE STATE

In the early Hindu polity, religious forces were at a considerable advantage. They had a virtual monopoly over spiritual dispensations. Brahmans enjoyed an exalted role as religious intermediaries and were also often responsible for the education of the ruling classes. Many of them exercised advisory ministerial or political functions. Since the other castes had no equivalent religious status in traditional Hinduism, political forces had no alternate source that could deliver widely accepted legitimacy. Political recognition required religious sanction and that sanction had only a single wellspring.

It was not too long, however, before this monopoly over the dispensation of religious endorsement was challenged. New religions began to arise. Between 500 B.C. and A.D. 1500, four significant

religious movements impacted on traditional Hindu society—Buddhism, Jainism, Islam, and Sikhism. Frequently, mass conversions took place and rulers now obtained legitimacy from non-Hindu religious sources. Inspired by the new faiths, great empires were established. Among them was the domain of the Emperor Asoka. In the third century B.C. his territories reached from the Himalayas to south-central India and were governed according to essentially Buddhist ideas.

Although Muslim rulers had governed large parts of India from about the ninth century A.D., Islamic penetration found its most powerful political expression in the Mogul Empire. Located in north India, the Mogul imperium was established in the name of Islam and encouraged conversion to that faith. The Mogul political base contracted and expanded according to the ability of successive rulers, but in one way or another it was maintained from the early sixteenth century until the British *raj* displaced it in 1857. Jains, Sikhs, and others also had influential positions in society and some leaders of these faiths administered substantial kingdoms. Each of them sought sanction from their own faiths, although they often governed largely Hindu populations. In turn, Hindu revivalism spawned political reactions against non-Hindu rulers and these responses were frequently presented as attempts to restore the integrity of Hinduism.

Three significant features emerge from this experience. First, the Hindu monopoly on religious expression was broken. Yet, wherever Hindu political forces existed, they still sought religious support as a legitimizing imprimatur. Second, religion now needed the state more than ever before. Many political conflicts were also religious wars and

7. Juan Mascaro, trans., *The Bhagavad Gita* (New York: Penguin Books, 1962), p. 51.

physical protection of religious places and priests was needed. This only the state could provide. Third, although non-Hindu forces were now important, they followed the pattern earlier established by Hindus. They, too, sought legitimacy through the approval of their respective religions. The religious content changed, but the legitimizing role of religion continued.

While we can observe this linkage between religion and politics, little is known about the precise dynamics of the church-state relationship in ancient India. Mutual reinforcement, exchanges of patronage, legal protection of religion—all this is recorded in the histories of those periods. However, we are less aware of the tensions and stresses, the demands and the remonstrances, the disputes about boundaries of authority that must have occurred. Occasionally, documents and folklore hint at strains in specific situations. Greedy priests and unjust kings sometimes made inappropriate demands that have been detailed. Yet, for the most part, the known record suggests a continuous and growing accommodation between religious and state authority founded on the seal of legitimacy and exchanged for protection and favor.

BRITISH COLONIALISM

Traditional patterns and accommodations underwent a major change with the consolidation of British power on the subcontinent and the advent of a new, displacing Christianity. Although Indian Christianity had existed since the first century A.D., it had never been an important political force, was very small in the number of its adherents, and was Indianized in culture. The same condition prevailed among those Indians whom missionaries had converted to Christianity in later centuries.

Now, however, a conquering Anglicized Christianity arrived with British colonialism. Unlike earlier religions that seeped into India from outside, this Christianity remained very much the belief system of the colonizer. Conversions were made and missionary work undertaken. Yet, the Anglicized Christianity that accompanied the British did not evoke a mass response in India and was not widely integrated into Indian culture. It was confined to British expatriates and a small group of Indians, mostly those who formed a supporting establishment for the colonial regime.

In its own way, Anglicized Christianity now became a legitimizing instrument for British rule. English officialdom was careful to preserve all the proprieties for its faith—the erection of churches, sanctification of public ceremonies, attendance at religious events. Large segments of public education, especially the more elite institutions, were directed by religious authorities. If the British *raj* could not Christianize the heathen, it made every effort to draw its Christianity into supporting its administration. The myth of a civilizing mission, so essential to the maintenance of British colonialism, was partially sustained by joining Christianity to empire.

The gradual takeover of assorted Indian kingdoms and their incorporation into a unified British Indian empire was finally completed by about the middle of the nineteenth century.[8] It was the

8. In August 1858, Queen Victoria signed the Government of India Act, by which the government of India was fully assumed by the British crown. The government-supervised administration of the British East India Company was now formally vested in the British government.

culmination of almost two centuries of British inroads that began with the efforts of the British East India Company in the seventeenth century. For the first time in its history, the whole of India was now subject to one political authority. The viceroy ruled the subcontinent, first from Calcutta and later from Delhi, in the name of the British sovereign and the British God. Two systems of administration operated within this viceregal structure. About 55 percent of Indian territory, containing about 70 percent of the population, was under direct British rule. The balance consisted of 562 princely states, which the British governed through local Hindu and Muslim rulers—the *rajas* and the *nawabs*. These rulers were traditional princes, who had accepted British suzerainty and who were supervised by the British.[9]

The role of Indian religions, especially Hinduism and Islam—the two major Indian faiths that had survived as politically legitimizing churches—now underwent a dramatic change. Christianity had displaced them as legitimizers of the polity. In the princely states, Hindu and Muslim rulers owed their existence to British authority, not to any local religious authority.[10] In directly administered areas the Anglican Church of England functioned as a kind of official state religion. Throughout India, government funds supported its religious endeavors.

LEGITIMIZING OPPOSITION TO THE STATE

Removed from their historic role as legitimizers of state power, Hinduism and Islam suffered the pains of disestablishment. They were now regarded by the British state as subordinate religions. Their relationship with governmental authority was attenuated, when it existed at all. Any political role was officially denied and efforts to achieve it were regarded with deep suspicion by the British.

As this decline in relation to state power was taking place, another legitimizing role was developing. Hinduism and Islam became the repositories for nationalism. Protest movements against British rule sought their approval and support. Invocation of religious blessings on these anticolonial efforts was regularly asked and readily given. Hindu and Muslim sentiment was, for example, a key contributory factor in the Great Mutiny of 1857, a major uprising against British rule.[11] Occasional promises by the British government, to respect non-Christian religions and guarantee their freedom of expression, did not have any significant impact on the anticolonial dispositions of Hinduism and Islam, dispositions that Christian missionary efforts did not improve.

The great Indian nationalists of the nineteenth century were not only political figures, but also religious revivalists or reformers. Most of them saw the liberation of India in both political and religious terms. Their close association with religion helped to legitimize their

9. Territorial and population data as of 1947, on the eve of Indian independence. For details of the British administration structure, see Urmila Phadnis, *Towards the Integration of Indian States* (Bombay: Asia Publishing House, 1968); V. P. Menon, *The Story of the Integration of the Indian States,* 3rd ed. (Calcutta: Orient Longman, 1961).

10. British authorities did not hesitate to remove Indian princes of whom they did not approve. These recalcitrants were usually replaced by more pliant members of their own princely families.

11. Christopher Hibbert, *The Great Mutiny— India 1857* (New York: Penguin Books, 1980).

nationalist aspirations in the public mind. Ram Mohan Roy founded the Brahma Sabha in 1828, Keshab Chandra Sen established the Prarthana Samaj in 1867, and Dayananda Saraswati began the Arya Samaj in 1875. Later leaders, Bal Gangadhar Tilak and Gopal Krishna Gokhale, inaugurated the Ganapati and Shivaji festivals and the Servants of India, respectively. All of them and other nationalists of this era drew some measure of their popular esteem from religious and allied activities.

By the end of the nineteenth century, the foundations of the modern movement for the independence of India were being laid. The Indian National Congress, originally a movement for greater self-government, was formed in 1885. While all this activity promised much for the future, it evoked little immediate political enthusiasm among the masses. In part, this was due to the limited goals that the nineteenth-century nationalists sought—reform of the existing system, moderate change within the imperial framework, a larger degree of home rule. This situation was, however, soon to change.

The catalyst of change was Mahatma Gandhi. Returning to India from South Africa in 1915, Gandhi soon dominated the Indian National Congress and became its master political strategist and paramount leader. Yet, he was far more than this. It was Gandhi who mobilized the Indian masses and harnessed them to the nationalist cause. A large part of his hold on these masses, especially on the Hindu majority, derived from their perception of him as a religious or semireligious sage. The very title *mahatma* ("great soul") implied this. In appearance, behavior, speech, and public persona, Gandhi was very much a Hindu incarnation.

Gandhi blended shrewd political tactics with a profound spiritual and moral philosophy. He spoke to the people in their own idiom and frequently invoked religious themes in support of his political efforts. Among these was *Ram Rajya*, "the rule of Ram." To Gandhi, this was a model of the righteous society, the revival of social morality and civic virtue. To his vast audiences, these calls for *Ram Rajya* symbolized the religious values of his message. Ram was an incarnation of Vishnu, one of the premier gods of Hinduism, and recourse to him provided religious legitimacy for the Gandhian movement. Mention of *karma, ahimsa, dharma,* and other Hindu concepts was frequent in Gandhi's public statements and provided an appealing and sanctifying aura to which the Hindu masses responded.

The Hindu context that surrounded much of Gandhi's ideas and activities gave religious sanction, but it also created some unintended consequences. The suspicions and fears of a substantial Muslim minority were aroused. Many Muslims saw a suggestion of Hindu theocracy in Gandhi's metaphors, doubts that were not allayed by his regularly proclaimed veneration for all faiths. His ecumenism did not soften Muslim feelings, and it alienated extremist Hindus, who felt that Gandhi was too accommodating of non-Hindus. And so, Islamic sentiment began to crystallize around the idea of separation. In its own way, Islam legitimized the nationalism of political separatists, leading to the eventual partition of the subcontinent on largely religious lines, and the creation of Pakistan.

On the eve of Indian independence in 1947, it was clear that religion had played a major inspirational and legitimizing role in the run up to freedom. Indeed, the primacy of religious sanction was such that many political leaders who used more secular appeals lost their challenges for leadership.[12] Disturbed at this, the Indian Communist leader M. N. Roy complained, "It is neither a philosopher nor a moralist who has become the idol of the Indian people. The masses pay their homage to a Mahatma—a source of revealed religion and agency of supernatural power."[13] An interesting thread of continuity in religion as a legitimizer of political authority had endured: once the legitimizer of Indian states and the historic political establishment, religion had become the legitimizer of Indian nationalism and political protest in more recent, colonial times.

THE NEW SECULAR STATE

Independence came to India in August 1947. The new state, created from the crucible of imperialism by the division of the British Indian empire, united a large part of the subcontinent under an Indian government. The creation of this polity, and events that occurred around that time, produced three fundamental changes in the atmosphere that were to influence the church-state relationship.

First, the division of the region into modern India and Pakistan drastically altered the religious mix of the territory that remained as India. Major vocal segments of the Muslim population of the old British Empire now had their own state of Pakistan. Neither Gandhi's vision of a common spirituality shared by all faiths nor Jawaharlal Nehru's idea that the bonds of modernization and nationalism would transcend the declining power of religion had proved salable to a large number of Muslims. India was left predominantly Hindu. Although significant minorities remained within the boundaries of the new India, Muslims and all other non-Hindus represented only about 20 percent of the people. This encouraged many of the more fundamentalist Hindus to expect a special place for Hinduism and special recognition for traditional Hindu social practices in the new state. These expectations were not, as we will see later, to be fulfilled.

Second, there was a wide and growing consensus that the new state should be democratic and egalitarian in its structure. The authoritarian experience of local monarchies and the colonial administration had left an unpopular legacy that Indians did not want to repeat. Most important political groups also agreed that the average citizen should be given representation in government and equal rights in society.

Third, the moral and political leadership of the country devolved on Nehru, the heir to Gandhi's mantle. Nehru, while accepting many of Gandhi's approaches to life and politics, was a very different man from his mentor in both thought and personality. Essentially agnostic in his spiritual beliefs, with little patience for traditional religious observances, he was drawn to modern liberal, scientific, and socialist thinking. Nehru's influence was dominant in the political field and his ideas formed the

---

12. This refers to Communists as well as those within the Congress movement. Both Rabindranath Tagore and Subas Chandra Bose contended with Gandhi, advocating ideas more secular than his. Neither could compete with Gandhi's popularity among the masses. On the Muslim side, even an essentially secular leader such as Mohammed Ali Jinnah was careful to invoke religious sanction for his political designs.

13. Quoted in Donald Eugene Smith, *India as a Secular State* (Princeton, NJ: Princeton University Press, 1963), p. 500.

bedrock of state policy during the period when he was prime minister of India, from 1947 to 1964.

The confluence of these three developments helped to shape major decisions that the new nation had to make about its character and its future. The principal decision-making forum was the Constituent Assembly, which engaged in the task of preparing a constitution for India. After two years of intense debate and drafting, the assembly adopted the Constitution of India on 26 November 1949. Two months later, in January 1950, these laws came into effect as the official charter of the new Republic of India.

The Indian Constitution, one of the longest and most comprehensive in the world, is a remarkable document for many reasons. Two of these are of special importance in the context of the church-state issue—the emplacement of democracy and the establishment of a secular form of government embracing the concept of equal civic rights for every Indian citizen.

The selection of democracy as the political system of India initiated a new method of legitimizing the authority of the state, a method different from that ever before experienced in India. Governments, the agents of the state, were now to be elected by universal balloting. This was to be the only determinant of their legitimacy. No longer was religious or any other sanction required. The basis of legitimacy, traditionally rooted in religion and continued in much that way during the colonial period, had undergone a dramatic shift. A radical principle was now written into law: the state was the only legitimate authority that could regulate society and change it through legislation.

The concept of excluding religion as a legitimizer of the state was taken a step further in Article 25(1) of the constitution: "subject to public order, morality and health . . . all persons are equally entitled to freedom of conscience and the right to freely profess, practice and propagate religion."

Speaking in 1950, Prime Minister Nehru, one of the principal architects of the secular state, declared, "The government of a country like India, with many religions that have secured great and devoted followings for generations, can never function satisfactorily in the modern age except on a secular basis."[14] Many traditionalists did not agree. They argued that Hinduism should receive a special place in the state, but Nehru and other secularists were able to resist this notion.

The Indian concept of secularism is somewhat different from the conventional definition of this ambiguous term. The *Oxford English Dictionary* states that secularism is "the doctrine that morality should be based solely on regard to the well-being of mankind in the present life, to the exclusion of all considerations drawn from belief in God or in a future state." Indian secularism, a definition shared by all religious and nonreligious believers, is based more on the idea of separation of church and state, on the freedom of all religions to coexist, on the absence of any favored position or recognition or preference for any one religion by the state, and on equal protection for all religions.

Nehru explained what a secular state was to be and how it would function in India:

What it means is that it is a state which honours all faiths equally and gives them

14. *The Hindu* (Madras), 13 Sept. 1950.

equal opportunities; that, as a state, it does not allow itself to be attached to one faith or religion, which then becomes the state religion. . . . In a country like India, no real nationalism can be built up except on the basis of secularity . . . narrow religious nationalisms are relics of a past age and are no longer relevant today.[15]

The absence of a privileged position for any religion and the rejection of a state religion effectively removed any official legitimizing role for religion in the Indian state. In doing this, India contrasted markedly with its neighbors, most of whom wrote constitutions that specifically recognized the links between the majority religion and the state.[16] Many modernists, in an excess of optimism, predicted that the Indian measures would soon see the rapid decline and eventual disappearance of religion in Indian politics. The failure of their hopes is discussed later.

Along with the secular thrust went egalitarian constitutional provisions that affected the ways in which religion or religiously derived tradition impacted on the people: equality before the law, guarantees of nondiscrimination because of caste, secular arbiters of the law such as courts of justice. Article 14 of the Indian Constitution holds that "the state shall not deny to any person equality before the law or the equal protection of the laws within the territory of India." Article 15(1) proclaims that "the state shall not discriminate against any citizen on grounds only of religion, race,

caste, sex, place of birth or any of them." Article 17 abolished untouchability—the practice of discrimination against underprivileged castes—and goes even further: "The enforcement of any disability arising out of Untouchability shall be an offense punishable in accordance with law." These were historic and pioneering steps. "The government of independent India is the first in the country's history that declared total war on untouchability," reported a *New York Times* correspondent.[17]

The British historian Percival Spear was equally enthused by these laws:

It represents the substitution of the idea of the individual with equal rights and duties as the unit of society and a society of such equal units, for the idea of groups of unequal individuals with varying rights and duties arranged in ascending order of magnitude. An egalitarian society of individuals has become the official basis of society instead of a hierarchy of under- and over-privileged groups.[18]

The idea of society composed of unequal individuals is, of course, a fundamental part of the traditional Indian heritage. It is explicitly stated and refined in the ancient source books of Hindu jurisprudence, such as the Laws of Manu.

The secular and egalitarian nature of the constitution was vigorously attacked by traditionalist Hindus and their spokesmen in the Constituent Assembly. Later, they strongly opposed almost all enabling legislation.[19]

15. Jawaharlal Nehru, Foreword, in Raghunath Singh, *Dharam Nirpeksh Raj* (New Delhi, 1961).

16. For example, the Constitutions of Pakistan (1956), Nepal (1959), and Burma (1961), all drafted around this time, provided for a special place in the state for Islam, Hinduism, and Buddhism, respectively.

17. A. M. Rosenthal, "India Spurs Fight to End Caste Bias," *New York Times,* 23 Feb. 1958.

18. Percival Spear, "Christian Higher Education in India," *International Review of Missions,* 40:87 (1951).

19. Many laws were enacted to give substance to the principles stated in the constitution. These included the Special Marriage Act of 1954; the Untouchability (Offenses) Act of 1955; the Hindu Marriage Bill, the Hindu Succession Bill, the

The massive authority of Nehru and his liberal supporters, however, prevailed in the assembly, in the Indian Parliament, and in the country. And so, a new framework of national law defined the legal and political body of the infant republic and set new parameters for church-state, political-religious interaction. It was a radical break with the traditions of the past, a major victory for those who wanted the separation of religion from politics, and a serious disappointment for those who wanted religion to be an official source of political and social legitimacy in the new state.

WORKING THE CONSTITUTION

The Republic of India has been a working reality for almost four decades. For most of that period, the government has been dominated by Jawaharlal Nehru until his death in 1964; his daughter, Indira Gandhi, prime minister from 1966 to 1977 and again from 1980 to 1984; and his grandson, Rajiv Gandhi, since 31 October 1984. Their political vehicle has been the Congress Party and their policies and perspectives have been strongly supportive of the secular nature of the state. During their stewardships, the secular structure of Indian government has been firmly maintained and religion has been excluded from any legitimizing role. As Indira Gandhi put it:

Religion has an important place in our culture, our society, and our personal beliefs and values. It has no special place in our state framework and no place in our politics. Our secularism never means opposition or indifference to religion. It means that all religions will receive equal recognition and respect, and that no one religion will have excep-

tional privilege or will influence government policy. The idea of an established religion or a government authorized by religion is abhorrent.[20]

The elimination of a legitimizing role for religion in the state has not, however, prevented religious issues from becoming important political issues. At the inception of the republic, Nehru's government sought to promote social justice and, as it did so, it created a paradox that has existed ever since. While the constitution and Nehru's policies outlawed caste discrimination, the government wanted to give special political protection to the outcaste untouchable Harijans. Consequently, the concept of special Harijan electorates was introduced—parliamentary constituencies reserved for these people.[21] Initially regarded as a temporary, ten-year measure, the reserved constituencies have become a permanent feature, their existence extended regularly by constitutional amendments. Currently, about 15 percent of the seats in the Indian Lok Sabha—the popularly elected House of the People—are so designated and most political parties endorse this system.

By standards of equity, the policy of reservation for the underprivileged is a fair approach. It provides representation for the most deprived segment of society—representation that it would

---

Hindu Minority and Guardianship Bill, the Hindu Adoptions and Maintenance Bill, all enacted in 1955 and 1956.

20. Statement made to me, New Delhi, 1 June 1984.

21. The reserved-constituencies system also exists in the legislatures of Indian states. It works in this way: whenever elections are held in these constituencies, the only candidates allowed are those from the scheduled groups, that is, from the underprivileged castes. The reservations are proportionate to the population of scheduled groups within the country—for national elections—or within any particular state. However, scheduled individuals are free to contest anywhere. See Articles 330, 332, and 334 of the Constitution of India.

not otherwise get. Yet, this system also provides official recognition only to the Hindu religion. No reserved seats were given to Muslims or other minority religions, and caste, after all, is based on Hindu social divisions. Any special caste representation enables those divisions to endure and become constitutionally entrenched.

Early amendments to the Indian Constitution granted further special protection to other deeply underprivileged castes and tribes. Their aim was to help sections of society in urgent need of assistance—the concept of protective discrimination for these scheduled communities. However, conversion from Hinduism to other religions often resulted in withdrawal of special status and its benefits. In effect underprivilege was defined by religion in this situation and preference given to the Hindu deprived. Various adjustments were made to resolve this problem; scholarships, economic aid, quotas for employment in government and for admission to colleges were extended to many other classes and communities seen as backward. Yet, even today, only those who belong to the untouchable segments of the Hindu and Sikh communities can qualify for this designation and for political benefits created for the scheduled castes. Thus, the pursuit of justice has sometimes caused continuing discrimination against other religions and has produced constitutionally implicit preferences for some.

These problems are the by-product of good intent and moral purpose. Although they contradict the strict ideal of separation of religion from the state, few will quarrel with their good intentions. In general, however, and with only a few other exceptions, the state has been able to prevent religion from having a significant legitimizing role.

However, religious issues continue to arise in modern Indian politics. Most major political crises that do not directly involve economic questions have a religious element. Taken as a whole, these crises represent efforts by religious groups or their political allies to gain some special protection, position, or recognition by the state for their own religion or its practices at either national or local levels of politics. Among the most controversial of these attempts have been moves to agitate for special laws regarding:

—prohibition of the sale of liquor;

—prevention of the slaughter of cows;

—bans on conversion from one religion to another;

—enhancement or reduction of special quotas for deprived social groups;

—establishment of exclusive privileges for Hinduism; and

—creation of exceptional privileges for Sikhs in the Punjab or for Sikhism in general.

For the most part, these issues have been sponsored by local forces—social or political. There has not, as yet, been any mass national movement on any single religiously oriented issue. Given the nature of Indian society, it is unlikely that these could arise. Yet, the political implications of localized or regionalized agitation can be serious. Politically interested groups, such as the once-vocal Hindu Mahasabha or the Jamaat-i-Islami or the Rashtriya Swayamsevak Sangh (RSS) or the Shiv Sena of Bombay, have directly or indirectly encouraged some of these happenings. Political parties like the Jana Sangh in the past or the current Bharatiya Janata Party have been suspected of politically advancing the cause of Hindu militancy. More recently, in 1982, the organization of the Virat Hindu Samaj, a self-proclaimed social movement to emphasize the interests of Hinduism, aroused the fears of many who saw it as an embryo religio-political party. Around this time, the rise of N. T. Rama Rao from film idol to chief minister of Andhra State and the success of his Telegu Desam Party was largely based on his capacity to project a god-king image—arousing fears of Hindu revivalism in south India. In the early 1980s, conversions from Hinduism to Islam, many of which took place among poorer segments of the population in a few regions such as Karnataka, generated a political reaction of hostility. However, none of these efforts showed indications of developing as wide, national movements.

On a national scale, the success of attempts to promote religious issues as political issues has produced minimal results in terms of laws or administrative regulations. While local or state governments have occasionally given in to pressures and have enacted such measures or have elected officials who have done so, the impact on the national scene has been more in controversy than in any serious breach of the secular nature of the state. By its own definition, that of being evenhanded to all religions and giving no special preference to any one faith, India has been largely true to its concept of secularism in the national polity.

PRESERVING SECULARISM

Why, despite intense local pressures, has this been so? The answer rests largely in the ideology of the political party that has governed India for 36 of its 39 years of independence—the Indian National Congress. Donald Eugene Smith, who examined secularism in the early days of the republic, writes:

The Indian National Congress has behind it a long tradition of non-communal nationalism and has on the whole been faithful to the ideal of the secular state since independence. It is the party to which the religious minorities (with the exception of the Sikhs) have instinctively looked for the protection of their interests; there is at least a clear ideal [secularism] which can be appealed to. There are elements of religious revivalism within Congress, but these are weak, very weak . . . political parties in India which directly challenge the secular state can claim but a [much smaller] amount of popular support.[22]

In general, political controversy on religious issues has come from opponents of national or state Congress governments. Either because of its ideology or because of the source of these pressures, Congress governments have resisted attempts to introduce religion into the political arena. On several occasions, Congress administrations have even called out the armed forces to enforce law and order in these situations.

While Congress policy has embraced and advanced the ideology of secularism, much credit for this attitude must be given to its leaders, particularly Jawaharlal Nehru and Indira Gandhi. Nehru was the great advocate of secularism and his influence on politics wove this idea into both party and government. His approach differs sharply from that of the leaders of neighboring states, which is perhaps why the contrast between India and these has been so great. Indira Gandhi accepted her father's policy totally, a theme reflected in the frequent references to secularism that are

---

22. Smith, *India as a Secular State*, pp. 494-95.

contained in so many of her public statements.

Toward the end of her life, somewhere between 1981 and 1984, Mrs. Gandhi was reportedly developing a more responsive relationship to Hinduism. Her political opponents alleged that she was orchestrating vote banks for electoral purposes; others claimed that this was part of her own spiritual growth. Whether there is truth in any of these speculations is a matter of conjecture. What is important is that her executive actions and policies did not waver from her commitment to the secular notion of India.

The culminating crisis of the Indira Gandhi era had a close connection with the issue of secularism. One perception of the problems in the Punjab is that they have resulted from the demands of a small, powerful religious community of Sikhs. In the making of the Indian union, Sikh nationalism was accommodated within the federal structure of the republic. Gradually, Sikh irredentism, a blend of communalist and religious sentiment, began to surface and expand. It found political expression in the Akali Dal Party and, as time passed, in other groups—all of which appealed to religious symbolism and leaders to establish their legitimacy among the Sikhs. The demands of the Sikh groups were always partly religious in content. While the extent of support for these groups among the Sikh people as a whole is uncertain, they did develop a sizable following—enough to create a virtual breakdown in civil administration in the Punjab in 1983-84. The most sacred of Sikh religious centers, the Golden Temple in Amritsar, became the headquarters for many militant Sikh organizations. Eventually, Prime Minister Indira Gandhi ordered the army into the temple and, while military success was assured, the action cost her life.

This is by no means the full story of the complex Sikh situation, but it indicates the level to which political temperature can rise when infused with religion. It also shows the commitment to secularism and national unity that Indira Gandhi had, a feeling largely shared by many in the Congress Party. Prime Minister Rajiv Gandhi has continued to indicate a strong attachment to these ideas and policies.

On the whole, secularism has served both India and the Congress Party well. The country has survived as an integrated unit and its large religious and ethnic minorities have been able to live relatively peacefully within the union. Any comparison with neighboring nations, all of which have similar minority components in their populations, indicates the advantages of Indian secularism over the problems minorities have had in Pakistan, Sri Lanka, Bangladesh, and Nepal. Except for the election in 1977, when robust family-planning programs alienated the minorities—especially Muslims—they have provided important support for the Congress. And, today, the Congress Party is widely perceived as the guardian of secularism and consequently the choice of both Hindus and non-Hindus who endorse this view.

THE RISING RELIGIOUS TIDE

Contrary to widespread expectations generated in the minds of many Indians around the time of independence, the adoption of secularism as state policy did not lead to a decline of religious involvement in politics. Initially, many forces appeared to validate this expectation. Industrialization, urbanization, expansion of Western values and life-styles, decline of the old Indian family system, growth of literacy and modern education—all these factors appeared to converge in Indian society to reinforce the general atmosphere of secularism in both personal and public life.

Political analysts saw the shift in the basis of state legitimacy from religion to the vote, the essence of constitutional democracy, as a critical element in the decline of religion in political affairs. Economists, especially those of socialist orientation who rode high in the Nehru years, saw the Planning Commission and its succession of five-year national economic plans as a rational path to development, a path producing a modern economy that would erode traditional social beliefs. Scientists predicted the death of God as modern technology became available. All these processes took place, but the expected results did not appear.

Six factors have contributed significantly to the continued presence of religion and its influence in political life. First, there is the structure of the Hindu spiritual world. Hindu belief and thought is a multilayered complexity allowing for the existence of many gods, many incarnations, many levels of truth. Consequently both modernization and tradition can exist together and the advance of one does not always mean the decline of the other. Thus, it is not unusual for Hindus to have an expanding consciousness of several different and, in the Western view, apparently conflicting understandings.

Second, religion continues to be a means for political gain. The deep feeling for religion in India has allowed ambitious or religious-minded public figures to make religion, or issues associated with it, an important factor in politics. Politicians of all faiths are well aware of the capacity for religious arousal and many, particularly those out of office, have used it for their ends, encouraging the tenacious loyalty to community and caste that retards full acceptance of the secular state.

Third, even though Muslims, Sikhs, and other minorities have made much progress in India, they remain insecure. Aware of their vulnerability, they tend to seek protection in group solidarity, the group being primarily based on religious affinity. They also often seek to articulate their viewpoints as religious communities, creating a resentment among the majority. They know that Hinduism is genuinely and generously absorptive, but Hinduism does not often dignify that which it assimilates or tolerates, often consigning it to a subordinate position of inferiority within the Hindu system. So, separate identity becomes important and a separate place in the political universe protects that identity.

Fourth, there is the nature of the development process to consider. Almost four decades of development have made a major impact on Indian society. Development is a process often accompanied by physical and/or emotional dislocation. In this context, religion becomes a center of certainty in a turbulent world—one of the few stable verities in an age of transition. At least in the short term, then, the development process has reinforced the religious nature of society.

Fifth, the character of political notables is changing. At independence and for a long while thereafter, both politics and public administration were dominated by an Anglicized coterie. The passage of that elite, the mobility increasingly available in government and business, and the impact of development itself have brought forth a group of notables whose orientation is much more indigenous. "Power is devolving from the Anglicized elite of the Nehru generation to the sons-of-the-soil, the driving force behind regional and religious agitation wracking India today . . . [They] see the world through the incense and colored powders of Hindu ritual."[23]

The last factor is the system of law. The Constitution of India declares, among its directive principles, that "the state shall endeavor to secure for its citizens a uniform civil code throughout the territory of India." Much progress has been made toward this end; however, several different systems of religious personal law still exist. For example, Hindus, Muslims, Christians, and members of some other groups, who are legally equal citizens of the same nation, are governed by or can opt for different inheritance laws. Muslims, in particular, see their laws as the fundamental core of Islam itself. This multiplicity of religious personal laws is directly in conflict with the essential concept of the secular state. Yet, to accelerate any further uniformity in the legal code would be deeply resented by all religions and has become extremely difficult to undertake. This tends to shape the thinking of large segments of society along sectarian lines.

These entrenchments of religion in private and public life continue to produce a tension that endures in the relationship between faith and state—a tension that time has not diminished. Indeed, it can well be argued that many recent developments at the regional or local level, some of which have been discussed earlier, indicate the emergence of a renewed challenge to the secular state.

THE FUTURE

While it is possible to document this assertion, it is also important to realize the extent to which the ideal of secularism has become part of the Indian political system. The legitimizing role of religion has dissolved, probably permanently. Efforts to restore it are only partial and center around securing privileges for religions or religious groups. National support for political parties advocating the rejection of secularism has been limited. There have been significant regional expressions of religion in politics, but none of them have seriously undermined the national commitment to a secular state.

Under what conditions could this commitment be shaken or destroyed? Given the population mix in India, such a challenge could only come from a Hindu assault. The experience of India as an independent nation-state suggests that it would take a major upheaval to produce this assault. Perhaps a full-scale and prolonged war with Pakistan, an uncontainable separatist movement in one of the regions or states, the rise of some megacharismatic Hindu leader, the disintegration of the Congress Party or its capture by Hindu fundamentalists, countrywide Hindu-Muslim riots— any or all of these events could produce an upsurge of Hindu chauvinism that could destroy or seriously threaten the secular nature of the state. While there are forces within India that would welcome this and have not given up on the idea of establishing a Hindu state, it is difficult to see such a happening in the immediate future.

23. Richard Nations, "Power and Paranoia," *Far Eastern Economic Review,* 18 Aug. 1984, p. 24.

The secular state is only one part, although an integral one, of the Indian democratic totality. It is now virtually impossible to separate secularism from democracy in India. Any departure from secularism at the national level will also probably be the end of democracy. It is even possible to conjecture that, should democracy terminate, any successor regimes would still have to maintain secularism. If India is to survive, in whatever political form the future may bring, the price of its existence as a nation-state with a diverse population may well be continued secularism. In that sense, secularism as part of the state structure may well outlast democracy, although democracy is unlikely to outlast secularism.

Finally, we should recognize that perfect secularism—the completely secular state—does not and probably cannot exist. As long as religion survives and concerns itself with public issues, there will be some overlap between church and state. In a poor, traditional country, such as India, the fringes of secularism will always be blurred. Yet the ideal established in 1950, when India's constitution became the national charter, is widely accepted, has been sustained through difficult periods, grown in inhospitable social soil, and is being implemented in a major way. The belief that it is essential for India's integrity and development is supported by a much greater number than those who oppose it. The vigor of its practice and the length of its endurance, rather than the perfection of its totality, is the touchstone of judgment about the success of the secular state in India. Any such evaluation of this unusual experiment in the relationship between church and state must leave us with a sense of optimism about its future.

Religion and State in Germany: West and East

By JÜRGEN MOLTMANN

ABSTRACT: The relationship between church and state in Germany is conditioned by the centuries-long history of state Christianity and also by the struggle for the independence of the churches over against the state. The churches won their critical power against the state's power in their opposition to Hitler's dictatorship and the totalitarian *Weltanschauung* of national socialism. Since the division of the two German states in 1961, a church in socialism has developed in the German Democratic Republic. It is willing both to resist the totalitarian claims of its society and also to join into a critical partnership with the state to develop domestic social politics and peace politics between nations. In the Federal Republic of Germany, the Catholic and Evangelical churches are further developing themselves along the lines of a church for the people (*Volkskirche*). This understanding of the nature of the church has been repeatedly placed into question since the development of the peace movement in 1981. A critical distance between the churches, on the one hand, and the claims and the political religion of the state, on the other, has consequently developed.

Jürgen Moltmann is a member of the Reformed Church in West Germany and professor of systematic theology at the University of Tubingen, West Germany. He received his doctoral degrees in 1952 and 1957 from the University of Göttingen, served as a pastor in Bremen from 1953 to 1958, and lectured as professor in Wuppertal and at the University of Bonn before he came to the University of Tübingen in 1967. He was guest professor at Duke University in 1967-68 and at Emory University in 1983. His major works include Theology of Hope *(1967);* The Crucified God *(1975);* The Trinity and the Kingdom of God *(1982); and* On Human Dignity *(1984).*

WHEN understood from a political perspective, the relationship between religion and state is determined by the struggle for public power by the churches and the struggle for religious legitimation by the state. When viewed from a religious perspective, the relationship between church and state is determined by the faith of the church and the credibility of church and state in a nation. The particularly Christian nature of the churches always comes into play in their relationship to the state.

The people measure both church and state according to their credibility. The church can survive persecution from the reigning political powers, and has done precisely this often enough. It perishes, however, with the contempt of the people. The government of a state can arrange itself with the hierarchy of a church. However, if it alienates itself from the people or becomes tyrannical, the state will perish. State and church, therefore, must, in their mutual relations, pay attention to the needs of the people whom they both must serve.

This requirement appears to me to be the lesson of the continual German *Kirchenkampf*, a struggle between church and state, in the past under the Hitler dictatorship, and in the present in the socialist state in East Germany and in the democratic state in West Germany.

THE COMMON HISTORY:
AUTONOMY AND RESISTANCE

Article 37 of the 1919 Weimar Constitution declared, "There is no established state church in Germany." Prior to this declaration, the churches in Germany had been state churches. The religious wars of the sixteenth and seventeenth century were ended with the law *cujus est regio ejus religio* ("whoever governs the region controls the religion"). As state churches, churches were a part of the state order: bishops were princes, princes were bishops; pastors and priests were civil servants; every citizen was at the same time a member of the state and the church. Religion was commonly practiced through both the state and the church. There was religious freedom only through the *jus emigrandi* ("right of emigration"). The religious ideology of the alliance of "throne and altar" dominated "the holy empire," the "Christian nation," and the "Christian West." The separation of church and state was really nothing more than a division of power within the common religion.

This alliance was dissolved when, in 1919, the throne of the German emperor was abolished and the first German democracy was founded. With this, the task before the churches was to become independent and take care of their own affairs without the help of the state. They remained privileged organizations, however, as so-called public corporations; they still hold the rights of religious education in the schools, of theological faculties in state universities, and of maintaining their own hospitals, kindergartens, and diaconal institutions. They must, however, arrange their relationship to the state themselves.

The Catholic Church established this relationship through concordats with the German state governments: in 1924 with Bavaria, in 1929 with Prussia, in 1932 with Baden, and on 20 July 1933 with the German Empire under Adolf Hitler. The Evangelical regional churches followed through with the signing of church contracts only after 1945. In 1955 they signed with Niedersachsen, in 1957 with Schleswig-Holstein, in 1960 with Hessen, and in 1962 with Rheinland-Pfalz. With these concordats and contracts, the religious ideology of the church for the people (*Volkskirche*) replaced the ideology of "throne and altar." The church became a church for all people, a pastoral church, a church of spiritual care, in short, the organized religion of German society. These churches concern themselves with fulfilling the various claims of society and thereby gain approval.

The German system of religion is, even today, a system of involuntary church affiliation. One is Catholic or Protestant by virtue of birth and becomes a Christian through infant baptism. Consequently, approximately 90 percent of the people in West Germany belong to a church and pay 10 percent of their income tax as church tax, but only 10 percent to 15 percent attend church regularly and remain active Christians.

Through the demise of the state church, the state was robbed of its religious legitimation and therefore had to legitimate itself secularly and through the democratic consensus of the people. This was not successful in the Weimar Democracy of 1919-33. The political religion of German nationalism required a new, authoritarian state.

In 1933, the political messianism of German national socialism fulfilled this demand with the establishment of the Third Reich under the führer: one people, one empire, one führer. This totalitarian state could not tolerate an autonomous church. The government attempted to infiltrate the churches through the national socialist movement. The movement held that German Christians demanded a unified church of the empire under a single bishop (*Reichsbischof*) obedient only to the führer. They falsely made Christianity into a German religion by discarding the Old Testament as a Jewish book and declaring Christ to be a racially pure Aryan.

This fraudulent transformation provoked the resistance of the Confessing Church, an Evangelical body. With the Barmen Declaration of 1934, the Confessing Church turned against these intrusions into the church. The Church Must Remain the Church was the motto of the Confessing Church in opposition to the totalitarian state and its new political religion. It was unclear whether this resistance was a purely self-defensive measure of the church, or whether it was also an attack on the inhuman German dictatorship in the name of its victims: the Jews and the politically oppressed. In the Catholic Church the defensive measures fared better because of its obedience to Rome. There were bishops and cardinals who were allied with Hitler, but there were also others who initiated resistance.

These experiences in the German conflict between church and state intensified the necessary struggle for the independence of the churches from the state. They revealed the continual, latent conflict between the religious ideologies of the state and the peculiarly Christian nature of the churches. They led the churches into solidarity with the victims of a religiously legitimated state power. Obviously, however, there is no possibility of resistance without the acceptance of the political, social, and cultural conditions within which the church exists, but this engagement demands the independent witness of the Christian faith and Christian life.

THE CHURCHES' ROLE IN
DIVIDED GERMANY, 1949-61

In the postwar era, from 1945 to 1961, the year in which the Berlin Wall was erected and the borders between

East and West Germany were closed, the churches were certainly the strongest organizations for the unity of the German people. The Evangelical Church in Germany (Evangelische Kirche in Deutschland [EKD]) was planned in Treysa in 1945 and founded in Eisenach in 1948. The EKD organizationally federated all of the regional churches in divided Germany, as the German states were then referred to. General synods, general assemblies, aid programs, and diaconal works built the connection between both parts of Germany. This pan-German activity was certainly bound up with the national desire for unity of the Germans of east and west, but was not ecclesiastically expressed in a nationalistic manner. It was formulated through the Stuttgart Confession of Guilt in 1945, which claimed that the common guilt of the war and of Auschwitz unifies the Germans in the east and west.

The vision of the newly reformed EKD in Germany in the postwar era was not the voluntary congregation of the Confessing Church in resistance, but the old church for the people, which is present in all strata of society. What occurred in the churches, as in the state after 1945, was no new beginning, but the restoration of the old relationships that were established before 1933. Much the same occurred in the Catholic Church. It was, however, with this concept of restoration that the churches failed in a divided Germany.

In 1949 the two German states were formed: the Federal Republic of Germany in the west and the German Democratic Republic in the east. The churches attempted to reinstate in both German states the relationships from the church for the people. They nominated delegates in both governments. As in the west, theological faculties were also inaugurated in the state universities in the east. Religiously affiliated hospitals and diaconal institutions were supported by the state in both countries.

The rearmament of the Federal Republic and the corresponding integration of the German Democratic Republic into the Warsaw Pact altered this symmetry. In 1957, the EKD signed a military chaplaincy contract with the Federal Republic that secured the presence of the church in the military and that brought the spiritual care of the soldiers into close connection with the inner guidance in the military. Because a corresponding military chaplaincy could not be allowed in the socialist army (*Volksarmee*), the government of the German Democratic Republic broke off its relationships with the EKD and dismissed its representative, Probst Grüber. From this point on, the churches in East and West Germany were forced to develop themselves separately. The churches in the Democratic Republic strove for their independence over and against the claims of Marxism-Leninism and of so-called real existing socialism. The churches in the Federal Republic engaged themselves more and more in fulfilling the religious claims of society and of the democratic nations in the Free World of the West.

In August 1961, Walter Ulbricht ordered the notorious Berlin Wall built in order to stop the stream of refugees from East to West Germany. As a result, the EKD was unable to function. Its synods and commissions could no longer convene. At the same time, the churches in the east were pressed to adjust to socialist ideology and to the socialist conditions. Pastoral groups and synods were infiltrated. The socialist youth initiation (*Jugendweihe*) was established to replace Christian confirmation. Christians in the schools and universities were discriminated against.

For some time, the Communist party followed the Czechoslovak model of a socialist state church. The ideologically proclaimed "dying away of religion" through the creation of all-encompassing, presumably liberating socialist conditions determined the church politics of the government in the Democratic Republic in the 1960s. Because of their close connection to the EKD and the regional churches in West Germany, the Christians in East Germany were considered disloyal and therefore untrustworthy. The West German support for the churches and Christians in the east, however, was not only religiously, but also strongly ideologically, motivated. The construction of the Berlin Wall in 1961 ended this support for the long term.

In 1969 the regional churches of the Democratic Republic formed their own, independent Union of Evangelical Churches (Bund evangelischer Kirchen). In 1971 this union was officially recognized by the government in the east. In 1972, in its synod in Leipzig, the union developed its own vision: a church in socialism. It no longer considered itself as part of the EKD organized in the west, but as an independent church. Real existing socialism was adopted as the ideological locale for Christian existence and church activity.

The church in socialism is not a socialist church, nor a church of socialism, but more the self-reliant Christian presence within a socialistically determined society. The church and the socialist state have now adjusted to each other, without mutual destruction. The Democratic Republic, for the church, is not a state system that will disappear after a treaty for the reunification of Germany is signed. The Christian church, for the state, is not an epiphenomenon of capitalism. Instead the new church politics of the Democratic Republic show that Marxists are ready to alter significantly the old Marxist critique of religion and to recognize that there will be original presuppositions for the church in mature socialism and also in the expected Communist society.

THE CHURCH IN SOCIALISM

Because atheistic Marxism-Leninism serves as the national ideology of the Democratic Republic, the division of church and state is nearly perfect. Article 39 of the Constitution of 1968-73 guarantees the religious freedom of every citizen and the independence of Christian churches and other religious communities. The churches no longer operate as public corporations. There are no church-state concordats, and the old church contracts with the German Empire have been rescinded. The churches, therefore, must support themselves through a voluntary church tax. Religious education can only be offered in church-owned buildings. There are still, however, theological faculties in state universities, church-affiliated hospitals, diaconal institutions for the handicapped, special times reserved on radio and television broadcasts, regional church assemblies with over 50,000 participants, and other privileges. These, however, are not contractually guaranteed, but result from dialogues between representatives of the churches and the state.

The social system of the Democratic Republic is organized around the principle of democratic centralism. In this, the totalitarian claims of the Party permeate all aspects of life. As individual organizations, only the churches have their autonomy preserved; democratic centralism has found its limits in the churches.

Since the founding and recognition of the Union of Evangelical Churches, the churches in the Democratic Republic can no longer be seen only as the extended arm of the West or as the remains of an already overcome capitalism. This has changed the religious politics and the church politics of the government. The attempts of the state and the Party to influence the churches decreased in the 1970s and ceased altogether in the 1980s. The Central Committee of the Party had already declared in 1971 that the state did not intend a socialization of the churches. On the other hand, the government, of course, wants the churches to participate in domestic politics and in the politics of peace between nations. Therefore, the government is openly ready to renounce the Marxist critique of religion and to downplay the atheism of the state ideology against the churches.

The decisive date for the new relationship between church and state was 6 March 1978, when the dialogue between the state chairman, Erich Honecker, and Bishop Albrecht Schönherr took place. This initial dialogue did not lead to a church contract with the state, but it created a certain partnership between state and church. The churches would receive room to operate within socialist society and would also have a certain right to participate in decision making in public affairs; the Christian citizens received the right to exist within socialism.

The antichurch polemic disappeared from the Party ideology, but, nevertheless, the control of the state and of society remained with the Party. Those who belong to the Party are bound to its

Marxist ideology. Christians, therefore, are excluded from Party membership and from leading positions in society.

Since 1978 the problems between church and state have been regulated through dialogues. The relationship between church and state thus remains open. Churches are only as strong as is the faith of Christians in the congregations.

Due to the various costs of belonging to a church, membership in the churches has sunk to approximately 30 percent of the population. The active presence of Christians in society, however, is even more distinctly recognizable. The church for the people (*Volkskirche*) has become a community church (*Gemeindekirche*). Peace politics and service to others are two of the areas in which a critical partnership between church and state has been achieved. In 1978 the churches protested against the requisite socialist military education in the schools and opposed it with their own program: Education for Peace. In 1981 the churches supported the spontaneously evolved youth peace movement Swords into Plowshares. The Party reacted cautiously to the churches' support.

Religion's accepted involvement in the public sphere was demonstrated conspicuously in the Karl Marx commemorative year, 1983. Chairman Honecker nominated himself chairman of the Martin Luther Committee and sponsored the festivals of the Martin Luther commemorative year.

In the realm of arms control, too, the presence of religion is felt. Over and against the progressing arms buildup in the camps of the North Atlantic Treaty Organization and the Warsaw Pact, the government of the Democratic Republic has publicly supported the improvement of relations between East and West Germany. In this regard, the common statements on peace and arms control published by the churches in the two Germanys have taken on certain weight.

The relationship between church and state in the Democratic Republic, then, is characterized by (1) the further division between church and state; (2) the newly won independence of the church over against the state; and (3) a critical solidarity of the churches with the politics of the state in the areas of peace politics and diaconal service to others in their society.

The churches have neither accommodated themselves to real existing socialism nor have they been thrust into a religious ghetto. They have maintained their identities as Christian churches and are publicly recognized as institutions in their own right.

THE CHURCH IN THE
WEST GERMAN DEMOCRACY

In contrast to the churches in socialist East Germany, the churches in West Germany have extensively integrated themselves into the democratic society. They continue to operate as churches for the people. Although the number of those leaving the churches is ever increasing, 90 percent of the people still belong to one or the other of the two main Christian confessions. In contrast to East Germany, where the number of Catholics is much smaller than the number of Protestants, in West Germany the numbers in each group are about equal. The Catholic Bishops Conference speaks out on public issues such as abortion, peace, unemployment, and ecological problems through pastoral letters based on Catholic social teaching. The Evangelical Church in West Germany speaks out through synods and through the church leadership of the EKD in the new form of memoranda (*Denkschriften*) on the problems of public and political life. Its basis is the prophetic mandate of the church. Although these pastoral letters and memoranda still betray a trace of unquestionable religious authority, they prompt ever more public, democratic discussion and receive public criticism.

The process of the democratization of the old state churches and churches for the people has, however, just begun, and it is a painful learning process for many representatives of the church hierarchies. Along with the state churches, the democratic state has also abandoned a corresponding state religion and thus has opened the door for religious pluralism. Nevertheless, there is still an ideology of the Free World infused with the religious elements present within this system. Deeply rooted anticommunism too easily leads this Western ideology to the political Manichaeism of good versus evil and to the apocalypse of a nuclear final battle.

The bitter experiences with terrorism in Europe led in the 1970s to an emphasis on what has been termed the fundamental consensus of all German citizens, found in the Constitution of the Federal Republic: a catalogue of fundamental values. This fundamental consensus had to be defended against terrorists, but it was also easily lifted up into a new German civil religion.

The churches were required to support, not criticize, this new religious foundation of the state. In the churches, that demand led to a new conflict between church and state—not about the question of terrorism, but about the question of peace. When, in 1981, new American nuclear missiles were stationed on West German soil at the request of the North Atlantic Treaty

Organization, massive protests from the people and from large numbers of Christians were the response. Both the Evangelical and Catholic Churches produced dialectical statements with the message that Christians should hope to secure peace both with weapons and without weapons. Through such statements, the churches could make allowances for both the military chaplaincy in the army and the new Christian-motivated peace movement.

The first break in the indecision engendered by the church for the people was made by the Reformed Church, which in 1981 declared the nuclear deterrence systems to be incompatible with the Christian faith. The synods of other Evangelical regional churches followed. The Union of Evangelical Churches in East Germany also rejected "the spirit, logic, and practice of nuclear deterrence systems."[1] The Catholic Bishops Conference in West Germany followed the American bishops' statement in this regard.

The pressure of Christian peace movements on church leadership is intense. If it is successful, then the basic relationship between church and state will be put into question. Church contracts and concordats, military chaplaincies, and the support of the religious ideology of the Western world must then be revised. The churches can no

1. Synod of the Union of Evangelical Churches, Hermannswerder, German Democratic Republic, Nov. 1983.

longer remain churches for the people. They must become confessing peace churches.

It is understandable that national representatives—primarily the conservative ones—have already warned the churches and attempted to use the church leadership to bring the Christian peace movement under control. Because the end of further construction of nuclear deterrence systems is not in sight, despite the intensive ongoing disarmament talks, the peace question becomes more and more a confessional question of the Christian faith.

The conflict in both Catholic and Protestant churches for the people in the Federal Republic will increase. It will create a new conflict between church and state. The political religion in West Germany demands loyalty and support of nuclear deterrence systems. The Christian witness demands the elimination of this threat of world annihilation and the creation of an active service for peace. The churches cannot straddle this issue, any more than the individual Christian can.

It is on the peace question that a new and astonishing accord has arisen between the churches in socialism and the churches in Western democracy. The community of churches in the two Germanys is a community on the border between the two world superpowers. It can take no other form than the common witness for the peace of humankind and the life of creation.

An Open Issue of Legitimacy: The State and the Church in Poland

By ZDZISLAWA WALASZEK

ABSTRACT: Since the founding of the Communist state in Poland, the growth of the institutionalized basis of Catholicism there has accelerated. This trend obviously reflects a continuing growth in the social base of support for Catholicism. This article presents church-state relations in terms of confrontation between the church and Communist rule, and it postulates that the Polish Roman Catholic Church has been transformed in the course of its coexistence with Communist rule and resembles very little the Catholic Church of the prewar period. The Roman Catholic Church serves as an alternative legitimate system within Communist Poland. It is an authority system that is not constitutionally recognized, but in real terms it functions as if it were and coexists with the Communist authorities. Moreover, in the eyes of the general public, the role of the Polish church is conditional upon the performance of the Communist regime. The church's authority extends beyond the spiritual and moral domain and directly enters politics and, more recently, the social and cultural life of local communities.

Zdzislawa Walaszek received her Ph.D. in sociology from the Johns Hopkins University in 1973. From 1974 to 1978 she was assistant professor of sociology at the University of Chicago; since 1974 she has been a research associate at the National Opinion Research Center. Her primary research concerns the study of the actions of individuals and groups as indicators of power distribution and has included a survey of registered Washington lobbyists. Dr. Walaszek has published several articles on general problems of power, influence, and authority, and she is currently working on a volume, Communism and National Sovereignty: The Case of Poland.

NOTE: This article is part of the author's work in progress *Communism and National Sovereignty: The Case of Poland.*

PROBLEMS of legitimation of authority have been central to intellectual pursuits since the time of Aristotle. An interesting post-Weberian contribution was made by Seymour Martin Lipset, who distinguishes between the effectiveness of political systems, which can be judged using instrumental criteria and related to the systems' performance, and their legitimacy, which is an evaluative criterion and refers to the public's perception of the systems' appropriateness and belief that the body politic of a system has the right to exercise political authority in given domains.[1] Depending on historical circumstances, effectiveness and legitimacy—as well as the absence of these—can characterize virtually any form of political organization. Moreover, the stability of political institutions, and their performance in both conflict and nonconflict situations, depends upon their effectiveness and their legitmacy.

LEGITIMACY AND EFFECTIVENESS

Although the distinction between effectiveness and legitimacy is heuristic and in real political life the two interact with one another, it is nevertheless a useful distinction for analytical purposes. For example, if society perceives that a system is legitimate, this perception can compensate—even after extended periods of time—for erroneous, inefficient, and ineffective policy decisions. Furthermore, citizens who perceive a system as legitimate will be more likely to acquiesce even to actions that are against their individual interests. Second, a high level of effectiveness in heeding the public interest and fulfilling individual expectations may purchase

some legitimacy for an initially illegitimate system, such as a revolutionary one. Finally, any legitimate system is subject to erosion and processes of delegitimation if in the long run the system proves to be ineffective. Hence, legitimacy needs to be re-earned constantly. No system can survive in the long run without being effective.

Effectiveness alone, however, without mechanisms that redress the ideology of legitimation, is not sufficient. Thus, in today's Poland, for example, even if the regime were capable of providing something comparable to goulash socialism, the society would not work hard enough—or, more generally, the society would not release its productive forces—unless some basic civil and human rights reforms were likely to follow. So what we observe in Poland on an unprecedented scale is an erosion of legitimacy of the political system. In this process of erosion of systemic legitimacy, the Polish Catholic Church has acquired the attributes of a political authority system.

Consider the postwar confrontation between the Communist authority on the one hand and the authority of the Polish church on the other. From the point of view of legitimation of their respective power bases and their institutional effectiveness, one can argue that the legitimacy of the regime in the eyes of the nation has never been fully resolved, whereas that of the church—a traditionally legitimated system—has not suffered an erosion of legitimacy. On the contrary, it is today, after the disfranchisement of Solidarity, the only supranational institution that has been granted full legitimation by the society at large.

In this quest for legitimacy Solidarity can be considered as the manifestation

1. Seymour Martin Lipset, *Political Man* (New York: Columbia University Press, 1959).

of societal aspirations in the political domain that were part of a broader manifestation of national aspirations embedded in the adherence of Poles to their Catholic Church. The institutionalization of the free trade-union movement as a legitimate system of representation within the existing Communist system forced the issue of the authority system into the open. What started as a regional union almost overnight evolved into an organized national movement. Solidarity became, in effect, the first institutionalized form of representation in the postwar era that has been fully legitimated by society.

The legitimation of Solidarity was accompanied by total withdrawal of whatever legitimacy there had been for the regime. The close bonds between the workers, peasants, intelligentsia, and clergy that emerged in 1980 were sustained even after the imposition of martial law, contrasting quite effectively with the compartmentalization of political segregation and alienation among the workers, peasants, and intelligentsia at the times of earlier crises in Poland, in 1948-49, 1956, 1968, 1970, and 1976. The unprecedented turning to the Polish church as the sole remaining repository of national aspirations manifests this societal alliance and normative opposition of each of the Polish strata. In this search for legitimacy, the society effectively politicized the institutional role of the church, and the church leaders ultimately entered the arena of politics.

Perhaps the best way to illustrate the complexity of the relations between the Roman Catholic Church and the Communist state in Poland is to present some simple statistical data. The figures in Table 1, which cover nearly half a century, show steady growth for the Polish Catholic Church. The expansion occurred in three dimensions: in institutional infrastructure, as measured by the number of places of worship; in active affiliation, seen in the number of parishes; and in human resources, as in the number of priests. This indicates that more people are served by the Catholic Church and that more people are willing to serve the church in a network that is both geographically expanded and more dense.

Given the fact that church-state relations are inherently unstable in a Communist system, and that Marxist ideology actively advocates disfranchisement of religion, the phenomenal growth of the Polish Catholic Church demonstrates an unconditional and noteworthy growth in the social basis of support for the Catholic religion. However, the Polish Roman Catholic Church was transformed in the course of its coexistence with Communist rule and resembles very little the Catholic Church of the prewar period.

The Communist state and the Catholic Church provided the society with different scenarios of choice. Thus, for example, while Communist rule introduced the doctrine of Marxism, the Catholic Church sustained the teachings of the normative system of Christian ethics; the Communists advocated internationalism, the Polish church patriotism; the Communists tried to purchase credibility through promise of future benefits, while the church not only offered hope but actively promoted the welfare of the people; the Communists implemented policies that initiated cyclical crises, and the church provided sanctuary for the victims of those crises. Hence, on balance, the Polish church came out the victor in each of these confrontations, which is evidenced by the extent of the Catholic allegiance of the

TABLE 1

INSTITUTIONAL GROWTH OF THE POLISH CATHOLIC CHURCH

	Places of Worship	Parishes	Priests
1937	7,251	5,170	11,348
1967	13,273	6,334	17,986
1970	13,392	6,376	18,151
1980	14,585	7,089	20,617

SOURCES: Stanislaw Markiewicz, *Panstwo i kosciol w Polsce* [The state and church in Poland] (Warsaw: KAW, 1984); Dionizy Tanalski, *Tendencje ideologiczne we wspolczesnej katolickiej mysli spolecznej i filozoficznej* [Ideological tendencies in the contemporary social and philosophical thought in Catholicism] (Warsaw: Kslazka i wiedza, 1984).

Polish nation. The extent of this allegiance should not, however, be interpreted as a new form of fundamentalism in Poland.

If Marxism continued to emphasize the ideals of collectivities, Christian teachings began to emphasize the ideals and values of individuals. Marxism saw Polish history through the prism of selective social movements, Polish Catholicism through the individual acts of people. Thus, in addition to providing an ongoing history lesson, the church defended the right of the nation to its own heritage and heroes.

From the defense of the individual moral right to hope and belief, or more generally the right to the choice of religious beliefs, it was a small step to the defense of earthbound rights of individuals vis-à-vis their state. Thus, by 1980 Poland had become the arena where the opposing concepts of national sovereignty, self-determination, and societal and state organizations openly collided.

Why was this quest for legitimacy important? The Soviet Union's primary gains as a result of World War II were not so much its geographical expansion through the annexation and acquisition of territories, but rather the establishment within the community of nations of a dominant nation's right to determine the internal makeup of the social and political system of a subjugated nation, without the appearance of an outright violation of the subjugated nation's sovereignty. Within a relatively short period of time after the war, the systemic independence of nations that found themselves within the Soviet sphere of influence was successfully eradicated. By 1948, the Soviet-style system was firmly established in most of the countries of central and eastern Europe. The establishment of Communist systems in those countries was begun under the banner of the progressive forces of mankind; and while maintaining a semblance of their territorial sovereignty, all of the countries became extensions of the Soviet Union. Furthermore, a postcolonial precedent was initiated within the international forum in which the nature of the political system became the key to a country's claim of independence. Thus, an independent, territorially sovereign postwar Poland, for example, was acceptable to the Soviet Union only insofar as it introduced a specific sociopolitical order, namely Communism patterned on the Soviet model. Consequently, outright domination based on military strength alone was subtly redefined, such that the territorial sovereignty of a country was preserved while ideology became an accepted tool of dominance.

The political system of Poland between the wars, especially during the 1930s, was nationalistic, militaristic, and authoritarian, but it was never totalitarian. Though badgered, the opposition parties operated legally except, eventually, the Communists, who were obliged to resort to the subterfuge of fronts. The trade unions and the press, although harassed, remained independent and active. Outspoken opponents of the government continued to teach at the universities and to publish their criticisms; the judiciary's autonomy from the administration was preserved; and the bureaucracy, while rigid, was technically competent. More generally, the prewar state was the last truly legitimate Polish state, despite its many and serious weaknesses. And it is precisely this attribute, this quality of legitimacy, that the contemporary Polish regime has never been able to earn in the eyes of the Polish public, despite four decades of ceaseless attempts. To implement the new system, an array of strategies has been used. This began as early as 1943, culminating with the founding of the Polish Committee of National Liberation in 1944. The final result was the establishment of a dominant totalitarian regime by 1948-49.

AMBIGUITY OF THE
COMMUNIST MANDATE

The quest for legitimacy involved two complementary strategies: military control and political control. Without reliance on force, the implementation of the political program would not have been possible; and force without an appealing sociopolitical platform and concrete postulates would not have been enough to pacify and to convince the

population. A synopsis of these strategies is quite informative.

Implementation of the Communist system was possible only with reliance on military force. Moreover, given the circumstances, such military force could not be overtly Soviet. With the departure of the Polish Army from the Soviet Union to join the Allies under the command of General Anders, actual control over Polish military forces eluded the Soviets. That situation, however, was soon remedied. By February 1943, under the aegis of the Union of Polish Patriots in the Soviet Union and the Polish Communists, together with close supervision by the Soviets, a second army was formed. This army, which was politically reliable, was to become the power base and the tool for social and political transformation in Poland. The nucleus of this so-called First Army was formed in Sielce on the Oka River.

Communist supervision of recruitment and training was very strict. In addition, the army was placed under the direct control of the Soviet military command. Thus, the entire policy of recruitment and appointments was implemented under the close scrutiny of the commanders of the Red Army. At the same time, such obvious and mundane things as supplies of food, arms, and ammunition had to be cleared through the Soviet channel. The key commanding posts of the Polish Army were given with Stalin's personal approval to the most reliable Polish Communists. The officer corps of the newly formed army was heavily populated by Soviet *Popy*, a nickname for Russians that were fulfilling the duties of the Poles. By the end of 1944 they constituted about 45 percent of the entire officer corps, or about 19,000 men, including 36 generals who commanded the major army units. Those were gradually replaced later by Polish officers trained in special schools and course programs in the Soviet Union.[2]

This control was further reinforced by the political apparatus in the army itself, which consisted of the Communist party representatives acting in the capacity of political officers. Those party plenipotentiaries were directly appointed by the Central Committee of the Polish Workers Party; many of them held positions as deputy commanders and were directly accountable to the army's Main Political Directorate, which was equivalent to the military department of the party's Central Committee. Despite this already extensive system of control, some other measures were also taken.[3]

This political and ideological supervision was further reinforced by the activities of two important controlling agencies: the army's Counter-Intelligence unit and the Soviet Narodnyi Komissariat Vnutrennikh Del (NKVD). Little is known about their activities, but we do know that the Polish Army's Counter-Intelligence was created from over 200 graduates of the Soviet Political School, located near Kuibishev, who then served as advisors, political officers, and military court judges. For example, with the advance of the Red Army to Poland the Soviet-trained Polish Army units were directly responsible for the arrest and kidnapping of the Polish underground's military and political leaders, the mass arrests and deportations to the Soviet Union of the soldiers of the Home Army, and the elimination of the underground radio stations.

Despite these precautions, what followed in the period of 1944-47 was something comparable to a civil war. By the end of September 1944, it was estimated that over 21,000 Home Army men had been arrested. Detention camps were set up. Many of the military and paramilitary units were subsequently dissolved by fiat when the Polish Home Army itself was officially dissolved by orders from the government in exile. Subsequently, there were two amnesties: one in 1945, with about 42,000 Home Army members surfacing from the underground; the other in 1947, with 60,000 people leaving the underground.

It should be recognized that complete political control over the armed forces was attained prior to the massive purges and political trials of the so-called Stalinist period. This control was, of course, further strengthened during the next few years, when many people were arrested, tortured, and sentenced because of their Home Army background. It was not until the crisis of 1956 that the veterans of the Home Army were rehabilitated

2. F. Zbigniewicz, "Rola Komunistow polskich w orgznizowaniu dzialalnosci LPP oraz polskich sil zbrojnych w ZSSR" [The role of Polish Communists in organizing the activities of LPP and Polish military forces in the Soviet Union], *Z pola walki,* no. 4, p. 16.

3. A. Polonsky and Bolesaw Drukier, *The Beginning of Communist Rule in Poland* (London: Routledge, 1980); Marian Kostecki, "Organizacyjna historia polski" [Organizational history of Poland] (Institute of Philosophy and Sociology, Polish Academy of Sciences, Warsaw, 1982). For example, in October 1944, the leaders of the Polish Workers Party established a special five-man Army Department within the Central Committee whose purpose was "to further strengthen the partisan [pro-Communist] elements in the army." Appointments of party officials to the military command and officers corps followed. Also, recruiting agencies were given more strict instructions to screen out "unreliable and hostile elements." This obvious political selection meant that recruitment slackened; in November 1944, 10,000 so-called patriots and party-appointed members were delegated to the army and the established schools for officers. Kostecki, "Organizacyjna historia polska."

and acknowledged for their fight against the Germans in World War II.

Political strategy

As indicated previously, reliance on military force in implementing the new regime was coupled with political strategy. One of the earliest strategies of legitimation of the Communist regime was that of imitation and appropriation of the symbolic aspects of the prewar democratic legacy. This strategy had serious consequences in the realm of domestic politics, creating further confusion amid the chaos that already existed toward the end of World War II. For example, with the founding of the Polish Communist party by the Communist International (Comintern), the name "Communist Party" was never used—the Communist regime concealed itself under the name of the Polish Workers Party. There were two reasons for this. One was the association of the term "Communist" with the embarrassing fate of the original Polish Communist Party; the other was the current level of popular support for Communists. The original prewar Polish Communist Party was dissolved in 1937 and its leadership and a significant portion of its membership subsequently were executed by order of Stalin and the Comintern on grounds of treason. The entire Polish Communist Party was effectively wiped out.

During the prewar period, the number of Communist deputies to the Seym— the Polish Parliament—was small. There were no Communist deputies between 1919 and 1922, six between 1922 and 1924, seven between 1928 and 1930, and four between 1930 and 1935—0.0 percent, 1.4 percent, 1.6 percent, and 0.9 percent of all deputies, respectively. Furthermore, not a single Polish govern-

ment from 1918 to 1945 ever had any Communists in the cabinet. The Communists have always been a negligible minority. Thus, reactivating a Polish Communist party became a tricky enterprise, since it could bring back memories of the Soviet-inspired demise of the original Communist party on the one hand, and the unpopularity of Communists with the nation on the other. Thus, the "Polish Workers Party" was born.

The Polish Workers Party, in its quest for dominance, created a parallel body destined to play a future part as a representative Polish parliamentary body. Following the advance of the Soviet army at the close of World War II, members of the party, at the express instigation of Stalin, hastily formed a provisional body with legislative powers. This body was formed secretly in Warsaw on 1 January 1944—a few days before the Red Army crossed the Polish-Soviet frontier near Sarny, Volhynia. The chosen name was "National Council of the Homeland" (Krajowa Rada Narodowa), an obvious copy of the two existing parliamentary substitutes connected with the Polish government in London: the National Council, the first session of which was held in Paris on 23 January 1940, and the Council of National Unity, formerly the Political Representation of the Homeland, set up by the underground in Poland in the winter of 1939-40. Much effort was spent on creating a pretense that the new body had wide popular support and that its founding was a result of grass-roots political activism on the part of the Polish masses.[4]

4. For example, the following so-called parties and groups were declared to have taken part in setting up the council: the Polish Workers Party, the Polish Workers' Socialist Party, the Peasant Party, the Committee of National Initiative, a

When the Red Army crossed the Bug River, the Polish Committee of National Liberation was set up by a decree of the National Council of the Homeland. The committee was designated to become the provisional executive authority "to head the nation's struggle for liberation and to secure its independence and the reestablishment of the Polish state." It published its political platform, which became known as the July Manifesto. The platform included a call for broad agricultural reform based on land redistribution without compensation to former owners of large estates, and it promised to reestablish a democratic political system as well as free elections after the war ended. Some aspects of the manifesto are extremely interesting as a means of creating an aura of legitimacy around the new Communist regime, as well as extricating the regime from the political legacy of the prewar period. The manifesto declared, "The émigré government in London and its agency in Poland is an illegal and self-styled authority, based on the illegal Fascist Constitution of April, 1935."[5]

By using the epithet "émigré," the committee's manifesto intended to emphasize the abandonment of the Polish nation by its government during a time of crisis in September 1939. However, the prewar Polish government, of which the London government was a legal continuation, left Poland in September 1939, as a result of two swift blows—the invasion from the west by the German Army, and the invasion from the east by the Red Army, a consequence of which was the fourth partition of Poland. The subsequent Polish governments led by Sikorski and Mikolajczyk, respectively, had to be formed on Allied soil, the former in 1939 in France, the latter after General Sikorski's tragic death in 1943. Although the executive powers resided physically in London, the Polish government had not been a fully émigré government almost since the beginning of the Nazi occupation of Poland. Its permanent underground administration, headed by a government delegate, had never left the country.[6] By using the term "agency" the manifesto attempted to underline both the derogatory and the minority status of the Polish government in Poland. However, this "agency" in reality covered the whole of the vast Polish underground administration: the Polish Homeland Political Representation, consisting of representatives of the four democratic parties and later renamed the Council of National Unity, a

---

group of nonparty democrats, the Underground Trades Union Movement, the Fighting Youth Association, a group of artisans' representatives, and representatives of the People's Guard, the People's Militia, the Peasants' Battalion, and the Regional Formations of the Home Army. *Wolna polska*, 24 May 1944. To emphasize the grassroots origin of the National Council of the Homeland, it was reported that the council was elected by the voivodeship—the highest administrative territorial unit in Poland—the district councils, and the local councils, which in turn had been elected by patriotic organizations. Ibid., 8 Feb. 1944. However, it was later reported that the voivodeship council of such an important region as Upper Silesia was created only at the beginning of May 1944—over four months after the National Council of the Homeland was founded! Ibid., 24 July 1944.

5. Wladyslaw Gomulka, "Ideologiczne zalozenia manifestu polskiego Komitetu wyzwole-

nia narodowego" [Ideological principles of the manifesto of the Committee of National Liberation], in *Artykuly i przemowienia* [Articles and speeches] (Warsaw: Ksiazka i wiedza, 1962).

6. For example, by the decree of 1 September 1942, the government delegate was admitted to the Polish government in the capacity of deputy premier, and three heads of the delegates' 13 administrative departments became cabinet ministers. *Polish Daily*, 15 Jan. 1944.

substitute for Parliament; the vast network of underground educational institutions, including post-secondary education; and the entire Home Army and affiliated underground organizations.

To charge the Polish government with being "an illegal and self-styled authority" in 1944 was tantamount to challenging the diplomatic recognition of that government over a period of several years by Great Britain, the United States, and all the Allied and neutral powers, not to mention its recognition for nearly two years by the Soviet Union.[7]

The most intriguing part of the manifesto is the attack on the 1935 constitution, and therefore implicit recognition of the 1921 constitution, by the committee. Why was this? The reasons were twofold. First, by challenging and in fact revoking the 1935 constitution, the committee *ipso facto* abolished the legal basis of the existing Polish government in London, thereby obliterating any form of government that had been a legitimate continuation of the prewar period. Second, the emphasis on adherence to the 1921 constitution, which could have been interpreted by a layperson as the continuation of the prewar democratic principles by the new political system, was in effect a ploy to create legal opportunities for transfer of powers to the Communists. The 1921 constitution provided for presidential power to be transferred under certain circumstances to the Speaker of the Seym. As indicated earlier, the Communist-sponsored National Council of the Homeland assumed the position of the Seym. Once in that position, the council's

Speaker, Mr. Boleslaw Bierut, could rise to the position of Poland's acting president—and that is effectively what happened.

To give the newly created system an appearance of reality, names of old and popular parties were revived and used to designate newly founded groups. To understand the originality of this strategy, a brief description of the political life of prewar Poland is necessary.

It is clear that the leaders of the later Communist party in Poland were only too conscious of the unpopularity of their doctrine among the Poles. However, the adoption of the new name, "Polish Workers Party," was in itself not enough. Poland had old political traditions of its own that included a strong attachment to parties that existed even prior to 1914, during the partition period in Prussian, Russian, and Austrian Poland. These parties had greatly contributed to the reestablishment of Polish independence and to the founding of the Polish state of 1918. Within the framework of the new system of power set up in Poland in 1945, unscrupulous use was made of the names of the prewar established parties in order to be able to document both continuity and support of all existing Polish political trends. The greatest possible use was made of the labels of two parties, the Polish Socialist Party and the Peasant Party. The newly created Polish Socialist Party, in terms of its platform and its leadership—apart from its remaining membership—had very little linkage with the original prewar party. Osobka-Morawski, the chairman of the Lublin Committee of National Liberation, became the chairman of the Polish Socialist Party. Similarly, the new Peasant Party had little if any relationship to the old one, despite a further attempt

---

7. Following the British-Polish Mutual Assistance Pact, the Polish government in London chose to collaborate with the USSR until the Soviet Union broke diplomatic relations on 25 April 1943, as a result of the Katyn investigation.

of political falsification in which its chairmanship was entrusted to Andrzej Witos, the half-brother of the great prewar peasant leader Wincenty Witos, twice a prime minister of Poland. However, when it became clear that no one was taken in by the same surname, and that a sharp distinction was being made between the two brothers, Andrzej Witos was simply thrown into the political dustbin.

A Democratic Party was also included in the new, allegedly pluralistic system. A party of that name had existed in prewar Poland, but it had been fairly new. Why that particular party was included at this point is not quite clear, as it did not have any long-standing tradition. Perhaps the name was supposed to suggest the democracy of the new system. Interestingly, three political parties that existed before the war were neither reactivated nor were their names utilized in the new structures for political life. Those included the National Democratic Party, the Jewish Zionist Party, and the Christian Democratic Party; the last was better known in Poland under its new name, the "Labor Party." The National Democratic Party, among whose founders were men such as Roman Dmowski, had for 40 years represented the views of the Polish right wing and had been one of the strongest parties in several Polish parliaments. The Christian Democratic Party, with a smaller following, represented the views of moderate social reformers as expressed in the famous papal encyclical *De Rerum Novarum*. Other strategies of pseudolegitimation of the Communist regime in Poland included the appropriation of the prewar press titles for the postwar propaganda effort.[8]

LEGITIMACY OF A COMMUNIST REGIME IN POLAND

The political spectrum of the period 1945-48 contained the Communist movement, under the auspices of the Polish Workers Party and backed by the Soviet Union; the illegal opposition, which contained the remaining units of the Home Army and other underground groups sponsored by the London government in exile; and the legal opposition, consisting of the three reactivated political parties mentioned earlier. First, the systematic eradication of illegal opposition eventually succeeded. The Communist government continued to consolidate its position. Then mock free elections and the departure of Mikolajczyk from Poland cleared the remnants of legal opposition. By 1947 the legal opposition was largely disfranchised. This successful eradication of legal opposition in Poland was marked by the merging of the Polish Socialist Party and the Polish Workers Party into a

---

8. For example, after the founding of the Committee of National Liberation in 1944 an official daily organ was started under the title *Rzeczpospolita,* a name strangely reminiscent of that of the official Polish underground movement, *Rzeczpospolita Polska.* Subsequently names of popular weeklies of various prewar Polish parties were appropriated, such as *Robotnik* [Worker] of the Polish Socialist Party and *Zielony sztandar* [Green flag], the publication of the Peasant Party, among others. This imitation extended even to the nonpolitical press. The children's weekly, for example, was *Plomyk* [The little flame], the reason being that in prewar Poland the Association of Teachers published a popular children's paper under that title. Despite the variety of titles and trends, these Communist papers were very much alike. The leading articles, editorials, political commentary, and anything else of importance appeared as a rule in all papers practically simultaneously, both in openly Communist papers and in papers alleged to represent the socialists, the peasants, and the democrats.

single entity, the Polish United Workers Party of today.

One of the hypotheses postulated here is that the initially gradual and then accelerated growth of the legitimation of the power of the church on the one hand, and the ongoing political crises in Poland on the other, go deeper and beyond the evident policy mistakes of different Communist leaderships. What we observe in Poland is an ongoing crisis of the legitimacy of the authority system. The roots of Polish postwar statehood and the ambiguity of the Communist mandate, as well as the form of the implementation of the system, meant that the regime lacked sufficient initial legitimacy. Given that lack, the regime was obliged to devote much of its energy to defending its own authority by concentrating on strategies for eradicating any challenges to that authority. Even the postwar Polish Workers Party, the established authority, was not immune from the coercion and repression that became necessary to maintaining a facade of pseudolegitimacy.

For example, a faction of the Polish Workers Party, and particularly Wladyslaw Gomulka, spoke of the "Polish road to socialism," the emphasis being that the shape of the Communist system in Poland should be determined by Polish traditions and history together with some of the Marxist principles. Thus, the Polish system should not be an exact replica of the Soviet system, which in many ways was incompatible with the Polish political culture.

In contrast, the Muscovites—the other party faction, led by Boleslaw Bierut—sought to establish a Stalinist regime from the outset. Bierut accused the "natives" of being "radishes," red on the outside and white within. The political blueprint advocated by the Muscovites contained a system of monopolies of power. The party would be run in a hierarchical fashion in which policy decisions came down from the Politburo to the Central Committee, then to district party offices, and finally to local cells in offices and factories. The central economic planning system would be essential to the management of the economy. Private ownership was not to be tolerated. The military and security sectors would be part of the centralized system of power. The media and any propaganda instruments would also be subject to the control of the party, as well as state institutions and organizations. This model also actively discouraged religion and sought to substitute for it the Communist axiology.

The two factions struggled for power in the provisional government. By 1948 the Muscovite faction gained ascendancy. The group became sufficiently strong to challenge the more traditional faction and impose a Stalinist-style pro-Soviet government. In 1948 the so-called nationalistic tendencies of the Polish United Workers Party were criticized by the Soviet Union, and in 1949 Gomulka, the leader of the Polish party, was arrested and subsequently jailed. During the following plenum of the party, Bierut became the president of Poland.[9] The shift of power toward the pro-Soviet faction resulted in changes in Polish political life. The Russian model was slavishly copied in every sphere. Polish economic decisions had to be endorsed by the Soviet leadership, and both foreign and domestic policies were shaped by the Moscow directives.

Adoption of the Soviet bureaucratic model as a result of the 1948-49 crisis

9. The further Sovietization of Poland was accelerated when Soviet Marshal Konstanty Rokossowski became the minister of defense and commander-in-chief of the Polish Army.

was to bear fruit later. Two major consequences should be distinguished, one being a drastic reduction in political support for the regime. In fact, this problem of legitimacy had been critically important to the society since 1944. The elections of 17 January 1947 that gave the so-called Democratic bloc—controlled by Communists—80.1 percent of the votes were rigged, and some sources estimate that approximately only 20 percent of the voters would have voted for the Democratic bloc.

This is not to deny that as the internal situation calmed down and the civil war subsided large segments of the population began to render support to the regime, particularly as the regime effectively concentrated on the task of rebuilding the war-shattered country. However, that support was based also on the assurance that democracy in Poland would be maintained and that Poland would be allowed to solve its problems in its own way. With the ascendancy to power of the pro-Soviet faction, the credibility of the regime was threatened. Moreover, the post-1948-49 leadership was no longer representative of the Polish people; rather, it issued Soviet-inspired policy decisions, and the overall legitimacy of the Communist-backed rule became openly questioned. Also, in the midst of events that followed later and in subsequent crises, the theme of the regime's legitimacy continued to haunt the authorities in question. For example, a survey conducted in 1980 by a team of sociologists from the Polish Academy of Sciences showed the following:

1. About 80 percent of the sample favored increased involvement of the church in public life.

2. Increased involvement of nonparty people in the exercise of power was favored by 92 percent of the sample.

3. Of those sampled, 80 percent wanted decision making in the most important matters to be in the hands of the local authorities and wanted a restriction of the prerogatives of the central authorities.

4. More freedom of speech and more freedom to circulate opinions critical of official policies were favored by 83 percent.[10]

This polycentric model of power reveals a remarkable image of political attitudes. After more than 37 years of Communist rule, less than 20 percent of the sampled population endorsed that rule. What legitimacy, then, did that regime have in 1948?

The other consequence of the 1948-49 crisis was the development of a system of bureaucratic socialism, directly borrowed from the Soviet model, that in addition to its obvious deficiencies was totally incompatible with Polish political culture and traditions. The Soviet model therefore could not be fully implemented in the Polish socioeconomic context. In many ways this veneer of Stalinism, totally incongruent with Polish traditions, gave rise to social forces that were to emerge later.

TRANSFER OF LEGITIMACY?

Within this political context, let us now consider the process by which the church began to be defined as the active repository of societally granted legitimacy. This is perhaps best illustrated by

10. Wladyslaw Adamski et al., *Polacy 1980* [Poles 1980] (Warsaw: Polish Academy of Sciences, Institute of Philosophy and Sociology, 1981).

the name given by society to Cardinal Stefan Wyszynski, the late primate of Poland, during the Stalinist period. He was called "Interrex." This stemmed from a long historical tradition dating from the time when Poland was an electoral monarchy. During the interregnum period—that is, between royal elections—the supreme power of the state rested in the hands of the primate of Poland. Hence, the popular perception of Cardinal Wyszynski as the interregnum supreme authority really indicated a collective perception of the tenuous legitimacy of the Communist regime. Although Cardinal Wyszynski never saw himself as the political leader of the nation, public opinion nevertheless saw him as such. This perception grew stronger over time, and Cardinal Wyszynski began to be seen as a political figure and a symbol of social yearnings and aspirations.[11]

Cardinal Wyszynski saw himself as the spiritual father of the nation—as both a religious and moral guide. This sense of spiritual fatherhood was directly derivative from the concept of "God our Father." In the societal perception, fatherhood was translated into political guidance as well and to some extent Cardinal Wyszynski was conscious of the need for normative leadership. This was well exemplified by his teachings, in which he set his religious mission in a historical context. His sermons on the deadly threats to the survival of Christianity should not be underestimated. He early recognized the nature of the political environment that led him to focus particularly on the materialism and antireligiousness of Communism. He had a deeply embedded faith that he was a missionary of God in a particular historical setting. Cardinal Wyszynski might not have been intentionally political, but he began to represent the political aspirations of the nation.

In his role as the spiritual father, Cardinal Wyszynski was extremely active in establishing and fostering extensive contacts with his flock. He visited parishes and religious orders, met with the old and the young, and actively participated in religious rituals not only in Warsaw but throughout the entire country. This sense of spiritual fatherhood and responsibility for the nation was exemplified by his form of addressing congregations as "my children" and by his repeated emphasis on the inseparability of the fate of the nation from the fate of its Catholic Church in the new historical reality.[12] This broad conception of spiritual leadership characterized the entire church hierarchy, from parish priests to cardinals, such as Cardinal Karol Wojtyla, Cardinal Franciszek Macharski, and Cardinal Jozef Glemp, and including the entire episcopate.

The progressive Stalinization of the sociopolitical life meant that society was attacked from all sides. Existing social bonds began to be questioned, along with family life, Polish spiritual identity, and cultural and national identity. The incompleteness of reforms after each crisis that followed de-Stalinization after 1956, and the workers' revolts of 1970 and 1976, meant that the gap between description and reality was growing wider. Stefan Nowak, in describing a high incidence of authoritarian and punitive attitudes in Polish society,

11. Andrzej Micewski, *Kardynal Wyszynski prymas i maz stanu* [Cardinal Wyszynski the primate and the statesman] (Paris: Societe d'editions internationales, 1982).

12. Ibid.

argues that it is a sign of deeply internalized collective repression.[13]

The Polish Roman Catholic Church quite perceptively sensed that collective repression and responded to it in its teachings. Thus, the concept of spiritual fatherhood of the nation extended to issues such as human dignity, freedom, and human rights. The church's teachings were not narrowly nationalistic, as some critics argue, but rather incorporated the concept of an open society in which freedom and human rights acquired centrality of values. As we shall see later, the specific policies of the Polish episcopate that developed over the years began as policies aimed at protecting the spiritual welfare of the nation, transcended into the political domain, and encompassed social and political welfare as well. This spiritual fatherhood—which extended well beyond matters of faith and incorporated and voiced national aspirations and consensus regarding matters of sovereignty, freedom, human rights, and societal rights to a better life—was the primary reason that the church acquired the power that it commands today. The church came to be perceived as an alternative authority system in the political domain. By becoming the guardian of the Polishness of Poland—that is, of its separate cultural and political identity and its democratic heritage—the church reinforced the bonds between the sense of national identity and Catholicism. It is no coincidence that Pope John Paul II, on the occasion of his first visit in Poland in June 1979, stressed that he rejoiced in all social achievements of Poland whatever the inspiration from which they came, but added that all

forms of colonialism were bad and that all alliances must be based on the individual interests of their member nations.

Nowhere else in Eastern Europe did the church's teachings focus so much on national sovereignty, dignity, freedom, and human rights, as well as on the inseparability of the nation from its church. The great laicization movement in Europe eluded and continues to elude Poland. As in Northern Ireland, the Catholic religion has become almost totally identified with the struggle for cultural survival and national independence.

This transfer of moral and, effectively, political leadership of the nation to the church in times of crisis is part of a historical tradition. The authority of the church is, of course, formally recognized as spiritual, but the intimate part the church played in Poland's patriotic struggle against partitions, in resistance to the Nazis, and in its active defense of traditional values and of its people after 1945 embued this authority with a political dimension. It was the Communists who were faced with the thankless task of trying to establish a lay state in Poland for the first time in history. But the Communists lacked the constituency of a liberal mass movement convinced of the necessity of separating church and state. They also lacked a constituency who believed in the Communist doctrine in which religion is seen as unnecessary once a person reaches a level of consciousness inspired by the advance of scientific socialism. Confronted with two powerful authoritarian creeds—Catholicism and Marxism—the society opted for its church. The religious spirit that accompanied the Solidarity movement indicated that the population did not accept the concept of a Communist-imposed lay society.

13. M. Marody et al., *Polacy 1980* [Poles 1980] (Warsaw: University of Warsaw, Institute of Sociology, 1983).

The election of Cardinal Karol Wojtyla, a man highly popular and respected in Poland, to the papal throne stunned and delighted the Poles. Given Polish history and beliefs, no other honor to the nation could be more satisfying. To the faithful, it was a divine sign of hope for tormented Poland. Non-Catholics and many rank-and-file party members showed their enthusiasm as a matter of Polish pride. Even the Polish Politburo sent its congratulations, which contained a message of socialism but contained some other elements as well: "For the first time in the history of the papal throne it is occupied by a son of the Polish nation, which is building the greatness and prosperity of its socialist fatherland with the unity and cooperation of all its citizens."[14] A familiar poem of Juliusz Slowacki, one of the great Polish poets during the partitioning in the nineteenth century, acquired an uncanny prophetic force: "Among the quarrelling, the Lord struck/On a mighty bell:/Lo, for a Slav Pope/He provided the throne/He shall spread love, as today the Powers/Spread weapons."

But in addition to the spiritual reaffirmation of the Polish Catholic creed, the election of the pope had an immediate political impact of further radicalizing the existing opposition of Polish society and radicalizing the Polish episcopate, which began to be discouraged with the policies of conciliation of Cardinal Wyszynski. The first papal visit to Poland was one great manifestation of love, loyalty, and solid Catholic allegiance. In the perception of the general public, the meeting between Edward Gierek, then leader of the Polish United Workers Party, and Pope John Paul II was a pairing of opposites. The pope was seen to be speaking from a position of strength in contrast to the shaky and insecure authority represented by Gierek. Although there had been no anti-Soviet or anti-Communist outbreaks during the visit, there was a growing general consensus afterwards that another great crisis of the regime was yet to come.

In the societal quest for legitimacy and expression of supranational collective will, the society found one solid institution: the Polish Catholic Church. It was the church that nurtured the simple monuments of Poland's nationalism and heritage. It was in the church that the Poles sensed their collective strength and regrouped. And it was this regrouped nation that launched the national insurrection of August 1980, that in the spirit of Christian teachings of nonviolence and forgiveness entirely avoided bloodshed and suppressed its deeply internalized hostility toward the Soviet Union. The national movement that developed under the protective umbrella provided by the workers was patriotic, pluralistic, egalitarian, democratic, implicitly anti-Communist, and Catholic.

When the strikes erupted in 1980, it was not surprising that the church provided the strikers with many of their symbols. As the protests spread, the church became the mediator between the state and the emerging Solidarity. On 7 September 1980, Solidarity received formal blessing from Cardinal Wyszynski during a visit paid to him by Lech Walesa. As the Solidarity movement—a movement entirely secular in nature—grew, the church's views became important in the development of a moderate line within Solidarity that dealt with tactics.

14. Neal Ascherson, *The Polish August: Self-Limiting Revolution* (New York: Penguin Books, 1981).

Following the death of Cardinal Wyszynski in May 1981, Archbishop Jozef Glemp, Wyszynski's long-time secretary, became his successor. Wyszynski's funeral was a grave and solemn occasion; there was a pervasive feeling that this was the end of a chapter of Polish postwar history during which nobody had protected the nation more than this man had.

Martial law and afterward

The dynamics that led to martial law can be easily understood when examining the unfolding of the Polish democratic revolution. On the one hand, once the Polish renewal process was initiated, it was bound to continue far beyond a series of economic strikes and evolve into a popular democratic movement. On the other hand, once the regime, or at least some of the powerful members of the regime, recognized this, they were bound to try to stop the process at all costs. On 11 and 12 December 1981, a meeting of the National Committee of Solidarity took place in Gdansk to debate a strategy for further action. On the night of 12 December the armed forces closed down telecommunications networks throughout the country, sealed off the main roads, and arrested national leaders of the union as well as experts, advisers, and other prominent intellectuals. In the early morning roadblocks were erected and cities were surrounded by police and the military. Trains and buses were stopped. On 13 December armed cars, tanks, and armed police vehicles patrolled the main cities, and early that morning martial law was proclaimed. The disintegration of the party as the government force, the cornerstone of Communist rule, meant that short of the army no other institution could assure that the Soviet model of state functioning could be sustained.

The imposition of martial law forced the Polish church to come out of its peacetime position and once again revert to its traditional role of protector and defender of the nation. Since the lifting of martial law, there have been some new developments that are as novel to the church episcopate as they are to General Wojciech Jaruzelski's regime, namely, an emergent active network of parishes whose functions extend far beyond spiritual counsel, and which had their origin during martial law. More generally, the Polish religious institutions once again assumed the role they fulfilled during the partition period. Since the church largely escaped the martial law restrictions, its institutional infrastructure provided a basis within which some form of organized resistance to martial law could emerge. Also, in the absence of communication networks, which were successfully closed down with the martial restrictions, Sunday sermons substituted for information centers. The churches in both urban and rural areas became the forum within which people gathered, manifested their opposition, exchanged information, and so on. Even with the lifting of martial law, the Polish churches are no longer a place solely designed for worship or religious rites, but serve as centers for nonreligious activities such as lectures, information exchange, and cultural events. In this, local parishes are very active.

The growing use of the local church network for nonreligious purposes is not only a problem for Jaruzelski's regime but for the Polish episcopate. To Jaruzelski's regime, the activating of local groups with leadership potential and the clustering of communities around their local churches means that a network of human activities outside the jurisdiction and control of authorities is sustained that continues to fuel social discontent.

To the Polish episcopate, whose interest is to preserve the sanctity of places of worship and maintain immunity from direct persecution, nonreligious utilization of the church's institutional base might prove to be a problem. Many of the parishes are run by young priests, and there are signs that the decisions of those priests on how to run their parishes might not necessarily coincide with the overall policy of the episcopate. The radicalization of the younger ranks of the priesthood in expressing their disapproval of the regime in conjunction with the grass-roots social pressure might jeopardize the already fragile truce between Jaruzelski's regime and the Polish episcopate. Furthermore, this widens the gap between the upper echelons of the church's hierarchy and the rank and file. The murder of the Reverend Popieluszko, other recent evidence of brutality directed against priests, break-ins into some local churches, and desecration and theft of religious objects—all those are signs that the Polish church might be heading toward troublesome times.

Finally, the clustering of societal activities around the local parish churches, not only in rural areas but also in metropolitan areas that are characterized by a great degree of initial anonymity, implies that the usefulness of an old sociological unit has been rediscovered in the nation—the local community. This is not to say that the opposition activities ceased in the industries; however, a national movement like Solidarity, derived from grass-roots activities within an industrial base, is less likely. Hence, the rediscovery of local communities in both urban and rural areas, based on residents that are within the domain of individual parishes, might provide an alternative network of social organization. And in this process the local priests, particularly those of the younger generation, might prove of crucial importance.

Once the Solidarity movement was suppressed, the church began to function as an authority system that is not constitutionally recognized, and it presently coexists with the Communist authorities. The church's authority extends beyond spiritual and moral domains and directly enters into the sphere of politics and more recently into the sphere of social and cultural life of local communities. The extensive social basis from which the church derives its strength can be objectively assessed, and it is nowhere comparable to the social basis upon which the Communist party rests its claims to governance.

The Russian Orthodox Church
and the Soviet State

By PHILIP WALTERS

ABSTRACT: The Constitution of the USSR guarantees religious freedom, but the ruling Communist Party actively encourages the disappearance of religion. In the 1930s there was comprehensive religious persecution, but despite the virtual disappearance of the Russian Orthodox Church as an institution, the believing population did not give up its faith. During World War II, Stalin adopted a new policy. He granted the churches a limited institutional existence, and in return church leaders have been expected to speak favorably of Soviet political and social realities. Only a proportion of the clergy is, however, fully acceptable to the government, and a significant number tries to serve the religious needs of its flock the best it can. The ordinary believer is treated as a second-class citizen. Individuals who try to make the plight of Soviet Christians known in the world at large or to bear witness to their faith in public can expect reprisals from the authorities.

Philip Walters received an M.A. in modern languages from Cambridge University and a Ph.D. from the London School of Economics. He was at Moscow University from 1974 to 1975. From 1976 to 1979 he was a research fellow at Corpus Christi College, Cambridge. Since 1979 he has worked at Keston College, a research and information center that deals with the situation for religious communities in Communist countries. Appointed there initially as a researcher on the Soviet Union, he is now research director, in charge of the development of the college's whole research program.

THE only country in the world in which it is illegal to be a religious believer is Albania. In all other countries with Marxist-Leninist governments, churches and other religious bodies function legally. At the same time, however, the ruling ideology in all these countries is intrinsically hostile to religious belief as a social phenomenon, and varying degrees of tension characterize relations between religion and the state.

THE STATE AS INSTRUMENT OF THE PARTY

The claim is often made that the Soviet Union has done more than most other states to guarantee freedom of religion by stipulating such freedom in its constitution. The present constitution does indeed state that citizens are free to profess any religion or no religion, and to engage in antireligious propaganda. The same constitution also states, however, that the basic liberties of an individual are granted "in the interests of the people and with the aim of strengthening and developing the socialist system" and "in accordance with the goals of the building of communism."[1] These conditions illustrate the fact that the Soviet Constitution is not the final court of appeal for those who feel their rights have been infringed. The organs of the Soviet state are subordinate to the policies of the Communist Party, which, since the Civil War of 1918-21, has been the only permitted political party and which reserves to itself the right to organize society in the interests of the proletariat. These interests have always been held to include the liberation of citizens from religious superstition.

During the last half-century of the Russian Empire, those of the so-called intelligentsia who were concerned with social and political reform were almost universally atheists, profoundly hostile to religion and particularly to the Russian Orthodox Church. The latter was established by law as the state church, supported financially by the government, and expected to use its influence to promote the stability of the czarist autocracy. It had very little administrative autonomy and, since 1721, when Peter the Great abolished the patriarchate, had in fact been under the control of the procurator of the Holy Synod, a government-appointed layman. Marxism took hold as the most fertile revolutionary doctrine in Russia during the 1890s; it was developed to suit Russian circumstances by Lenin, who had a deep personal antipathy toward religion, asserting not only, as Marx did, that religion is a symptom of humanity's enslaved state, but that it is a weapon that the oppressive classes can use to preserve their power: "Marxism always regards . . . all religious organizations as organs of bourgeois reaction, serving to defend exploitation and stupefy the working class."[2]

SOVIET ANTIRELIGIOUS ACTIVITY: THE FIRST PHASE

Soon after the Bolsheviks came to power they began directing legislation against established religion. The Decree on Separation of Church from State of 23 January 1918 declared all churches

---

1. USSR, Constitution of 1979, arts. 50 and 51.

2. V. I. Lenin, "Ob otnoshenii rabochei partii k religii" (1909), in *Polnoe sobranie sochinenii,* 5th ed. (Moscow, 1961), 17:416.

separated both from the state and from the educational system, and it deprived the churches of the right to hold property and of legal entity. The most devastating effect of this legislation would obviously have been on the wealth and privilege of the Russian Orthodox Church. Until the later 1920s, in fact, non-Orthodox sects and churches that had been disadvantaged under the empire enjoyed greater freedom than they had ever known. The Seventh-Day Adventists, for example, undertook a successful period of missionary activity from 1919 to 1926, by which time they had doubled their membership and were allowed to publish three newspapers.

During the early 1920s, the new Soviet government continued its confrontation with the Orthodox Church. A major pretext was that during the famines that followed the Civil War, the church had allegedly refused to surrender its valuables to be sold to help the starving and had also allegedly given support to anti-Soviet groups abroad. Patriarch Tikhon, who in 1918 had denounced the Bolshevik regime, was indicted in May 1922 and released in June 1923, after which he agreed to express his loyalty to the Soviet regime and his determination never again to interfere in political matters. He died in 1925, leaving a testament confirming this attitude toward the Soviet state. The authorities required more, however, and continued to imprison Tikhon's nominated successors. The second of these, Metropolitan Sergi (Stragorodsky), was released in 1927 and in July of that year issued a declaration of loyalty to the Soviet Union, "whose joys and successes are our joys and successes, and whose setbacks are our setbacks." Even this move from passive loyalty to a position of positive support for all Soviet policies did not reconcile the Soviet government to the church, however, and comprehensive persecution of the church continued throughout the 1930s.

THE 1929 LEGISLATION ON RELIGION

A decisive shift in Soviet policy toward religion became apparent at the end of the 1920s. From then until the outbreak of World War II, persecution was to be directed indiscriminately and comprehensively at all religions and churches. Symptomatic of the new policy was the important Law on Religious Associations of 1929. This is the basic Soviet law defining religious freedom and is still in force today.[3] Rather than attacking the institutional superstructure of the churches, it wiped the slate clean and defined the basic framework in which religious citizens could set about securing their right to worship. The law states that in any locality, a group of at least 20 adults, a *dvadtsatka*, may seek permission from the local authorities to use a registered building for the performance of their cult. It is important to realize that worship in a duly registered building is the only right accorded to religious believers under Soviet law.

Evangelizing, educating young people in religion, producing and distributing religious literature, organizing any kind of religious activity outside a registered building, and using the donations of the faithful to finance libraries, medical care, and other welfare work are all either illegal or actively discouraged. Church institutions are tolerated by the government for pragmatic purposes rather then specifically allowed by

3. It was revised, but not substantially altered, in 1975.

law. There is no legal basis for the existence of permanent theological schools or monasteries, although some denominations have them; nor for the official publications that some denominations produce; nor for hierarchs or central representative bodies. Jews and Roman Catholics are, in fact, denied the latter.

THE LIVING CHURCH

During the 1920s, in the course of its struggle with the Orthodox Church, the Soviet government had attempted to set up a rival organization, the Living Church.[4] Unlike the patriarchal church, the Living Church was dedicated to the full support of Soviet power and claimed that the Bolshevik program embodied essentially Christian aspirations. Many of those in the Living Church leadership had been associated before the 1917 revolution with the movement for church reform and with Christian socialist activity; but others had been involved in organizations such as the Black Hundreds and the League of Russian People, which were dedicated to supporting the czarist status quo. The motives of the latter seem to have been to stay on the winning side. The mixture of impulses that engendered the Living Church and the preoccupations of its leadership certainly failed to inspire mass support among ordinary Orthodox Christians. The realization that a popular base was

absent must have been behind the Soviet government's abandonment of total support for the Living Church during the mid-1920s in favor of a policy of divide and rule, allowing the rival church factions to fight each other while continuing to persecute religion in general.

Two important consequences of the encounter between the Living Church and the patriarchal church have continued to color relations between the Soviet state and the Russian Orthodox Church to the present day. The Soviet government must accommodate itself to the fact that a substantial minority of Soviet citizens—numbering approximately 50 million at the present time—remains stubbornly loyal to the church. For its part, the church has been sensitive, certainly from the time of Metropolitan Sergi's 1927 declaration, to the need both to declare overt loyalty to the policies of the Soviet state and at the same time to attempt to keep its internal organization free from state interference and to preserve its spiritual integrity. The Living Church had compromised its own integrity, with fatal results from the point of view of the average believer.[5]

STALIN'S VOLTE-FACE

By 1939 the Russian Orthodox Church had virtually ceased to exist as an institution. Only about 2000 churches remained open, as compared with a prerevolutionary total of 46,000, and four bishops remained at liberty. Thousands of clergy and laypeople were in

---

4. The most comprehensive, if unstructured, account of the Living Church movement is to be found in A. Levitin and V. Shavrov, *Ocherki po istorii russkoi tserkovnoi smuty* (Küsnacht, Switzerland: Glaube in der 2 Welt, 1977). See also Dimitry Pospielovsky, *The Russian Church under the Soviet Regime 1917-1982,* 2 vols. (New York: St. Vladimir's Seminary Press, 1984), pp. 43-92; A. Krasnov-Levitin, *Likhie gody 1925-1941* (Paris: YMCA Press, 1977); Philip Walters, "The Living

Church 1922-1946," *Religion in Communist Lands*, 6(4):235-43 (Winter 1976).

5. See William C. Fletcher, *A Study in Survival: The Church in Russia 1927-1943* (London: SPCK, 1965).

labor camps. Disconcertingly for the government, however, the loyalty of the Soviet public to the virtually nonexistent church remained substantial.[6]

The outbreak of World War II saw a major reorientation of the Soviet government's attitude toward the Orthodox and other churches as institutions in Soviet society. When Hitler violated the Nazi-Soviet pact in 1941 and invaded the USSR, Stalin was taken completely by surprise; the first to appeal to the patriotic spirit of the Soviet people and to call on them to resist the fascist aggressor was Metropolitan Sergi. Meanwhile, underlining the continuing potential vitality of the church on Soviet soil, a remarkable revival of religious activity was taking place in the areas of the western Soviet Union passing under Nazi control.[7]

In September 1943, Stalin met Sergi in the Kremlin. Shortly afterward Sergi was elected patriarch of the church; a government Council for the Affairs of the Russian Orthodox Church was set up to deal directly with the church hierarchy; churches began to be reopened; the number of clergy grew steadily; theological schools and monasteries began to function again; and the church was allowed to publish an official journal.

6. In the mid-1930s the head of the Union of Militant Godless indicated that some 57 percent of the Soviet population remained believers. The results of the 1937 census, which contained a question on religious affiliation, were suppressed, and the question did not reappear in the census of 1939.

7. See Wassilij Alexeev and Theofanis G. Stavrou, *The Great Revival: The Russian Church under German Occupation* (Minneapolis, MN: Burgess, 1976); Wassilij Alexeev and Keith Armes, "German Intelligence: Religious Revival in Soviet Territory," *Religion in Communist Lands,* 5(1):27-37 (Spring 1977); and ibid., 5(2):109-16 (Summer 1977).

Church support for Soviet policies

In return for these concessions, the church was expected to endorse the war effort. After the war, the government continued the same policy, and now the church was called upon to consolidate its influence over the Orthodox churches in the Eastern European countries, which were then falling under Soviet control. After 1948, a new field presented itself in which the state could continue to make use of the church: the promotion of the concept of peace as a peculiarly Soviet aim in the postwar world. The Christian Peace Conference was founded in Czechoslovakia in 1958, and Soviet church leaders played an influential role in its debates.

The Orthodox Church continues to participate in peace debates throughout the world and to host such debates at home. The Soviet government benefits from the impression given that the church is an autonomous institution within Soviet society giving voluntary endorsement to aspects of Soviet foreign policy. Another way in which the church can serve Soviet interests in the world arena is in helping to build up a favorable image of Soviet domestic conditions and in particular in insisting that real religious freedom does indeed exist in the Soviet Union. Representatives of the Russian Orthodox Church at the World Council of Churches—of which the Russian church has been a member since 1961—have been able on numerous occasions to conceal the extent of antireligious activity in the USSR. They have defused protests sent out of the USSR by those persecuted for their faith by characterizing their authors as unrepresentative of the Soviet Christian community or motivated by anti-Soviet political sentiments.

It is important to remember that the new policy toward the churches initiated by Stalin involved no new legislation. It was a pragmatic policy and depended on a liberal interpretation of the Law of 1929. What is more, the new policy of concessions was directed toward the churches as institutions and did not represent a softening of the policy of the Communist Party toward religion as such. Antireligious education and propaganda continued at greater or lesser intensity throughout the period under discussion; and they continue to the present day along with the policy of institutional accommodation previously described. The discontinuity between the two images of the church—an image of ceremony, freedom, and influence for foreign consumption, and an image, until recently only partially glimpsed, of a persecuted and deprived church within the Soviet Union itself—continues to confuse observers of the Soviet scene who have not briefed themselves sufficiently on the complexities of the religious situation in that country.

*Restrictions on the
church's activity at home*

As we have seen, the range of activities permitted to the church within the Soviet Union is very narrow. Although church leaders travel abroad addressing themselves primarily to political issues, in the course of their pastoral activities at home these same men, and the rest of the priests and bishops, are in effect forbidden to touch on any contemporary issues at all, whether social or political. A secret report by V. Furov, deputy to the chairman of the state's Council for Religious Affairs, received in the West in the 1970s, makes revealing reading.[8]

Bishops are appointed only after the candidates have been investigated by the council. The council's employees systematically interview priests and monitor their activities: "all political work with the clergy is carried on in the interests of the state" and is aimed "not only at keeping them within the bounds of the law, but at diminishing their activity and limiting their influence on believers." "If a priest gives sermons, they must be strictly Orthodox in content, containing expositions of the Gospel or Epistles in the spirit of the Church Fathers and Teachers. Sermons must contain no political or social issues or examples." Teaching materials used in the church's academies and seminaries, as well as by the staff themselves, are similarly systematically investigated. A basic assumption behind the work of the council can be taken to be that "the clergy of the Orthodox Church, although loyal to the Soviet state, still remains a body with an ideology which is incompatible with our world view."

*The church's defense
of its internal affairs*

Despite systematic interference by the Council for Religious Affairs in the internal life of the Russian Orthodox Church—an interference difficult to reconcile with the legally defined "separation of church from state"—the church

---

8. A photocopy of the report is in the archives of Keston College, Kent, United Kingdom. Parts of the report have been published in Russian under the title "Iz otcheta soveta po delam religii —chlenam TsK KPSS," in *Vestnik RKhD* (Paris), no. 130, pp. 275-344 (1979); ibid., no. 131, pp. 362-72 (1980); and ibid., no. 132, pp. 197-205 (1980). For translations of extracts in English, see *Orthodox Monitor,* nos. 9-10, pp. 58-80 (July-Dec. 1980). Extracts from the report have also appeared as *Rapport secret au comité central sur l'etat de l'eglise en URSS* (Paris: Seuil, 1980).

leadership has generally remained conscious of the need to try to defend its inner life from too much secular control. When theological educational establishments were opened, the church immediately began to make selection procedures and the examination system as strict as possible to improve the quality of the students. The caliber of priests has consistently improved. Over the last 15 years the seminaries have more than doubled their intake. When the secular authorities have proved unwilling to allow new places of worship to be opened, the church has used ingenious means to provide improved worship facilities—for example, by supposedly repairing already existing churches, after which they often emerge considerably expanded in size. The church hierarchy has attempted with varying success to resist state pressure on various monasteries and has also attempted to protect a number of prominent religious dissidents who have incurred the state's anger.[9]

The state, meanwhile, is concerned to keep the church's autonomy in organizing its internal affairs as limited as possible. Above all, it is concerned to ensure that the church should never feel that its cooperation with the state is based on specifically Christian principles, and to make it quite clear that a Soviet Christian's loyalty to the state is in spite of, rather than a consequence of, his or her Christian convictions. A church leader once stated that the church cooperated with the state in order "to persuade the state to recognize the church legally as part of the national social organism and to make its peace with her, recognizing in her a positive moral role and force in the state."[10] Patriarch Pimen (Izvekov) showed a more realistic understanding of the state's expectations in an interview in 1978: "In putting into practice its religious life the Russian Orthodox Church is guided by the teachings of the Gospel of Our Lord Jesus Christ . . . but in their activities in society and at work the Orthodox Christians in our country, like all believers within the Soviet Union, follow the principles which were proclaimed sixty years ago when Soviet power was established in Russia."[11]

The bishops of the church: a spectrum of response

The Furov report divides the bishops of the Orthodox Church into three categories reflecting the degrees of trust that the secular authorities place in their reliability. The first category includes the patriarch and 16 other bishops who "confirm in word and deed not only their loyalty but also a patriotic devotion to socialist society"; the second includes 23 bishops who are loyal to the state but also try to revivify the inner spiritual life of the church; and the third includes 17 bishops who "try to evade the laws on religious cults." It is interesting that the late Metropolitan Nikodim

9. Father Dimitri Dudko was at first moved from church to church rather than suspended from his priestly functions. Father Gleb Yakunin, although suspended as a priest by the patriarch in 1965, was later given the post of reader, and it seems that in 1978 or 1979 an offer may have been made to him by the church to reinstate him as a priest, an offer that Father Gleb allegedly turned down. Father Vasili Fonchenkov, a member of Father Gleb's Christian Committee for the Defense of Believers' Rights, was removed from his position as a professor at the Moscow Theological Academy, but he still functions as a parish priest.

10. D. Pospielovsky, "Mitropolit Nikodim i ego vremya," *Posev,* no. 2, p. 21 (Feb. 1979).

11. "Intervyu svyateishego patriarkha moskovskogo i vseya Rusi Pimena: V sluzhenii miru na zemle vidim velikuyu tsel svoyu," *Golos rodiny,* no. 5 (Feb. 1978).

is placed in the second category. For years, as head of the External Church Relations Department of the Russian Orthodox Church, he was responsible for presenting abroad a favorable image of Soviet religious reality. He demonstrated, evidently in a similar way to a large number of bishops, an ability to combine service to the state on one level with a real Christian zeal in his pastoral work.

KHRUSHCHEV'S ANTIRELIGIOUS CAMPAIGN AND THE BIRTH OF DISSENT

The Stalinist policy of accommodation of the church continued throughout the 1940s and 1950s. In 1959, however, Khrushchev launched an unexpected and savage antireligious campaign that lasted five years and profoundly jolted any confidence the churches may have built up in the possibility of permanent peaceful and mutually beneficial coexistence with the government. Two-thirds of the 20,000 churches then legally operating were closed down, and priests and believers arrested. No change in the law was involved; the letter of the existing law sufficed to justify the campaign as a return to "Leninist legality."[12]

The traumatic shock of the Khrushchev campaign to the religious community in the Soviet Union catalyzed what has developed into the so-called dissident movement of the last 20 years.

12. On the campaign as a whole, see Michael Bourdeaux, *Patriarch and Prophets: Persecution of the Russian Orthodox Church Today* (Oxford: Mowbrays, 1970); idem, "The Black Quinquennium: The Russian Orthodox Church 1959-1964," *Religion in Communist Lands,* 9(1-2):18-23 (Spring 1981); Donald A. Lowrie and William C. Fletcher, "Khrushchev's Religious Policy 1959-64," in *Aspects of Religion in the Soviet Union 1917-1967,* ed. Richard H. Marshall (Chicago: University of Chicago Press, 1971), pp. 131-55.

In 1961, state pressure on the leadership of the Baptist Church to impose severe restrictions on the range of acceptable religious activities of its members led to a split within that church and the formation of the *Initsiativniki,* or "unregistered Baptists," under the leadership of Pastor Georgi Vins. As the name implies, this substantial minority chose for itself the freedom of the outlaw, renouncing any accommodation to the state in favor of religious liberty.

A similar split did not take place in the Orthodox Church, but several strands of dissent became apparent. Certain priests and laymen, including Aleksandr Solzhenitsyn, began to criticize the leadership of their church for excessively supine attitudes in the face of state pressure and exhorted the leadership to be more bold for the sake of the health of the church. Other activists began to champion the rights of believers where these were infringed, appealing not only to the Soviet Constitution, but also to international agreements on human and religious rights that the Soviet Union had ratified. This movement received a great impetus after the Soviet Union ratified the Helsinki Final Act in 1975. Father Gleb Yakunin founded the Christian Committee for the Defense of Believers' Rights in the USSR in 1976, and the committee sent to the West over 3000 pages of documentation of cases of abuse of believers' rights before Father Gleb was arrested in 1979 and sentenced to 10 years' deprivation of liberty for "anti-Soviet agitation and propaganda."

Another strand in the Orthodox dissent movement has been one of self-education in the church's spiritual traditions among certain groups of young people, particularly in the major cities, who are trying to relate their faith directly to the problems of their daily life in Soviet society. Study such as this, as we have seen, is viewed by the secular authorities with deep suspicion. The Christian Seminar on Problems of the Religious Renaissance was founded in 1974 by the young convert Aleksandr Ogorodnikov. He and other young people prominently involved are now in labor camps as a direct consequence of their attempt at self-education in the faith.

STATE POLICY SINCE 1964

Since 1964 there has been no attempt to launch another comprehensive attack against religion; rather, there has been a return to the situation that obtained from 1943 to 1959. The state is prepared to grant the churches some concessions and a visible presence in society in return for vocal support for Soviet policies by church leaders. At the same time it has kept up antireligious education and propaganda and has also remained consistently hostile to any manifestations of religious creativity, initiative, or revival coming from the ranks of the ordinary priests and believers.

Until the later 1970s, it was evidently the preferred state policy to encourage the church leadership to discipline its own dissidents, but since 1978-79 there has been a shift in favor of direct intervention by the state's security organs. At that time the number of arrests of unofficial religious activists began to increase sharply, as did the number of arrests of human rights activists and those involved in nationalist movements. The number of Christians in the USSR known to us in the West who have been imprisoned for their religious activity increased from 180 in June 1979 to almost 400 by October 1982.

Under Presidents Yuri Andropov and Konstantin Chernenko the situation for the religious community as a whole, as for all dissenters, continued to deteriorate. Andropov had been head of the KGB, the Soviet security apparatus, until shortly before becoming Soviet leader and he was known to be no liberal in ideological matters; Chernenko spoke warmly on at least one major occasion of the need to protect the ideological purity of young people against the pernicious taint of religion. There has been an increasing tendency in the Soviet media to see behind all religious revival phenomena in the Soviet Union the hand of foreign anti-Soviet activists. Several pieces of legislation have made it more difficult for Soviet citizens to receive material aid from abroad and even to offer hospitality to foreigners without fearing they may be breaking the law. An alteration in the regulations concerning labor camps has made it possible for prisoners to be re-tried before the end of their sentences for violating camp discipline, and at least one prominent religious dissident has been sentenced to a further labor-camp term in this way. It is too soon to tell whether Mikhail Gorbachev will have any new initiatives to propose in dealing with the religious community in the Soviet Union. To date there seems to be no change in the policy of more of the same.

*Conditions for
ordinary believers*

Recent official Soviet estimates reached the conclusion that perhaps a fifth of the Soviet population are active religious believers. Soviet antireligious activities have been ineffective in eradicating religious faith; yet such activities continue systematically at a local level, and it is fair to say that all religious believers are effectively second-class citizens. Atheist education is compulsory from kindergarten onward, and antireligious propaganda is ubiquitous at places of work and recreation.[13] Religious believers who fall foul of the authorities are liable to defamation in the press without right of reply. They may find it difficult to locate adequate housing or to obtain permission to live in a particular city. Their lives and property may be threatened by local antireligious activists. They will find it difficult to obtain more than the most menial jobs. If they have responsible jobs or are receiving higher education and are discovered to be believers, they will probably be dismissed. For more troublesome religious activists, arrest and trial under various articles of the penal code are possible outcomes.

Two articles of the Soviet Constitution punishing illegal religious activity are worded so vaguely as to be readily to hand in almost all circumstances. Other useful articles are those that punish "parasitism," in the case of believers who cannot find anyone to employ them, and "hooliganism," often in connection with alleged resistance offered to those carrying out searches in believers' homes.

Longer sentences accompany such political charges as "slandering the Soviet system"[14] and "anti-Soviet agitation and propaganda."[15] These latter are most often used in connection with unofficial religious literature, typewritten *samizdat* journals, and petitions drawing attention to instances of religious discrimination. The charge will be framed on the assumption that religious

believers should concern themselves simply with worship, as specified by law, and that expressing an independent opinion on any other subject is a politically disloyal activity. Finally, there remains the threat of compulsory detention in a psychiatric hospital; religious activists are often diagnosed as suffering from schizophrenia. The advantage to the authorities is that such confinement is for an indefinite term—until the doctors pronounce the patient cured.

The consequences of zeal

The Russian Orthodox Church exists in the Soviet Union as a visible institution, and visitors to the major cities are regularly and easily impressed by the magnificence of liturgical worship and the fact that the churches are full. Their impressions that the church has won and retained a measure of freedom and influence in an atheist society are confirmed by the very high-profile activity of church leaders representing their country at international gatherings or hosting conferences at home at which no expense is spared.

Yet the Russian Orthodox Church is in fact deeply deprived and its opportunity for making a creative Christian contribution within Soviet society itself virtually nonexistent. What the Soviet authorities would ideally like is a church with a hierarchy but no believers.

As an example of what can happen when a priest of the church is too successful in his Christian witness, we may take the case of Father Aleksandr Pivovarov. He was trained in the theological seminary in Odessa and ordained a priest in 1960. He had graduated with distinction, but refused offers to take up an academic post at the academy since he felt his calling to be that of a parish priest. He was accordingly given a par-

13. David E. Powell, *Anti-Religious Propaganda in the Soviet Union* (Cambridge, MA: MIT Press, 1975).
14. RSFSR, Criminal Code, art. 190-1.
15. Ibid., art. 70.

ish in Siberia, where he rapidly became known and respected for his deep faith and exceptional preaching.

As a result of his sermons on the subject of the Resurrection, Father Aleksandr came to the attention of the secular authorities and was subjected to a year's investigation for "inciting fanaticism in the masses by spreading delusions." He was libeled in the press. Despite difficulties normally attending the building of new churches, he succeeded in having one new church and two baptismal chapels built in his area. He was by now subject to regular house searches and interrogations. Nevertheless, in 1975 the authorities of the Russian Orthodox Church appointed him secretary to the archbishop of Novosibirsk. In April 1982 he was implicated in a case being brought against certain Christians in Moscow who were producing unofficial religious literature; he had been distributing this literature among his parishioners. He was dismissed from his post, given no employment for six months, and then sent to the northernmost parish of the diocese. In 1983 he was arrested and tried for "engaging in an illegal trade." The allegation was that in connection with the distribution of religious literature his motivation had been financial greed. He was sentenced to four years in a strict-regime labor camp.

CONCLUSION

Although the churches in the Soviet Union exist under severe restrictions, they nevertheless continue to constitute a unique phenomenon. They are the only legally existing institutions that are not directly inspired and organized by the Communist Party. As such, they continue to attract all those who for any reason are inclined to question the Party's doctrinal infallibility and even those who are critical of aspects of the Party's social and political agenda.

In Poland, the Catholic Church and the teachings of the Polish pope were of central importance in the genesis of the Solidarity movement, with its political and social involvement. While it would be simplistic to expect similar developments in the Soviet Union, at least under the present conditions, the potential importance of the churches as factors in the future political and social development of that country should not be underestimated.

Religion in
Post-Mao China

By MERLE GOLDMAN

ABSTRACT: Increased interest in religion in post-Mao China stems from disillusionment with Marxism-Leninism-Maoism and the destructiveness of the Cultural Revolution. Young people, in particular, are searching for a new belief system. Equally important, the Deng Xiaoping leadership is willing to tolerate religious practices and to rebuild religious institutions. Its seemingly benign policy does not stem from a greater appreciation of religion, but from the desire to exert tighter control over religion. The repression of the Cultural Revolution had driven religion underground, outside the Party's control; thus, the Deng leadership's policy of religious tolerance is to lure religious believers from private to public worship, where the Party can reassert its control. Its religious tolerance is also aimed at winning the cooperation of relatively well-educated Christian converts and the assistance of Western nations in its drive for economic modernization.

Merle Goldman is professor of history at Boston University. Her latest book is China's Intellectuals: Advise and Dissent.

WHETHER in Confucian China or in the People's Republic of China (PRC), religion has always been regulated by the state. Unlike other great civilizations, Chinese civilization did not originate a great system of religious thought. Whereas the indigenous Daoism in its philosophical form sought intellectual, psychological, and aesthetic harmony with nature, its popular form became a folk religion with many deities and spirits inhabiting mountains, rivers, stones, and trees, which peasants believed affected one's fate. Because adherents of philosophical Daoism protested the systematizing of their beliefs and because peasants were unable to write about theirs, Daoism did not develop a formal theology. Ancestor worship, another indigenous practice, sought security in the hereafter, but went no further. Buddhism from India was influential at various times, and Christianity and Islam were influential in specific areas, but none of these religions built sufficiently strong institutions or political power to shape China's civilization in the way that Confucianism has dominated China ideologically as well as politically for thousands of years.

Although some practices of Confucianism may be interpreted as religious in nature, Confucianism was more a moral and political philosophy than a religion. Its morality did not originate in revelation but in the teachings of Confucius. Occasionally the Confucian state suppressed religious groups, as it did the Buddhists from 841 to 845, but for the most part it tolerated religions, including foreign ones, as long as they did not threaten the ruling state with disaffection and rebellion. Secret societies, which generally professed some form of messianic Buddhism, Daoism, or Chris-

tianity, were left alone. They were suppressed only when they exploded into revolt.

Since religious beliefs were diffused through society by the family and village, and lacked strong institutions and theological systems that could compete with Confucianism, state tolerance extended to a variety of religious beliefs. The exclusivity of religious belief, common in the West, was not part of Chinese civilization. Religious tolerance fulfilled a need in the Confucian state because it permitted a response to the ultimate questions of life—suffering, frustration, death—with which Confucianism was not concerned. Thus, most Chinese sought help from the gods and spirits in all or any religions that could help them in time of need. Their religion was an eclectic mixture of Daoism, Buddhism, ancestor worship, and a bit of animism.

RELIGION IN THE MAO ZEDONG ERA

When in the late nineteenth century China confronted the militarily powerful West, its tolerance of competitive beliefs, particularly Christianity, quickly faded. Missionaries and their converts, who were regarded as agents of the Western powers, were attacked and persecuted by officials and mobilized peasants. However, in the interim from the fall of the Qing in 1911 until the establishment of the PRC in 1949, when China was virtually governmentless or governed by weak governments, most religions, including Christianity, operated relatively freely. But with the Chinese Communists' consolidation of authority over the whole of China in the early 1950s, an intolerance of religious beliefs, reminiscent of the late Qing period, resumed and intensified. In addition to viewing religion from the Chinese nationalist perspective, they also viewed it from Marxism-Leninism, which saw religion as a hangover from feudal and bourgeois societies, in which the ruling classes used it to control and exploit the people. Using the standard Marxist opprobrium, they labeled religion the "opiate of the people," a social ill that must be cured.

The Communist regime was particularly hostile to Christianity. Although Christian missionaries had founded modern hospitals, the major universities, and hundreds of high schools, primary schools, and women's schools, the Chinese Communist Party, as its ideology dictated, regarded missionaries as the most invidious representatives of the Western imperialism that had humiliated China. Christians were not even 1 percent of China's population—700,000 Protestants and almost 3 million Roman Catholics—but the Party almost immediately imprisoned or expelled foreign missionaries. Of the Christian denominations, Roman Catholics were the most persecuted because their religion mandated allegiance to Rome, which recognized Taiwan. Even more important, the Party regarded the Roman allegiance as a challenge to its own supremacy. In 1957 the regime appointed a number of bishops without the Vatican's permission and arrested those who opposed the Party's usurpation of the Vatican's authority.

The regime was more tolerant toward Buddhism, which, with over 100 million adherents and a half million monks and nuns, was the most popular religion among China's peasants. Because Buddhism was not centrally organized, the Party—through land reform—was able to whittle away its local temples and monasteries by depriving them of means

of support. Monks and nuns were returned to secular life. A similar pattern was followed with the Daoists, who in many areas were merged with the Buddhists.

Islam, which had first come to China with the trade caravans along the old silk route of Central Asia, was treated more leniently than the Christian religions. Because Islam took root in China before the Chinese asserted control over their northern frontier, the Party treated it more as an indigenous religion, whereas Christianity was brought in by foreign missionaries. More important, because its 20 to 30 million believers lived primarily along the strategic areas in northwest China, which bordered the Soviet Union, and had more religious and ethnic identification with their Uighur, Kazakh, and Mongolian kinsmen across the border than with the regime in Beijing, the Party was more careful not to alienate them. Thus, while Christians were not allowed to celebrate Christmas and Easter, the Muslims were permitted to celebrate their holidays, such as Ramadan.

Despite its negative view of religion and its weakening of already weak religious institutions, the Party in its early years did not abolish religion by administrative orders or by force. Rather, it sought to control religion and create an environment in which religion would be regarded as a superstition or an anachronism that would eventually disappear. It sought to supplant religion with the deification of Mao and the Party, the study of Marxism-Leninism, and the rituals of criticism and public confession of political sins. Some religious doctrines were reinterpreted in Marxist-Leninist terms. Buddhist enlightenment, for example, was not to be gained by rebirth in the Western Paradise but by improving life on earth.

The Party created a number of institutions in order to control religious matters. It established the Bureau of Religious Affairs as its liaison with religious groups to whom the bureau conveyed the Party's policies, values, and ideology. The Party also established national associations of each religious group—Protestant, Catholic, Buddhist, Daoist, and Muslim. The associations might have been led by religious leaders, but they were actually controlled by Party officials. In addition, Christians had to be members of the Three Self Movement—self-support, self-government, self-propaganda—which had nothing to do with self-sufficiency, but which was another effort to cut off Christian groups from contact with the West. Severence meant that the Chinese government, rather than overseas religious organizations, would support them and give them guidance. If one did not accept the authority of these Party front organizations, he or she would be imprisoned, which happened particularly to a number of Chinese Christian clergy.

The first violent clash between the regime and a religious order came when Tibetans rebelled in 1959 after the regime had repeatedly broken an agreement that allowed Tibetans to follow Lamaism, a branch of Buddhism. Perhaps because Lamaism was much more interwoven with the ethnic, social, and cultural life of the Tibetans than the other religious orders were among other ethnic groups and the Chinese, the regime was less willing to tolerate its observance. It brutally suppressed the uprising, and the Dalai Lama, Tibet's supreme religious and secular figure, fled to India.

China's treatment of other religious groups also became less tolerant in 1959, the time of the Great Leap Forward, a massive campaign to have China reach Communism quickly. But it was not until the Cultural Revolution, from 1966 to 1976, that the regime moved from a policy of gradually repressing religion to one of extinguishing it altogether. One of the fundamental goals of this extreme radical movement, launched by Mao, was the total extinction of religion as part of the effort to build a totally new revolutionary culture. In bursts of nihilistic fury, gangs of Red Guards destroyed churches, temples, and mosques; burned scriptures; smashed relics; and tortured, killed, and imprisoned clergy and laity. The study of the Bible, the Koran, and sutras was forbidden. The Bureau of Religious Affairs and the various religious associations were dismantled and their leaders persecuted.

Organized religion was destroyed, but the religion could not be. Religious believers retreated into their homes to worship secretly with their families and friends. An American clergyman, Donald MacInnis, director of the China Program of the National Council of Churches, who traveled to China in 1974, reported that there was no sign of religious practice. But during this time, in private dwellings in villages and cities throughout China, religious believers were clandestinely meeting together in small groups to read scripture and exchange views on religious matters.

RELIGION UNDER THE DENG XIAOPING LEADERSHIP

After the return of Deng Xiaoping to full power in the late 1970s and the appointment of Hu Yaobang as general secretary of the Party and Zhao Ziyang as prime minister, the regime moved away from the Cultural Revolution's destructive approach to religion and revived the more tolerant approach of traditional China. Although all four constitutions of the PRC guarantee freedom of religion, the 1975 and 1978 versions, preceding Deng's ascent to the leadership, assert the freedom "to propagate atheism." In the 1982 version that right was deleted. In fact, Article 36 reads, "No state organization, social organization, or individual should force any citizen to believe or not believe in religion." These sentiments are more in line with the 1954 constitution, although Chinese Communist history has demonstrated that the Chinese constitution does not prevent China's leaders from ignoring it when they wish.

Nevertheless, as in the early days of the Communist regime, the Deng leadership accepted the fact that religious expression was too deeply embedded to be rooted out by directive or force. In fact, the past persecutions, chaos, random terror, and insecurity of the Cultural Revolution had intensified religious belief and even increased the numbers who sought solace in religion. Even though the regime attempted to explain that the Cultural Revolution was an aberration, perpetrated by Mao and the Gang of Four, many saw it as evolving from Marxism-Leninism. This view led to disillusionment with the ideology and a search for something to replace it. Even some former Red Guards, who were among the attacked as well as the attackers in the Cultural Revolution, turned to religion in the search for a deeper meaning to their lives. Some became interested in religion because of curiosity, others because of conviction. Whatever the reasons, even the official figures for the number of Christians in China increased. The number of Roman Catholics—3 million—remained about the same as in 1949, but the Protestant count increased from 700,000 to 3 million. Unofficially, some evangelical groups outside China put the number of Christians at anywhere from 20 to 50 million.

As the Deng leadership relaxed control and opened up to the outside world, there was initially a period in which religionists explored different forms of worship, testing the limits of the Party's tolerance. Some made contact with fellow worshipers abroad and sought to bring in large numbers of religious books. Some house churches came out into the open and conducted public services. When William Hinton in 1980 returned to Long Bow in Shanxi, the village whose takeover by the Chinese Communists in the 1940s he depicted in his book *Fanshen,* he found the same number of Roman Catholic families— 150—as there had been in 1947, before the Communists closed the church and drove out the priest. The families were holding mass again, in one of the houses. The church had been suppressed but not extinguished, as he had believed. It had been quiescent until conditions allowed it to reemerge, with the faith of its followers seemingly intact.

State tolerance

The Deng leadership's tolerance and even encouragement of public worship did not mean that it had a new appreciation of religion, a policy of religious freedom, or a desire for more religious believers. Rather, it recognized that the Party's harsh, repressive policies had driven religion underground and outside its control. Thus, it rebuilt churches, temples, and mosques, reprinted religious books, revived religious periodicals, and reopened theological seminaries to lure and even coerce believers from their secret gatherings, where it had no control, to public worship, where it could reassert its control.

The policy of religious tolerance was also intended to promote internal and international policies. Even though Christian converts officially constituted less than 1 percent of the population, they were relatively well educated and had the skills that the Deng leadership needed for its economic modernization. By offering them religious tolerance, it sought to win their cooperation in this effort. It also sought to project an image of religious tolerance to the outside world in the expectation that such an image would help obtain Western aid.

Ironically, the Party's tolerance and reinstitutionalization of religion led to a retightening rather than a loosening of the reins on religion. It resurrected the religious front organizations, which had been destroyed in the Cultural Revolution. They were organized on national, provincial, and local levels with Party-appointed leaders in charge. In addition to the revival of the Christian Patriotic Association, the Three Self Movement of the 1950s was also reactivated. Discussions of religion were brought under official auspices by channeling them into the revived official religious journals, such as the Protestant *Tian feng (Heavenly Wind)* and the *Chinese Catholic Church*.

Similarly, the training of clergy that had continued on a private, tutorial basis because of the destruction of theological education in the Cultural Revolution was also brought under official control with the restoration of theological seminaries in which political study was required. The formalization of religious education was meant to produce leaders who would guide religion along Party-directed lines. The Nanjing Theological Seminary, which had been the major center for training church leaders,

was reopened in 1981 and was made a center of religious study at Nanjing University. Protestant and Catholic seminaries were opened in other major cities along the coast. The Buddhist academy in Beijing was reopened, and young people could study here to become monks as long as they had their parents' permission. Young Men's and Young Women's Christian Associations (YMCAs and YWCAs) in Shanghai, Beijing, Guangzhou, and Tianjin reactivated programs to help reestablish supervision over young people, who were believed to make up about one-third of the Christian adherents.

The Bureau of Religious Affairs was reestablished in 1979 to act once again as the liaison between the government and religious denominations. Cases of religious discrimination and infringement on religious freedom were to be brought before the bureau, but its ability to act on such matters was compromised by the fact that it was also the Party's agency for coordinating and enforcing the Party's authority.

With these developments, the deinstitutionalization and spontaneous gatherings and sharing of religious experiences that had been conducted informally in homes and communities for almost 15 years were gradually ended as the Party reestablished its controls over China's religious denominations.

As in the 1950s, the Deng leadership was ostensibly more supportive of Islam than of Christianity. The number of Muslims had increased since the fifties. Officially China has 10 million followers of Islam; unofficially it is closer to 20 or 30 million. In the province of Xinjiang alone, which borders on the Soviet Union, there are 12,000 mosques and 15,000 clergy.[1]

1. *New York Times,* 15 June 1983.

Because the Muslim areas were close to the Soviet Union and because the Party wished to avoid the resurgence of Islamic fundamentalism that was sweeping the Middle East, the Party was especially concerned about its Muslim population. Moreover, the Cultural Revolution had discredited not only religion but also China's national minorities, demoralizing Muslim communities. Thus, the Party reopened mosques and Muslim seminaries even earlier than the churches in an effort to mollify as well as control the minorities. A small number of Muslims were even allowed to make pilgrimages to Mecca. Yet, at the same time that the regime bestowed these privileges in order to maintain stability along its long border with the Soviet Union, it also sent in millions of Han Chinese to the border regions in order to dilute the concentration of Muslims. While seemingly benign, the Party's policy toward Islam, as toward Christianity, was to tighten political control.

Besides the strategic and political reasons, the Party's reestablishment of religious institutions was also to gain tourist dollars. This is most blatantly demonstrated in its restoration of Buddhist and Daoist temples destroyed during the Cultural Revolution and in the refurbishing of Buddhist and Daoist sculptures, paintings, rubbings from stone inscriptions, and classics that are displayed in temples. Alongside the famous Lapuleng Monastery in Gansu, a hotel designed in the ancient architectural style and modern-style Tibetan yurts were built to accommodate tourists. Besides earning hard currency from tourists, the regime opened these religious showcases to show its professed tolerance of religious belief to the outside world. Consequently, religious belief is practiced more openly in tourist cities than in the interior.

These may be token gestures, but as invariably happens whenever the Party allows a degree of individual, intellectual, or religious expression, it cannot altogether control the response. Thus, at a meeting in April 1985 of the Chinese People's Political Consultative Conference, a gathering of intellectuals and professionals, the deputy secretary of the Chinese Academy of Social Sciences, Zhao Fusan, rejected the Marxist assertion that religion was the "opiate" of the people. Rather, he insisted that it was "an integral part" of culture and civilization; such unorthodox views had not yet been allowed in public forums. Moreover, visitors to China report that Buddhist temples are popping up all over the countryside and that Buddhist worshipers burn incense sticks and paper money. There has also been a reemergence in the countryside of sorcerers, wizards, witches, and fortune tellers who claim to exorcise evil spirits. The regime has repeatedly issued directives to religious believers to distinguish between religion and superstition.

Unauthorized religion

Despite the Party's effort to channel all religious activities into Party-supervised organizations, unsupervised religious practice continues in house churches. Even the Party's Protestant spokesman, K. H. Ting, head of the Nanjing Theological Seminary, said publicly in 1980 that some Christians found informal groups "much more spiritually satisfying than a large congregation."[2] He expressed the hope that Christians would continue to be able to

2. *China and Ourselves,* Newsletter of the Canadian China Programme, p. 9 (May 1980).

pray both in their homes and in their churches. He implied that private worship satisfied a certain need that politicized religious practice did not.

Officially, home gatherings were permitted if the participants registered with the authorities. But if the participants registered, then the gatherings would come under some form of official surveillance. Moreover, an internal Party document of 2 April 1982 directed that the clergy could only "propagate theism and religious doctrine in legal places." The document also implied that those who gather in homes have ulterior motives: "They gather together in a disorderly manner under the pretext of 'holding religious services in their homes.' " Since such happenings not only take away from production, but also supposedly disturb public order, provincial officials were directed "to exercise control over these improper gatherings."[3] But in order not to antagonize religious believers, the document urged officials not to call such gatherings illegal but rather to reduce their number gradually. Their method should reflect the Party's overall policy of weaning believers gradually from their religious faith, not through forceful means but through a limited tolerance.

This relatively lenient approach, however, does not appear to have reduced the number of religious believers. It is difficult to estimate the number of house churches and their adherents, but various Christian groups in Hong Kong estimate that there are about 10,000 unofficial church meeting places, mostly in the countryside.[4] One visitor, traveling through Henan, reported praying with worshipers who ranged in number from a dozen in homes to several hundreds in a courtyard. There were even reports of very large meetings in caverns.[5] The ability to conduct such religious services depends upon the local cadre. Some cadres do not interfere; others harass house worshipers. The worshipers usually meet at night after work and are conducted in prayer by their own, rather than official, leaders. Sometimes they are led by an itinerant preacher, tape recorders, or even religious broadcasts from abroad, primarily from Hong Kong.

In fact, the Party's internal document on religion acknowledged that the attraction to religion had increased rather than decreased. It asked, "Why has Protestantism developed so quickly in the past two or three years?" It frankly recognized that the disillusionment caused by the Cultural Revolution had evoked interest in religion because people "feel that they are ideologically empty and therefore accept religious belief as spiritual sustenance and enjoyment."[6] To counter the attraction of religion, the document urged intensified ideological education and improved economic conditions so as to enrich cultural and economic life. It was particularly concerned with the attraction of religion to Party members and to youth, and it directed that any Communist Party or Communist Youth League members who partake in religious activities should be dismissed from the Party and the youth league. The document in no way acknowledged that some people might want spiritual sustenance for reasons beyond political ideology and the material world.

3. Internal Party document, in *Issues and Studies* (Taiwan), p. 89 (Oct. 1983).

4. *China and the Church Today* (Hong Kong), p. 4 (Sept.-Oct. 1982).

5. *Pray for China* (Hong Kong), p. 2 (Oct. 1984).

6. *Issues and Studies,* p. 90 (Oct. 1983).

The suppression of the organizers of unauthorized religious gatherings was carried out in the context of the campaign against spiritual pollution, a drive against Western influence launched in the fall of 1983. Like the intellectuals, religious believers also suffered periodic repressions that repeatedly interrupted the Deng leadership's relative liberalization. China's president, Li Xiannian—in an interview with the Archbishop of Canterbury, Robert Runcie, in December 1983—insisted that the spiritual pollution campaign was against faulty thinking in culture, the arts, and ideology, but not against religion. The campaign, however, did activate leftists on the local level who used it to resume attacks on churches and religious believers. This kind of activity was soon stopped by the leadership, who feared the disruption to the economy of another Cultural Revolution and the suspension of Western aid. However, the leadership allowed and even encouraged the crackdown on those who conducted unauthorized religious services. There were reports from the second half of 1983 into 1984 of leaders of house churches who were arrested for refusing to join government-sponsored Christian organizations and for possessing Bibles that had not been officially published by the Three Self Movement. In Guangzhou in December 1983, for example, 10 house-church leaders were either arrested or interrogated by the Public Security Bureau.[7] In the drive against crime launched in the summer of 1983, just before the spiritual pollution campaign, officials arrested unaffiliated Christians in order to fulfill their arrest quotas, further intensifying the pressure on Christians. The spiritual pollution and crime drives became intertwined in the attack on religious believers and the unaffiliated.

As under Mao, Roman Catholics were treated more severely than the other religious denominations. Catholics whose first loyalty was to Rome rather than to the Party received especially harsh treatment. As did other religionists, Roman Catholics held services in private gatherings rather than in official churches. Even before the spiritual pollution campaign, conflict had arisen again over the relationship of China's Roman Catholics to the Vatican. Bishop Ding Yiming of Guangdong had been imprisoned for 22 years because he had refused to break with the pope, but in October 1980 he was chosen as the Guangdong Catholic bishop. The pope, John Paul II, supposedly in the belief that he was confirming the Chinese choice, appointed Ding the archbishop of Guangdong in June 1982. But the Catholic Patriotic Association, speaking for the Party, charged the Vatican with "rude interference in the sovereign affairs of the Chinese church."[8] Thus, instead of improving the relationship, the pope's action aggravated it further.

In March 1983, four elderly priests who had refused to break with the Vatican or to join the Patriotic Catholic Association were arrested and given terms of up to 15 years for "colluding" with foreign countries. Of the four, Bishop Geng Pinwei was the most well known. He had been imprisoned under similar charges in 1955 and released briefly after the Deng leadership took over, but he died in prison in 1984.

At the same time that the Party was repressing those loyal to the Vatican, it

---

7. *China and the Church Today*, p. 2 (July-Aug. 1984).

8. *Far Eastern Econonic Review*, 10 July 1981, p. 30.

convened a showcase conference of Catholic priests, nuns, and laypersons who declared their determination against becoming an "appendage" to the Vatican and their independence of any foreign power.

As in its treatment of the intellectuals, the Party's treatment of religious believers, whether under Mao or Deng, follows a cyclical pattern of succeeding periods of tightening and loosening of Party controls. Periods of repression are succeeded by periods of relative relaxation. After the spiritual pollution campaign, as the Party attempted again to win the cooperation of intellectuals in late 1984 and early 1985, it also relaxed its control over religious believers. Alongside its calls for "freedom of literature and art," it also called for "freedom of religious beliefs." The party sought to ingratiate itself once more with converts and the Western nations in order to further its modernization. It also sought to bring above ground again worshipers who had gone underground during the spiritual pollution campaign in order to reestablish its control over them.

The newspaper of the intellectuals, *Guangming ribao (Guangming Daily)*, in February 1985 acknowledged that the hold of religion was so deeply embedded in the lives of its believers that "this powerful traditional force and ideology will by no means be eliminated along with the old system."[9] It again called for dealing with religion by means of patient ideological education and continued economic development rather than by repression. The regime's belief that cooperation and unity are prerequisites for modernization even led it to recommend an end to atheistic propaganda among religious believers for fear of provoking clashes between believers and nonbelievers. Again the Party's renewed tolerance did not stem from a greater appreciation of religion but from its manipulation of religion to further its drive for economic modernization.

RELIGION IN CHINA'S FUTURE

Although overall the Deng leadership has treated religion more tolerantly than did the Mao leadership, its approach still follows the Maoist pattern: religion is used for political purposes. When the regime relaxes its controls over the population, there is more tolerance of religious belief; when the regime increases its control over the population, there is more repression of religion. As long as reform-minded leaders think that opening to the outside world and toleration of religious belief can help China's modernization, the relatively benign treatment of religion may continue. But there is no guarantee that the reformers themselves will not change their views of reform or that leftists who are less concerned with openness or individual interests will not return. Even among the reform leaders, there are more orthodox Marxist-Leninists who believe that the relaxation and openness to the outside world have gone too far. Periodically they assert themselves within the present leadership, as was seen in the spiritual pollution campaign. If the reformers as well as the more orthodox leaders were to perceive that religion could become an alternative to Marxism-Leninism, the limits of tolerance might be sharply narrowed.

What the PRC's experience with religion has proven is that despite tremendous political, ideological, and even violent pressure, religion does not die. It

9. *Guangming ribao* [Guangming daily], 18 Feb. 1985.

can be suppressed, but it reemerges when the pressures are lifted. If anything, repression strengthens religious faith and gains new adherents.

What explains the tenacity of religion under such difficult circumstances? Most obvious is that the ideologies of Marxism-Leninism and Mao do not answer the questions about human existence or give the kind of meaning to life that some people desire. The post-Mao religious resurgence demonstrates that the secular ideologies did not meet people's spiritual needs. When people were being arbitrarily persecuted and killed, when families suffered grief and despair in the Cultural Revolution, the Party's ideology could not provide spiritual help. On the contrary, its ideology was held responsible for the tragedies that had befallen them. Religion had not withered away, as Marx had predicted; it had intensified, a phenomenon further revealing the ideologies' inadequacies. The inability of Marxism-Leninism to deal with anything beyond the temporal world and its disregard of the inner being deepened the hold of religion on those who were already religious and attracted those who were looking for spiritual answers.

The Deng leadership recognizes that the Party had underestimated the power of religious faith. Its establishment of an Institute for Research on World Religions at the Academy of Social Sciences does not necessarily signify a positive view of religion, but it does signify a recognition of the influence of religion on political affairs. Despite the leadership's acknowledgment of the tenacity of religion and its policy of toleration, its ultimate goal remains the abolition of religion, not through administrative means, as after 1957, or through force, as in the Cultural Revolution, but through ideological education and economic development. However, as is true in other areas of life, the means to an end sometimes become the end. The longer the Party's limited toleration continues, the greater the possibility that the public expression of religious faith within official parameters will in time become an end in itself and a way of life in the People's Republic of China.

Book Department

INTERNATIONAL RELATIONS AND POLITICS

GARDNER, LLOYD C. *A Covenant with Power: America and World Order from Wilson to Reagan.* Pp. xv, 251. New York: Oxford University Press, 1984. $22.95.

The central concern with which this book begins—the relationship between liberalism as a precept for U.S. policy and the consequences of wielding power—is an important and interesting one. Until Woodrow Wilson, Gardner argues, a cardinal principle of the Republic had been freedom from foreign entanglements and the power politics of the old world. Wilson broke with this in the hope of helping to construct a world more conducive to liberalism and hence the well-being of the United States. Succeeding presidents down to the present have continued to do the same with results of varying gravity. In essence the defense of liberal values, including those of free trade and capitalist economic organization, required the use of power, power that can and has been abused such that it threatens to undermine what it set out to protect.

Unfortunately the argument of the book is not always easy to follow or indeed to discern, particularly toward the end, where Gardner catalogues the decline of American power and depicts President Reagan as Ahab sailing the *Pequod* to ruin. There is no convincing connection between this allusion, which will appeal to many, and what precedes it. In many ways the book reads like a stream of consciousness in which the beginning and end or even the thread is not readily apparent. The book would have been improved by being much more tightly structured around an agenda of clearly spelled-out questions. As it is, the theme changes and has to be continually teased out, only to be gradually lost.

Another shortcoming is the lack of references. Gardner explains, in an endnote, that he did not want footnotes to burden his purpose of writing a series of essays or think pieces in which he drew on more than 20 years of research. Footnotes are often overdone and tiresome and there is no doubt that Gardner knows his stuff very well. Nevertheless in this book there are numerous assertions and quotes that demand substantiation and references. The absence of them is frustrating and a serious impairment to the use of the book.

This is not to say the book is without value. For some readers it will be a rich source of suggestions and a starting point as to how successive leaders have seen the role of the United States in world order. Even so it is a pity that out of the mass of historical detail there emerge no generalizations that might shed light on the present.

PAUL KEAL

Australian National University
Canberra

GAWTHROP, LOUIS C. *Public Sector Management, Systems, and Ethics.* Pp. 173. Bloomington: Indiana University Press, 1984. $22.50.

The Aristotelian thesis that politics and ethics are inextricably entwined comes to mind in reading Louis Gawthrop's latest contribution to the literature of public administration. He unites public management, systems theory, and ethical considerations into an integrated, but altered, metasystem. He perceives the impending bicentennial commemorating the adoption of the Constitution as an auspicious occasion for redesigning an administrative order that is "capable of enhancing or inhibiting the ... citizen's role in government and the government's role in society."

At the outset, he cites Max Weber's bureaucratic model for decision making and problem solving, which guarantees administrative responsibility, continuity, and control. However, he quickly acknowledges that the Weberian blueprint underserves society's needs whenever the external forces pressing for change overwhelm the public sector manager's expertise. In such situations, new strategies are demanded.

In the world according to Gawthrop, administrators must be prepared to think and act independently, critically, and constructively. He exhorts them to approach public issues through a systems framework and an ethical perspective. He concedes the potential danger in assuming that every corporal carries an officer's baton in his knapsack, but he is prepared to take the risk. As a result, the reader must also be willing to examine the implications inherent in Gawthrop's acceptance of personal values and

bureaucratic discretion as major guides to public policy implementation. I am tempted to ask, What are the acceptable parameters for allowing individual morals to influence access to abortions, withdrawal of life-support systems, or the use of deadly force to subdue civilian populations? Whose managerial innovations and whose social values will prevail?

In subsequent chapters, Gawthrop deplores the tendency of public managers to compromise private virtues for the sake of pragmatism, consensus, or conformity to the rules of the game. The status quo is perpetuated by "ethics of civility" that discourage debate and the quest for purposeful goals. He deplores blind obedience to a system and maintains that social equity is as important as operating efficiency.

Gawthrop wishes to redesign the system so that professionals will be held accountable for their actions and free to search for just solutions without the impediments of structural authority or institutional boundaries. One might question his abiding faith in this new order of public managers as the deputies of the citizenry. Unlike elected officials, appointed administrators are not accountable to the voters. Furthermore, below the level of exempt positions, bureaucrats are removable only after demonstrated proof of malfeasance, misfeasance, or nonfeasance. In bypassing the nexus between elected officials and their constituents and transferring the linkage to administrators, Gawthrop alters the nature of representative government.

Unfortunately, the work seems caught in a time warp—circa 1980. While the book traces the phenomenal proliferation of federal programs during the 1960s and 1970s, there is no discussion of the relationship between the New Federalism and discretionary ethics. He simply suggests that the government may be ready to abandon some projects, but he is not convinced that the pendulum will swing back to its opposite extreme.

His scholarship and credentials are impeccable. As editor in chief of *Public Administration Review* and professor of public affairs at Indiana University, Gawthrop shows full mastery of the literature in the field. The richness and diversity of his sources are striking. The notes and quotations are drawn from political science, history, sociology, economics, philosophy, theology, psychiatry, and other disciplines. He weaves them together in a cogent and impressive manner in espousing a comprehensive approach to the public policy process.

LEONARD P. STAVISKY
Columbia University
New York City

HOLSTI, OLE R. and JAMES N. ROSENAU. *American Leadership in World Affairs: Vietnam and the Breakdown of Consensus.* Pp. xvi, 301. Winchester, MA: Allen and Unwin, 1984. $28.50. Paperbound, $9.95.

JONSSON, CHRISTER. *Superpower: Comparing American and Soviet Foreign Policy.* Pp. viii, 248. New York: St. Martin's Press, 1984. $25.00.

Although both of these books deal with contemporary international politics, they are based on quite different assumptions about why states behave as they do. They also employ quite different methodologies. Yet they each encounter similar or related logical problems, and their conclusions are not totally dissimilar. It is instructive to compare them.

Holsti and Rosenau report on their 1976 and 1980 surveys of American foreign policy leaders, some of whom hold official governmental positions. Their book persuasively argues that the Vietnam war was a watershed event because the way in which leaders viewed that war at its inception, while it was in progress, and in retrospect has had a profound impact on their general views toward foreign policy. The book maintains that Vietnam shattered the consensus among American leaders concerning foreign policy and that it is unlikely that a consensus will be reestablished easily or quickly. Holsti and Rosenau obviously assume that what American leaders think is an important factor shaping United States foreign policy. Their book, based on extensive, sophisticated analyses of the large body of empirical data gained through their surveys, is a model of scholarship and an important contribution to the literature.

Jonsson, on the basis of an analysis of existing literature, argues that the United States and the Soviet Union pursue similar foreign policies, especially toward the Third World. He tests and illustrates this argument by comparing U.S. and Soviet policies concerning aid to Third World countries, the continuing crisis in the Middle East, and efforts to prevent the proliferation of nuclear weapons. He attributes the similarities in the policies of the two countries to their superpower status, arguing that the United States acts and that the Soviet Union then emulates U.S. actions. He attributes differences in the two countries' policies to the considerably greater economic strength of the United States compared to the Soviet Union. The assumption on which Jonsson's argument is based is that a state's position in the structure of the global political system is the fundamental factor shaping its foreign policy.

Both books are interesting and enhance the understanding of contemporary international affairs. That the books leave fundamental issues unresolved is more a comment on the unsatisfactory state of theory about how the foreign policy behavior of states is shaped than a criticism of the books. With respect to the Holsti and Rosenau book the reader must take it on faith that the differences among the American leaders' views, many of which are small despite being statistically significant and which exist alongside substantial agreement on numerous points, affect what the United States does in international affairs. With respect to Jonsson's book, the reader must accept as an act of faith that those who make the decisions that determine the foreign policy of the United States and the Soviet Union base their decisions on a concept of the role of a superpower.

The arguments presented in the two books encounter similar difficulties caused by an absence of information. Because no survey was conducted in the earlier post-World War II years that is comparable to those that Holsti and Rosenau have conducted since 1976, these two authors are unable to demonstrate conclusively that there are more differences among the foreign policy attitudes of American leaders now than there were before the Vietnam war. By looking only at the policies of the United States and the Soviet Union, Jonsson cannot demonstrate that the policies of these two countries are unique. Do other states that are great, but not of superpower status, behave similarly?

Both books caution against projecting trends from the past into the future. For Holsti and Rosenau the question is the forging of a new consensus among U.S. leaders on what the country's role in world affairs should be. For Jonsson the question is what superpowers should do when their power, relative to the power of others, is diminished. That such methodologically dissimilar books should raise such basically similar questions about the future suggests that they have indeed identified a key issue, one that merits sustained, thoughtful attention.

HAROLD K. JACOBSON

University of Michigan
Ann Arbor

KUSNITZ, LEONARD A. *Public Opinion and Foreign Policy: America's China Policy, 1949-1979.* Pp. xii, 191. Westport, CT: Greenwood Press, 1984. $29.95.

WATANABE, PAUL Y. *Ethnic Groups, Congress, and American Foreign Policy: The Politics of the Turkish Arms Embargo.* Pp. xvi, 228. Westport, CT: Greenwood Press, 1984. $29.95.

"Public opinion . . . greatly affected Washington's policies toward the People's Republic of China." So concludes Leonard Kusnitz after examining U.S. policy on China from 1949 to 1979. But did it? Kusnitz attempts to demonstrate a link between public opinion and foreign policy by comparing the China policy of sequential administrations with the prevailing opinions on various China-related issues, such as whether the People's Republic of China should be admitted to the United Nations. But his approach raises some difficulties. First, there is no operational definition of "public opinion." Sometimes poll data are given—often in inconsistent form—but so are newspaper editorials, long considered unreliable indicators of public opinion. Moreover the salience of the China issues is never discussed effectively; thus, the reader never knows how strongly opinions are held or how much information lies behind them. Indeed, it is quite possible that the various administrations studied by Kusnitz were themselves responsible for affecting public opinion to support their chosen China policies, but Kusnitz does not explore this possibility thoroughly, despite strong support for it in previous literature. Finally, the reader does not learn from memoirs or documents very much about how presidents since 1949 have felt either constrained from or goaded into a China policy that they themselves would not have chosen on their own.

Paul Watanabe does somewhat better in his study of the Greek American response to the Turkish invasion of Cyprus in 1974. He explores first the role of ethnic group consciousness and then focuses on Congress as a target for ethnic group expression of policy preferences. He points out that Congress is the logical organ for ethnic group political contact given its diverse makeup and its divisions, which permit localized ethnic groups to link up with particular members in ways that would be impossible at the executive level.

Greek Americans were galvanized into political action not only by the Turkish invasion of Cyprus, but also by the perception that the Ford administration had handled the crisis poorly and was tilting toward Turkey after the fall of the Greek junta, whose actions precipitated the crisis.

In the end, though, Congress is not able to affect U. S. policy much—initial legislation supporting an arms embargo against Turkey was vetoed by Ford, and a watered-down compromise resulted. In short, Greek American activism failed to affect U.S. policies significantly, largely because it was directed through that branch of government whose ability to direct the course of foreign policy is quite limited.

Watanabe takes a long time to apply the introductory material to his study—it only comes together in chapter 6—and some of the material on Congress reads too much like a primer. But the book fills a gap in the literature on the role of ethnic politics and foreign policy, and it is important for that purpose.

In fairness to both Kusnitz and Watanabe, the field of public opinion and foreign policy is a difficult one in which to work—the linkages between the two areas are difficult to demonstrate. Unfortunately neither book really is able to overcome this long-standing problem.

DAVID S. SORENSON

Denison University
Granville
Ohio

Ohio State University
Columbus

SMITH, R. B. *An International History of the Vietnam War.* Vol. 1, *Revolution versus Containment, 1955-61.* Pp. xiii, 301. (New York: St. Martin's Press, 1984. $25.00.

Revolution versus Containment, 1955-61 is the first volume of R. B. Smith's four-volume series, *An International History of the Vietnam War.* To be published later are volume 2, *The Struggle for Southeast Asia, 1961-66;* volume 3, *War versus Detente, 1966-71;* and volume 4, *The Denouement, 1971-76.*

The theme of volume 1, and presumably of the volumes to follow as well, is that the Vietnam war was merely one element in the global power game and that to assess the war

properly it must be studied that way. In short, Smith puts the war in the context of U.S. foreign policy and the strategy and tactics of the Communist nations. The latter are generally coordinated well in the early years, says Smith, but are less so as the Sino-Soviet dispute develops; that dispute is itself a major factor influencing Hanoi's decisions and the course of the war.

In my mind this is the proper approach to the study of the Vietnam war, though it is not the easiest and most authors have been prone to look for analytic approaches in Vietnamese history, Communist ideology, the impact of bureaucracy on U.S. foreign policy decision making, and so forth. Thus this book is unique. Moreover, Smith does a good job at picking the most relevant variables in international politics—it being impossible to examine all of them—and relates them deftly to the course of the war at any given time.

Smith is writing from the vantage point of the elapse of ten years since the end of the war. He is therefore able to introduce a number of facts, and interpretations thereof, from newly declassifed documents. He is also able to glean some information from recent retrospective statements made by Communist leaders about the war. These new revelations, however, are generally not as startling as one might think or as the author would have the reader believe; rather they simply confirm in most cases what earlier historians have already said or guessed.

Smith's conclusion in this volume is that U.S.-Soviet relations and events elsewhere, namely the Cuba fiasco, led President Kennedy to adopt a policy of counterinsurgency, which in turn led to America's involvement in the war. Smith argues that the evidence indicates that Kennedy had no intention at the time, however, that counterinsurgency should be followed by a U.S. commitment to fight with large numbers of troops, as occurred during the Johnson administration.

Volume 1 of *An International History of the Vietnam War* is well organized and readable. It is interesting in the sense that putting a puzzle together fascinates the player. The most outstanding feature of the book is that Smith relates a myriad of global events to the war. To give just one example, he notes that events in Cuba, Algeria, and Iraq in 1958 led to a national liberation movement that helped Hanoi. Finally, he looks closely at the big players: Washington, Moscow, and Peking.

This book is recommended to anyone with an interest in the Vietnam war and/or international politics. I, for one, look forward to the next three volumes.

JOHN F. COPPER

Rhodes College
Memphis
Tennessee

SUTER, KEITH *An International Law of Guerrilla Warfare: The Global Politics of Law Making*. Pp. xii, 192. New York: St. Martin's Press, 1984. $27.50.

In terms of international law, war no longer exists: the most recent declaration of war—and the last, in Suter's view—was that of the Soviet Union against Japan 40 years ago. Since then, hostilities have been "armed conflicts" not falling under the Geneva and Hague Conventions. In 1967, Sean McBride of the International Commission of Jurists began a crusade to bring contemporary conflicts under the umbrella of international law. He was able to get a resolution to that effect passed at the 1968 U.N. Conference on Human Rights. Thereafter the United Nations referred it to the International Red Cross; apparently because its own efforts in 1957 to effect fundamental change had aborted, the Red Cross meekly pressed only for additional protocols to the now irrelevant conventions. Its diplomatic conferences were nearly wrecked on the question of special status for national liberation movements, but eventually conventional cool heads prevailed and in 1977 the additional protocols were agreed upon and have slowly begun since to gain acceptance by nation-states.

As its subtitle indicates, *An International Law of Guerrilla Warfare* concerns politics, not law as such—politics among nations, between nations and nongovernmental organizations, and among nongovernmental agencies. Suter—"since 1982 . . . President of the UN Association of Australia," the blurb tells us—participated in some unspecified capacity in the process, and it is the process that interests him, not some abstract play for power among nations. He certainly shows that ignorance, timidity, accident, and irresponsibility played huge roles in explaining why the mountain of concern in 1968 bore the mouse of two ineffectual additional protocols to two quite meaningless conventions. But his topic is not guerrilla warfare at all; it is the overall movement for reform of the law of armed conflict, with only asides as to the particular irrelevance of the end result to guerrilla movements. Suter's separate arguments—that the entire process was a farce and that guerrilla warfare is particularly badly covered by the end result—are not clearly distinguished from each other. Nor does Suter's prose do justice to the tale he tells: lists of factors end up within lists of factors, and lines of argument get confused by narrative; some editor should have relegated much of the text to footnotes. As it is, a fascinating tale is rendered painful to decipher and the book can be recommended only to the serious student of international politicking or international law—but not of guerrilla activity, about which the book says nothing—because only for them is the profit worth the pain.

RICHARD SIGWALT

Howard University
Washington, D.C.

BAKHASH, SHAUL. *The Reign of the Ayatollahs: Iran and the Islamic Revolution.*
Pp. x, 276. New York: Basic Books, 1984.
$18.95.

YODFAT, ARYEH H. *The Soviet Union and
Revolutionary Iran.* Pp. 168. New York:
St. Martin's Press, 1984. $25.00.

These two books complement each other:
one gives a detailed account of the internal
tensions of a revolutionary state; the other
studies this turbulent apparatus in one of its
most important external relations.

Bakhash goes to the heartland of revolutionary Iran—to Tehran—and produces an
exquisite account of the inner dynamics of
the postrevolutionary period. His chapters
are organized around some prominent men
of the revolution: Khomeini, Bazargan, and
Bani-Sadr. Other chapters, rich in firsthand
knowledge, deal with such characteristic sig-
nifiers as the Constitution of the Islamic
Republic, economics, land reform, and the
consolidation of power through terror.

Bakhash has a keen journalistic eye for
details; he gives his narrative an authentic
flavor that only a participant observer could
achieve. The short chapter entitled "The Collapse of the Old Order" provides a brief
account of the political events leading up to
the revolutionary upheavals. The chapter on
Khomeini covers his political activities from
Qum to Neuphle-le-Château. Here, despite
an accurate description of the revolutionary
leader's courses of action, Bakhash fails to
use his perceptive observations to provide us
with some insights into the character of the
most enigmatic figure of the revolution. The
chapter on Bazargan, on the contrary, cap-
tures the liberal and ineffective nature of this
old politician's disastrous administration.
Bakhash also covers the two controversial
issues of postrevolutionary land distribution
and economics with detailed accuracy. But
perhaps the most important chapter of the
book is the one that examines the Islamic
Republic's use of terror in consolidating its

power. Here Bakhash successfully portrays
the shrewd political acumen of the clerics in
the position of power.

The weakness of the book arises precisely
from its strength. Bakhash wants to capture
the immediacy of the revolution. He should
have kept this theme steady throughout his
book. When he ventures to make statements
about historical significance or sociological
implications he plunges deeply into untested
waters. In one instance, for example, he sees
the revolution as a "cataclysmic event which
has resulted in an extensive transformation
of the country's political, social, and economic structure." There are essentially two
problems with such understandings of the
revolution: (1) many prerevolutionary traits
are carried forward in the postrevolutionary
period; and (2) many seemingly revolutionary courses of action are merely intensifica-
tions of developments already dormant in
the old regime.

Politically, no major change affected the
state apparatus, and except for some artificial changes in the top echelons, the bureaucratic organizations stayed the same. The
post-Constitutional Revolution's social structure continued to hold together the Iranian
society. The massive emigration of the com-
prador bourgeoisie was almost immediately
compensated by the rejuvenation of the
traditional—*bazar*—merchant class. The bureaucratic middle class remained virtually
untouched. Despite massive mobilization
and politicization of the lower class—proletariat, *lumpenproletariat*, peasantry, and
the like—its plight and social conditions did
not effectively change after the revolution.
The political elite simply was relocated from
the Resurgence Party to the Islamic Republic Party, and from the Niavaran Palace to
the Jamaran Headquarter. Economically,
no major change affected the infrastructure.
Despite artificial Islamization of the banking
system, nationalization of international
trade, and coordination of industries, the
quasi-capitalistic nature of the old regime,
along with the sanctity of private property,
effectively continued.

On a fundamental sociocultural level,
many revolutionary developments had their

antecedents in the old regime. The totalitarian measures of the present regime in eliminating or assimilating independent social institutions—such as the universities, the judicial system, and the artistic and literary associations—are predicated chiefly on similar policies of the previous regime. Lacking institutional legitimacy, the present regime is following the old one in its exclusive resort to the use of physical force in securing its power.

The reign of ayatollahs, as Bakhash so ably shows, is certainly a new phase in the continuing saga of posttraditional Iranian society. As a political event of considerable magnitude, however, the Iranian revolution falls much too short of drastically redirecting either the time-honored continuity of cultural paradigms or the rapid rationalization and atomization of the Iranian social structure and individual character.

Yodfat's volume is a comprehensive study of the Russo-Iranian relationship from roughly the end of the czarist regimes to the present time. The bulk of the study, however, centers around the Iranian revolution of 1979 and the vicissitudes of the Soviet policies toward the new regime. The first two chapters that deal with the aggressive expansion of czarist Russia in Central Asia and the Soviet interventionist policy in the 1917-53 period do not add anything significant to what has already been covered extensively in F. S. Fatemi's *U.S.S.R. in Iran,* Marvin Entner's *Russo-Persian Commercial Relations, 1828-1914,* or George Lenczowski's *Russia and the West in Iran, 1918-1948.* But the significance of Yodfat's volume is more in its pioneering study of postrevolutionary Iran in one of that country's most important areas in its foreign relations. We are provided with a rare opportunity to observe the dynamic fluctuations of a turbulent state interacting with a superpower.

Following the tumultuous events of 1979, there are perhaps three crucial loci at which Soviet-Iranian relations culminate: (1) the establishment of the Islamic Republic in Iran, considered against the Muslim population of the Soviet Union; (2) the resurgence of the Tudeh Party in the postrevolutionary period, examined with regard to this party's pro-Soviet lines; and (3) the Soviet occupation of Afghanistan, understood in terms of both the Muslim population of this country and its Western border with the Islamic Republic. Yodfat's study covers the first point with detailed accuracy, but leaves the issue of Soviet Muslims effectively untouched, except for one short passage. It deals with the second point scantily but sufficiently. The treatment of the Afghanistan occupation is rich with details but fails to explore the occupation's significance either for Iran or for the Soviet Union. Instead Yodfat brings a wealth of information, meticulously collected from various journals, magazines, news reports, radio broadcasts, and other sources to follow Soviet-Iranian relations during the Iran-Iraq war.

Yodfat's study successfully follows the Soviets' incessant attempt, through either direct intervention or the agency of the Tudeh Party, to secure their interests—political and otherwise—in a country they consider a major diplomatic battlefield between themselves and the other superpower.

HAMID DABASHI

University of Pennsylvania
Philadelphia

BAXTER, CRAIG. *Bangladesh: A New Nation in an Old Setting.* Pp. xii, 130. Boulder, CO: Westview Press, 1984. $16.50.

For anyone seeking an introduction to Bangladesh, this is the book to read. Scholars and educators anticipating a sojourn in Bangladesh, government servants and members of the business community newly assigned to it, or, indeed, anyone with travel to Bangladesh in his or her future, but having little or no knowledge about the country, should find Baxter's slim but meaty and eminently readable book an excellent point of departure. By the same token, the volume's brevity combined with its scholarly substance and lively style makes it quite worth assigning for introductory survey or advanced courses on South Asia, the Islamic world, or Asia more generally—for which reason I hope that the publishers will consider producing a less expensive paperbound edition.

Baxter has brought to the book the uncommon combination of his extensive experience as an American foreign service officer, whose career in that capacity has included many years in South Asia—in India and Pakistan as well as in Bangladesh—and the expertise of a scholar trained at the University of Pennsylvania in modern South Asian political history and government, with a goodly number of respected academic publications to his credit. The result is a work well grounded in scholarship, buttressed by the well-tempered, balanced, and practical judgments emblematic of the seasoned diplomat.

Beginning with a chapter on geography and social demographics, the book amply covers the full range of topics one expects to find in an introductory country survey. The three historical background chapters, recounting the earliest known periods through Bangladesh independence in 1971, are remarkable for Baxter's uncanny ability to boil down the immense complexity of events and personalities and highlight the major points. Baxter engagingly renders the British and Pakistani periods of Bangladesh's modern history, providing capsule summaries that at once provide the basics of what the introductory reader needs to know and the informed reader can review with profit. The chapter on Bangladesh politics since its independence to mid-1984—through the first two years of the current Ershad regime—is replete with more detail. Perhaps mindful of how easily one unfamiliar with Bangladesh can become bogged down in trying to follow the twists and turns, the storm and fury, of the country's recent political history, Baxter provides a chronological summary that can be referred to in studying the chapter. There

follows a clear and informative account of the nation's civil and military administration and a review of its problems of economic and social development. The final chapter on Bangladesh's foreign relations provides an excellent overview of the subject, tracing a theme that Baxter has elsewhere articulated: how a country with multitudinous problems, but little national power, maneuvers its way to security in the international political system.

The professional political or social scientist will not find in this book any treatment of theoretical issues to which Bangladesh data might be possibly related, nor is this the sort of work that aims at presenting new research and examining the implications thereof. In addition, the book could have used a more explicit analytical framework as context for the narration of a nation's experience. Such, however, is neither the purpose of the author nor of the series of works in which Westview has published it. As suggested, the book does provide essential information that is important as background for anyone contemplating research for which Bangladesh data will be gathered or might be useful. Scholars who have worked in or who specialize in Bangladesh should have no quarrel with factual accuracy, although those who have been critical of the country's political and economic development, and especially of whatever role the United States may be seen to have played therein, may take issue with some of Baxter's emphases and interpretations. Certain of the more unsavory aspects of the coups d'etat that brought Ziaur Rahman to power in 1975, for example, as well as problems during his leadership of the country until 1981, have been downplayed, and Baxter's generally positive evaluation of this important figure as representing "the politics of hope" might not find universal accord among Bangladesh scholars.

This volume is intended primarily for the more general reader. Gracefully written, deftly summarizing a massive amount of material, illustrated with a set of well-chosen photographs, conveniently indexed, and providing useful chapter-by-chapter bibliographic suggestions for further reading, this book serves both the reader and the country about which it is written extremely well.

PETER J. BERTOCCI

Oakland University
Rochester
Michigan

MASAHIDE, SHIBUSAWA. *Japan and the Asian Pacific Region: Profile of Change.* Pp. 185. New York: St. Martin's Press, 1984. $25.00.

OZAKE, ROBERT S. and WALTER ARNOLD. *Japan's Foreign Relations: A Global Search for Economic Security.* Pp. xiv, 226. Boulder, CO: Westview Press, 1985. $35.00. Paperbound, $13.95.

In an effort to analyze and describe the implications of Japan's economic miracle for its foreign relations, the two volumes under review approach their subject in quite different ways; yet at the same time they complement each other and expand on certain topics that neither study covers completely.

Shibusawa Masahide's study, *Japan and the Asian Pacific Region,* is a historical account of Japan's rise from the ashes of war to its prominence in economic affairs. Although Japan is the central focus, Masahide gives more pages to putting it into historical perspective, thus deflecting the reader away from Japan to events and decisions elsewhere to which Japan must respond. Thus the reader will find himself or herself reviewing the cold war, the hot wars of Korea and Vietnam, and the rise of the People's Republic of China. In all this, Masahide breaks no new ground; however, by drawing extensively upon Japanese sources, he indirectly supports the accepted interpretation by Western scholars of the course of events in Asia since World War II.

Readers unfamiliar with the international aspects of Japan's economic miracle will find Masahide's discussion of "economism"—the emphasis on economic growth and foreign trade over other aspects of traditional international goals—both brief and informative. Beginning with a discussion of how the Japanese came to adopt this strategy and how it has been modified over the years, the reader with a limited background will find it useful as a basis from which to go more deeply into the policy that influences all other aspects of Japan's relations with the world.

It is at this point that Robert S. Ozaki and Walter Arnold's *Japan's Foreign Relations* intersects with Masahide's book. Under their editorship, a respected group of Japanese and Western scholars contributed essays on Japan's economic relations with particular countries or regions. The essays are somewhat uneven in their treatment of their specific topics, and this inconsistency reflects, in part, the degree to which Japan is involved with the specific country or region. Although each essayist gives a few paragraphs to post-World War II relations between Japan and his subject area, all primarily are concerned with the present state of economic relations and what the immediate future will hold. By reading this volume along with Masahide's, the reader will gain insight into the meaning of economism and how it is working in its present form.

But even together, the two books leave a huge gap in their coverage of Japan's foreign relations. As the strongest economic power in Asia, Japan will be forced to extend its political influence, and even potential military power, as other Asian and world powers become economic rivals to Japan. As the United States fights for markets and the cry for protectionism grows in some areas of that nation, as China modernizes and becomes a rival, and as the other Asian nations, from Korea to Thailand, develop more balanced economies, Japan finds itself in a changing world. How it is beginning to cope and to prepare for these changes are only hinted at, and the interested reader will have to look elsewhere for possible answers and insights, as these volumes do not really address such questions.

JOSEF SILVERSTEIN

Rutgers University
New Brunswick
New Jersey

MATTIONE, RICHARD P. *OPEC's Investments and the International Financial System*. Pp. xi, 201. Washington, DC: Brookings Institution, 1985. $26.95. Paperbound, $9.95.

Speculation about the oil revenues of the Organization of Petroleum Exporting Countries (OPEC) has oscillated almost as violently as the price of petroleum. The OPEC surpluses of the 1970s were seen as a dire threat to the Western economic systems. Recently the downturn in prices has spawned pessimism about the stability of many OPEC nations. Richard Mattione has done yeoman's work in ferreting out the realities of OPEC's revenues and investments, and the effect on world finances.

To do this he has had to analyze a wide spectrum of materials, because the statistics themselves have political overtones and are not always readily available. After a historical review of the anticipated threat caused by the oil bonanza, he takes up individually the various investment strategies of OPEC members. The division is striking within OPEC between high-absorbing nations that soak up revenues and low-absorbing nations that because of small populations really do have extra cash. The high absorbers in OPEC are Algeria, Ecuador, Gabon, Indonesia, Iran, Iraq, Nigeria, and Venezuela. The low absorbers are Kuwait, Libya, Qatar, Saudi Arabia, and the United Arab Emirates.

What the figures reveal is really a rather tame story. Far from acquiring control of vital sectors of the Western economy, the OPEC countries have generally pursued conservative, middle-of-the-road policies resulting in considerable diversity for their portfolios. No Machiavellian plot emerges.

Chapters on OPEC foreign aid and Arab banks are useful and again there is little for millenarians to get excited about. The aid has gone to over 90 different countries, with the bulk of it to Arab nations. The OPEC banks play a role in international markets but are not at all comparable in size or operations to the leading Western banks. Decisions do reflect OPEC political orientations but the major considerations are decidedly economic.

It is, then, a much less sensational tale than some have suggested. Mattione deserves full credit for being the first to lay rumor to rest by providing this solid reference book on where the money came from and where it went. He sums up, "The current oil market glut has largely removed earlier fears that ever-increasing foreign investments by OPEC members would pose a serious threat to the West."

PAUL J. RICH

Training and Development
   Department
State of Qatar
Doha

MUNSON, HENRY, Jr., recorder, trans., and ed., *The House of Si Abd Allah: The Oral History of a Moroccan Family*. Pp. xxi, 280. New Haven, CT: Yale University Press, 1984. $19.95.

Scholarship and the general public in the West sorely need accurate primary sources portraying the world view of Third World peoples in general and ordinary Muslims in particular. Henry Munson's portraits of three generations of a nonelite Moroccan family, through the eyes of two of its living members, address this need. Historians' growing interest in nonelite social history, as well as the manifest need for greater comprehension of Muslim goals and values on the part of American policymakers and the politically active public, should establish a varied audience for a book of this type. Munson's book is interestingly constructed, using interviews with two cousins to delineate portraits of other family members, as well as to contrast the viewpoints of these two individuals on a variety of topics, especially Moroccan history, the impact of colonialism and guest-worker migration on Moroccan culture and society, and the importance of religion as the basis for meaningful action in Muslims' individual lives. Munson chose his informants for their contrasting views: the elder, a traditionally educated and oriented male, and the younger, his female cousin, who left school in her teens in Morocco but eventually migrated to the United States, continued her education, and married an American academic. Both are Muslims, deeply troubled by the erosion of Moroccan values and social life due to the colonial experience and subsequent economic and cultural domination from the Christian West, but Munson illustrates both gross and subtle differences in their attitudes toward these issues. The jargon-free 50-page introduction, grounded in Geertzian views of religion and society, should appeal to non-specialists seeking primary information about the life of ordinary Moroccans.

The worthiness of his project and the straightforwardness of its organization notwithstanding, Munson's work presents problems for the oral historian or folklorist. In recent years, oral historians, following folklorists' lead, have increasingly concerned themselves with the performative aspects of "texts," the fact that an interview occurs between two people and that the speaker's utterances are shaped, both in form and in content, by what he or she deems appropriate for the listener—the historian—to hear. Ronald Grele, dean of American oral historians, wrote in 1975, "The representation of reality is as significant an event in the culture as the reality itself" [*American Quarterly,* 27(3): 287]. He demonstrated the crucial significance of a microcultural feature, the relationship between interviewer and interviewee, in shaping information and rhetoric in oral history interviews. Munson as editor-translator intentionally expunged his own presence from his presentation of interviews, and what is worse, he interpolated statements from his female source, which she asserted were "typical" of her male cousin, to fill "lacunae" in the man's own testimony. These interpolations are not identified in the text. By obscuring, in translation and editing, the presumably problematic relationship between Munson as a representative of the oppressive culture and his male interviewee—who is reporting his sense of

oppression, among other things—and by allowing one informant to put words in the mouth of another, Munson seriously fails as an oral historian. This is particularly frustrating, in that some interview segments appear well served in his translation, powerfully revealing and moving, such as al-Hajj Muhammad's statement on the experience of prayer. Because of this odd mixture, while the book will help to inform nonspecialists concerning Moroccans' world views, to the sociolinguistically concerned folklorist or historian, it proves disappointing as an oral history.

MARGARET A. MILLS
University of Pennsylvania
Philadelphia

SCHULZ, DONALD E. and DOUGLAS H. GRAHAM, eds. *Revolution and Counterrevolution in Central America and the Caribbean.* Pp. xv, 555. Boulder, CO: Westview Press, 1984. $35.00. Paperbound, $14.95.

GRABENDORFF, WOLF, HEINRICH-W. KRUMWIEDE, and JORG TODT, eds. *Political Change in Central America.* Pp. 312. Boulder, CO: Westview Press, 1984. No price.

By now—May 1985—I have accumulated a good-sized shelf full of multiauthored volumes on contemporary Central America, all of them written after 1981. Within this growing library I consider the two books under review to be among the best in terms of the quality of information and analyses, the breadth of topics covered, and the incisiveness of policy questions raised, if not answered to anyone's full satisfaction. The perspectives of almost all the authors lie within American liberalism and West European social democracy; such a concentration is not surprising in the case of *Political Change,* which grew out of two international colloquia organized by the Friedrich Ebert Foundation of the West German Social Democratic Party. There is, then, no brief, or peace, for the Reagan administration's approaches to the region.

Each volume raises and seeks to answer three main questions: What is the political situation in Central America? How did the Central American crisis or crises arise? And what should the non-Communist external actors do about Central America, and why? Of course all the authors do not agree on the answers, but here I will attempt to illustrate the predominant positions. Guatemala is a "counterrevolutionary state" based on state terrorism. El Salvador is experiencing class warfare after a decades-long cycle of "reactionary despotism" and timid reformism. In Honduras, the military dominates weak civilian institutions that fail to adequately represent the population. In Nicaragua, the Sandinista hegemonist intent may or may not move into a Marxist-Leninist single-party dictatorship.

How did these states arrive at their present condition? Each volume examines the changing roles of the major actors, sometimes specifically, sometimes within country studies. Internal actors include the military, the civilian oligarchies, the Roman Catholic church, the emergent middle sectors and proletariat, and the peasantry. Externally, there is especially the United States, which is perceived essentially as a firm ally of the most reactionary domestic forces. The external Communists—Cuba and the USSR—play subsidiary roles, at best, in the development of the crises, but they fish cautiously in the troubled waters once these are stirred up. *Revolution and Counterrevolution* is particularly revealing of the economic dimensions of the crises, an issue that *Political Change* largely ignores as a separate independent variable.

What is to be done, especially by the United States? The authors are in broad agreement that the United States should adapt to change in the Third World. Among other things, American support of the status quo forces exacerbates their intransigence, runs counter to the increasing complexity of those societies, and deepens the crises even if there are temporary victories over the forces of change—in areas where the status quo is horrendous for the large majority of Central Americans, and when the temporary victories are won in ever-widening pools of blood.

Revolution and Counterrevolution is a better introduction to Central America if only because its greater length allows the region's complexities and policy issues to be more fully explored—and despite the waste of space on peripheral, even if excellent, digressions into Costa Rica and the Caribbean, which are quite distinct matters. I have adopted *Revolution and Counterrevolution* with some success for an undergraduate course with intelligent but uninformed students. On the other hand, *Political Change* tends to pose more interesting questions and to be more schematic in its analyses and recommendations.

In short, both of the books under review are among the best in their field. To read both is to be reasonably well informed and to be alerted to most of the important questions. What both lack is a hard-nosed, right-wing, *Realpolitik* perspective that discounts the lives of the Central Americans and is willing to employ consistently whatever force is required to maintain our "sons of bitches"—in Franklin Roosevelt's words—in power. Sadly, I am somewhat persuaded by at least the medium-term likelihood of success of such a policy. The Afrikaners, whether in South Africa, the White House, or Central America, may indeed have an important point.

Both books are available in paperback.

DONALD HINDLEY

Brandeis University
Waltham
Massachusetts

SOLINGER, DOROTHY J. *Chinese Business under Socialism—The Politics of Domestic Commerce 1949-1980.* Pp. xiv, 368. Berkeley: University of California Press, 1984. No price.

Since little is known about and no thorough investigation has been conducted on the domestic commercial scene of the People's Republic of China (PRC), Dorothy J. Solinger set out to describe the subject within the framework of the socialist state plan, the ideological conflicts among the political elite, and the technological foundation for marketing in an underdeveloped economy. The material presented was based on archival research, supplemented by Solinger's two trips to the PRC in 1978 and 1979 and to Hong Kong in the autumn of 1979. Parts of the book have appeared elsewhere.

The book may appear too technical to the average reader but it is exceedingly informative for the China specialist, whether a political scientist or an economist. Instead of resorting to the commonplace dichotomy of Chinese politics into leftist and rightist approach, Solinger devised, with much ingenuity, an analytical framework of "three tendencies," namely the radical, the bureaucrat, and the marketeer. Chinese political economy is thus interpreted as the dynamic interplay of these three counterbalancing forces. Further, Solinger divided the period of contemporary China between 1949 to 1979 into six periods of policymaking: the post-Mao era (1976-80), the Cultural Revolution (1966-76), readjustment (1961-65), the Great Leap Forward (1958-60), the First Five-Year Plan (1952-57), and the period of recovery (1949-52). Other writers on Chinese political development have used similar periodizations in their works. Originality, however, lies in Solinger's application of political concepts to describe China's domestic commerce, which others naively assume do not exist because of the PRC's epousal of Marxism-Leninism as the state's guiding political ideology.

Solinger predicted that China's business, despite the current open-door policy, would still remain the same—"an essentially state-run affair." Whenever there is an excessive reliance upon market forces, as seems to have been the case since 1980, mechanisms would be put into play to redress the balance, swinging the economy back to state planning. To that extent, the Confucian paradigm of cyclic changes has a common denominator with and fits in aptly with Solinger's analysis.

FRANKIE FOOK-LUN LEUNG
Chinese University of Hong Kong

YAGER, JOSEPH A. *The Energy Balance in Northeast Asia.* Pp. xiv, 249. Washington, DC: Brookings Institution, 1984. $28.95. Paperbound, $10.95.

Three non-communist countries of Northeast Asia—Japan, South Korea, and Taiwan—have emerged as important industrial countries and exporters of manufactured goods. The expansion of their economies, with some of the highest growth rates in the world, has been made possible through reliance on imported fuels. Japan imports more energy than any other country; South Korea and Taiwan are also major energy importers. As part of a series of Brookings Foreign Policy Studies, Joseph A. Yager, an energy economist, has analyzed past energy developments in Northeast Asia for the light they may shed on problems in other energy-importing areas and on future international energy trade. Yager, with the research assistance of Shelley M. Matsuba, uses the energy-balance approach to analyze the supply and disposition of energy in each country and to compare the energy experiences of Japan, in particular, with those of three other non-communist industrial nations: the United States, France, and West Germany.

The book is structured chronologically to review energy developments in the three Northeast Asian countries in the 1960s and 1970s and the impact of the rise of world oil prices since 1973, and to project possible future energy requirements and their implications. The central finding of the book is that energy requirements of the Northeast Asian countries, especially South Korea and Taiwan, are likely to increase at a more rapid rate than those of other major industrialized countries because of higher economic growth rates, and that Northeast Asia will therefore account for an increasing share of the international energy market. Yager and Matsuba find that, as a result of the oil crises of 1973-74 and 1979-80, the opportunities to substitute other fuels for oil have already been taken, and that oil consumption is now concentrated in such sectors as transportation and petrochemicals in which the possibilities of substitution are limited. In keeping with projected economic expansion, the total consumption of oil is therefore likely to increase, although the relative dependence on oil is expected to decline. In all three countries, a larger proportion of total energy supplies is expected to be derived from nuclear power. Of other fossil fuels, the share of coal is likely to increase in the energy balance of Taiwan, and liquefied natural gas in that of Japan and ultimately South Korea. Yager and Matsuba review the potential sources of energy imports in considerable detail, although I probably would have liked to see more comprehensive discussion of the prospects of increased supplies from Siberia, which is sometimes touted as a potential purveyor of energy goods to this part of the world.

THEODORE SHABAD

Soviet Geography
New York City

EUROPE

DAWISHA, KAREN. *The Kremlin and the Prague Spring*. Pp. xiv, 426. Berkeley: University of California Press, 1985. $34.50.

It is very appropriate that this book has appeared in a series—the International Crisis Behavior Series—supervised by Michael Brecher, the chief guru of international crisis behavior, with whom Dawisha, a lecturer in politics at Southampton University, conducts a respectful dialogue as one does with a revered master: *sic dicit philosophus*. The followers of international crisis behavior resemble physicians inspecting patients, who are, in this case, the top echelon of Soviet manipulators of power. They believe that the causes of political behavior under stress could be established, the course of illness charted, all to be explained by an intelligent combination of interpretive skills. Dawisha has listed 51 Soviet politburo decisions reached between 22 March and 25 August 1968, which is certainly the highest count ever reached anywhere. She has also listed 15 "alternatives," which are really options and choices arranged in a chronological order.

Dawisha's achievements are not only quantitative. Her remarkable book is rich in discussing theoretical models and in the detailed analysis of assumed responses by individual Soviet leaders. She has also carefully followed the track of ongoing Soviet-U.S. negotiations, helped by access to some formerly classified U.S. intelligence documents. The emphasis, however, is on the Kremlin, not on the Hradčany Castle in Prague. Dawisha admits not being interested in the Prague Spring per se. Internal forces of the Czech reform movement are contemplated merely as objects of Soviet manipulation. In this sense her book can be considered as an antidote to Gordon Skilling's unrivaled *Czechoslovakia's Interrupted Revolution*.

However, when it comes to confronting hard facts of the crucial meeting between the Czechoslovak leaders and the Soviet politburo on 25 August, known to us from the fascinating account by Zdeněk Mlynář *Mráz přichází z Kremlu* (1978), Dawisha, for the sake of preserving the balanced pattern of her theoretical analysis, lets all the steam escape from the boiler. This is a pity because here we have, for the first time since Milovan Djilas's testimonies, another direct account from the Kremlin kitchen of decision making. Brezhnev, namely, was telling Dubcek point-blank that "the matter of utmost importance" that led the Soviets to invade Czechoslovakia was the desire to preserve the results of World War II, won at the cost of 20 million Russian lives, and that nothing would force the Soviets to give up the conquered territory in Europe—not even a threat of another world war. Although Dawisha returns to the Soviet "blood debt" argument later, comparing it with Brecher's "Holocaust syndrome" that exercised such a pervasive influence on Israeli decision makers in the wars of 1967 and 1973, she considers the Hungarian experience of 1956 more relevant to the Soviet handling of the Czechosolvak crisis of 1968.

MILAN L. HAUNER
Foreign Policy Research Institute
Philadelphia
Pennsylvania

FELDMAN, LILY GARDNER. *The Special Relationship between West Germany and Israel.* Pp. xix, 330. Boston: George Allen & Unwin, 1984. $35.00.

This is a superb study, carefully planned, beautifully researched, ably organized, and well written. In many ways it is an exemplary work of scholarship presenting an altogether new and welcome analysis of an important development in recent history.

The bilateral relationship of friendship and mutual support after World War II between Germans and Jews is an extraordinary story. On the one side there is the successor state to the abominable Hitler regime, its people guilt ridden and seeking to wipe away the shame and ignominy of Nazism. On the other side is the newly created state of Israel, its people haunted by the memory of the Holocaust. Both sides seek simultaneously to establish their legitimacy in the family of nations, in the process of which the Bonn republic and Israel turn to each other. "In one of history's greatest ironies," reads the book jacket, "West Germany looked to Israel for the Nazi victims to acknowledge the moral acceptance of the successor state and Israel looked to West Germany as the lone industrial state with both the means and the will to provide a measure of economic security."

Several main points emerge from this fine analysis of German-Israeli relations. The bilaterial relationship has been special since 1952 and continues today. It is based on a long history of mutual awareness between Germans and Jews and is shaped by the altogether negative psychological trauma of the Holocaust. Most important, psychological factors have been expressed on both sides and frequently in terms of morality. The policy relationship is pragmatic: Israel desperately needed economic rejuvenation, while Germany sought political rehabilitation. Each country shows preference to the other in defense, economics, science, technology, and culture. Bonn's special relationships with other countries—France and the United States—do not in general conflict with its relationship with Israel. German-Israeli ties are challenged by Arab countries, which fail to comprehend the binding character of the special relationship; German-Israeli connections have endured crises over policy toward the Arab world.

These main points are handled with convincing detail, including careful statistics. There is only one minor flaw, although Feldman may well disagree. In the latter part of her book Feldman attempts to set the implementation of postwar German and Israeli policies in the context of a general theory of bilateral ties between states, as advocated by Winston Churchill and Henry Kissinger among others. This shifting of gears could have been reserved for another study, for which Feldman is well qualified. As presented here in strictly limited space, it does not quite gel. By no means, however, does this personal predilection detract from what is really a first-rate, admirable piece of research.

LOUIS L. SNYDER
City University of New York

JENSON, JANE and GEORGE ROSS. *The View from Inside: A French Communist Cell in Crisis.* Pp. x, 345. Berkeley: University of California Press, 1984. $28.50.

The View from Inside, by two North American students of the labor movement, is an account, from the point of view of the ordinary members, of a period of intense controversy within the Parti communiste français (PCF). Covering the year 1978-79, this study provides an interesting account of the conflict between the two major currents in the PCF: the Eurocommunist and ouvrier-ist groups. This book is unique, moreover, in the literature in English on the PCF in that it is an example of participant observation or, more simply put, good reportage, rather than, say, the statistical study or structural analysis that animates the more conventional literature on the subject.

In the spring of 1978 two scholars, one Canadian and one American, joined a cell of the PCF in the Paris South area, part of the PCF's traditional red belt. They remained with this group, which they named, aptly enough, Cellule Danielle Casanova—there are at least half a dozen such groups in the PCF—until the Twenty-third Congress the following year, attending cell and section meetings and closely following the life of its militants.

The electoral failures of the PCF in the preceding period, largely to the benefit of the Parti socialiste, provoked a crisis of policy within the PCF, with the leadership adopting a militant and, some would say, sectarian policy that it tried to impose on a membership that, in large part, was Eurocommunist in orientation. This was closely tied to the questions that a growing women's movement within the party raised, the party's first open debate—at long last—on the legacy of Stalin, and the problems, always acute in the PCF, on the respective weights to be given democracy and centralism in a democratic centralist party. Those familiar with PCF history will not be surprised at who won, the movement for change at the base being effectively stifled.

Part of the analytical work in the study is concerned with the strategy of decline analysis of the PCF leadership that, even if imposed without discussion and false in the political conclusions it draws, is still closer to the economic reality of France than is the approach of the Eurocommunists.

A great part of the merit of this book comes from its irrepressible charm. The characters that animate its pages come alive, and we are left with an image, quite human, of Monique or Pierre, one that lingers and that no amount of statistical data on elec-toral behavior can provide and that gives us some substantial insight into the enigmatic interior of the PCF.

MURRAY SMITH

Verdun
Quebec
Canada

KAHLER, MILES. *Decolonization in Britain and France: The Domestic Consequences of International Relations.* Pp. xiv, 426. Princeton, NJ: Princeton University Press, 1984. $40.00. Paperbound, $9.95.

The efforts of the British and the French in decolonization have frequently been compared by students of decolonization. The primary focus of these studies has been the impact of the decolonization process on the colonies. The wrenching experience that the loss of colonies was for the French and the British cannot be underestimated, especially since it came at a time when the two nations were having difficulty adjusting to their decline of power and prestige.

Kahler's book addresses the issues of decolonization and domestic politics in France and Britain. Initially, Kahler relates decolonization to the study of international relations by means of a particularly useful examination of the world political economy and interdependence approaches. He then turns to his main themes, which involve a discussion of political parties and ideologies, economic actors such as interest groups and large corporations, and the populations of the empires and the states, including colonial administrators and the military.

The contrast between Conservatives in France and Britain and the French Socialists and the British Labour Party regarding decolonization is effectively drawn. The fact that DeGaulle was able to limit the damage from decolonization, which under any circumstances would have occurred, is appropriately emphasized. The same is true of the flexibility that the British Conservatives showed in facing the loss of the colonies. In dealing with Socialist parties, Kahler argues that the British Labour Party was unified, uncharacteristically, on the issue of decolonization and behaved ideologically. Also, the sad history of the post-World War II French Socialists, led by opportunists such as Guy Mollet, is presented in a way that is particularly cogent in view of the party's behavior in the past decade.

In approaching the economies of the colonies and their relationships to metropolitan politics, Kahler evaluates the role of major corporations. He makes a distinction between sectors developed before World War II, such as agriculture, mining, and concessionaires, and those involving commerce, banking, and manufacturing, which appeared mostly after the war. Emphasis is placed on the way different firms acted in the complex politics of decolonization.

An excellent presentation of the colonial populations as mainstream political actors is offered. Factors such as the intensity of resistance of the European settlers and their representative roles as compared to those of the native populations are described. Also, the coalitions these Europeans were able to develop with power holders within the military and colonial administrations are set forth.

Defining his terms clearly and addressing theoretical questions, Kahler is successful in relating international relations and domestic politics to decolonization. Furthermore, he offers useful insights into British and French political behavior.

STEPHEN P. KOFF

Syracuse University
New York

MOSSE, GEORGE L. *Nationalism and Sexuality: Respectability and Abnormal Sexuality in Modern Europe*. Pp. viii, 232. New York: Howard Fertig, 1985. $29.50.

Focusing primarily on Pietist Germany and, to a lesser extent, on Evangelical England, George Mosse, an eminent cultural historian, describes in this work how the simultaneous emergence of respectability and nationalism, both cross-class movements, during the late eighteenth and early nineteenth centuries determined modern definitions of sexual morality. Moreover, by noting how the middle class successfully asserted its ideal of respectability over what it considered the lazy lower classes and profligate aristocracy, Mosse emphasizes the significance of cultural vis-à-vis economic and political forces in shaping modern European history and in contributing to the rise of fascism.

Mosse discusses the contemporaneous movements of respectability and nationalism as manifestations of a quest for rootedness and community in the face of the threatening disorder of modernism and urbanism. He interprets this quest as essentially a search for the immutability of a paradise lost. In fact, he states that "nationalism, racism, and bourgeois society all sought to base themselves on nature in order to partake in its immutability." Spiritually, integration with nature meant a unity of body and soul and an outward beauty stripped of passion and pointing instead to an inner purity of the mind. Socially, it meant assigning everyone an unambiguous place in life, man and woman, normal and abnormal, native and foreigner.

The stereotype of the virtuous, the natural, and the normal was contrasted to the stereotype of the menacing outsider, depicted as the "ugly human being of modernity" found in the city, who was unable to control his or her passions. The distinction between normality and abnormality basic to modern respectability became a question of sickness and health, as physicians took over from the clergy the roles of definer and keeper of normality. As nationalism converged with respectability, those of ascribed deviant status, namely Jews, were lumped together and attributed the same characteristics as those of achieved deviant status, particularly the sexually disreputable. Some physicians not only legitimated the new ideal of respectability but also lent support to racism. While some outsiders participated in countercultural movements, such as the decadence movement, most sought acceptance by emphasizing their respectability, whether by proving their masculinity or femininity, their patriotism, or even their racism.

Mosse discusses the alliance between respectability and nationalism in controlling sexuality and defining outsiders, but he does not clearly explicate the relationship between the two movements themselves. On the one hand, he seems to indicate that the passive, so-called feminine values of respectability and rootedness provided the necessary cohesion for the development of the active, so-called masculine values of nationalism and war. Not only did respectability abet nationalism by condemning masturbation and homosexuality, which were perceived as sapping man's virility and as endangering Germany's military strength, but also, through its indispensable agent, the family, it preserved sexual role differentiation and encouraged population growth important to the growing power of the state. On the other hand, Mosse seems to indicate that "nationalism . . . supported respectability against the chaos of the modern age," not only by direct political means, but also by providing a new basis for solidarity and by refocusing attention away from passion and sexuality to an identification with the national community. Nationalism and war became antidotes to the egoism spawned in part by bourgeois economic norms themselves. As everything, including sexuality, became subordinated to the fatherland, the preoccupation with one's own manliness was projected onto the strength of the nation. Male bonding (*Männerbund*), which had immanent within it homoeroticism, was transformed, albeit precariously, into a friendship based on mutual love for nation. *Männerbund* in autonomous friendships gave way to the *Männerstaat*, which was reinforced as the camaraderie of the trenches of World War I gave young men their experience with community.

By principally analyzing literature and iconography, Mosse has provided an insightful interpretation of the evolution of modern definitions of respectability and abnormal sexuality. In using this approach, however, he has not clearly described the interplay between respectability and nationalism, and he has not, as he acknowledges, seriously examined respectability as an instrument in the ascendency of the middle class in the embourgeoisment of all society.

STANLEY K. SHERNOCK
Norwich University
Northfield
Vermont

POSEN, BARRY R. *The Sources of Military Doctrine: France, Britain, and Germany between the World Wars.* Pp. 283. Ithaca, NY: Cornell University Press, 1984. $32.50.

This is an impressive study that brings together theory and history as is rarely done: the use of theory to enhance our understanding of the past, and of historical reality to test the explanatory power of theory. There is much more to Posen's work than its title suggests. It is a book on international politics and strategy that examines the causes of state behavior at the national and international levels; explains and compares the grand strategies and military doctrines of Britain, France, and Germany during the interwar years; and explores the relative usefulness of organization theory and balance-of-power theory in the context of what is known about the period of "the second Thirty Years War."

Posen begins with the laudable effort to define and refine the concept of military doctrine as a critical subcomponent of grand strategy—"that collection of military, economic and political means and ends with which a state attempts to achieve security." Military doctrine, as he uses the term, deals specifically with military means and how they are employed. Posen identifies three crucial analytical elements of doctrine: its offensive, defensive, or deterrent characteristics; its capacity to integrate political aims; and its innovative or stagnant qualities. He examines these aspects of doctrine in terms of organization and balance-of-power theories, as well as the traditional considerations of geography and technology.

With his theoretical framework thus laid out, Posen proceeds to apply it in four comparative case studies. Focusing on the battles of 1940, he probes the reasons for the two great victories and the one humiliating defeat. Unlike the often complex social, political, or military-technological explanations offered by historians, Posen's is startlingly simple: "Each battle was won by the side that had prepared for it." Hitler won the Battle of France because the German army had developed an innovative, aggressive military doctrine, the *Blitzkrieg*, in accordance with Germany's industrial and military resources; the French army was defeated because its doctrine was defensive, stagnant, and aimed at spreading the cost of French security among uncooperative allies; the Royal Air Force won the Battle of Britain because politicians insisted that a reluctant brass develop an innovative and well-integrated air defense in Fighter Command. The deceptive simplicity of these explanations turns into elaborate analysis in three subsequent case studies of French, British, and German grand strategies and military doctrines. They constitute the heart of Posen's effort in which political-military goals, and plans to effectuate them, are illuminated by means of such analytical categories as distribution of power, environmental constraints and incentives, organizational influences, and aspects of innovation and integration; and in which the specific propositions of organization theory and balance-of-power theory are applied to discern which theory better explains and predicts what actually happened.

The results of this labor offer insightful reading in an important part of interwar European history. Although Posen makes no startling additions to or revisions of the English-language literature he consulted, he does sharpen the focus on the important elements of what he calls the "political-military, means-ends chain" of national security decision making. He also clarifies the utility of two prominent theories of state behavior and international politics, concluding that organization theory and balance-of-power theory yield "more persuasive and comprehensive explanations" than traditional propositions regarding geography and technology, and that balance-of-power theory is the "slightly more powerful tool" of the two for the study of military doctrine. In sum, this is an imaginatively conceived and well-executed work that makes instructive reading for anyone interested in international relations and security affairs.

J. H. HOFFMAN

Creighton University
Omaha
Nebraska

UNITED STATES

COHEN, ELIOT A. *Citizens and Soldiers: The Dilemmas of Military Service.* Pp. 227. Ithaca, NY: Cornell University Press, 1985. $22.50.

In this book Cohen focuses on the political dilemmas that face a world power such as the United States in being able to deal effectively with the diverse military situations of both total war and small wars. While preparedness for such very different types of warfare requires different military manpower policies, the United States in recent decades has been unable to effectively deal with the contrasting political dilemma posed by the beliefs that all should serve their nation—the egalitarian argument—but with minimum interruption to personal life and freedom—the liberal argument. Because the liberal argument has largely prevailed since World War II, we have developed no durable system of military service. Consequently, argues Cohen, we are not adequately prepared for either small wars of some duration or, especially, total wars.

Cohen organizes his book into nine chapters. In the first chapter he conceptually distinguishes eight different military manpower service systems that vary by method of recruitment, length of service, and military purpose. In chapter 2 he describes how these different systems evolved in different nations between 1776 and 1914. In chapters 3 and 4 he analyzes how the eight major military service systems are variously suited for both total wars and small wars. In chapters 5 and 6 he gives detailed attention to military manpower recruitment and conscription ideologies in democratic societies following the key precept that military institutions are fundamentally political institutions highly subject to debate. In chapters 7 and 8 he traces the debate from 1940 to 1980 over which military manpower policy should prevail in the United States. He gives particular attention to the political and economic ideologies that gave rise to the all-volunteer force in the United States and the military weaknesses of that type of force today, such as the low quality of its recruits and its critical limitations for a total war. The final chapter reviews the fundamental dilemma between preparedness for war, the conflicting values of national service and personal freedom, and possible military manpower solutions for the United States.

Cohen's dispassionate and detailed analysis of the factors that shape military manpower policies is a scholarly contribution that not only aids our understanding of the political, historical, economic, and military factors that shape them but also informs us of key factors that need to be considered in altering military manpower policies in the future. Furthermore, the book is good reading.

DUANE STROMAN

Juniata College
Huntingdon
Pennsylvania

FAUSOLD, MARTIN L. *The Presidency of Herbert C. Hoover*. Pp. xii, 292. Lawrence: University Press of Kansas, 1985. $22.50.

Herbert Hoover's commitment to his belief in ordered freedom, rooted in his Quaker heritage and strengthened through every stage of his pre-presidential career,

became the essence of his presidency. That presidency was a failed one, so judged by every constituency that matters—Hoover's own associates of independent stature, the majority of Americans for a half century, and virtually all historians from the thirties to the present. Martin L. Fausold, who admires Hoover's values, policies, and efforts to combat the Great Depression, provides us with a convincing argument for the creditability of Hoover's reform and antidepression efforts and a convincing explanation for his failure. His is the best book on the Hoover presidency.

Fausold demonstrates both that Hoover's belief in ordered freedom reflected his Quaker values and upbringing and that it informed his policies and programs as president. Quakerism is perhaps the most individualistic of faiths, but it espouses a disciplined individualism within a community of shared values and aspirations. Hoover's associationalism, his goal of establishing a corporatist balance among government, labor, and capital, had at its core a pronounced individualism. Hoover recognized the importance of, and indeed fostered, organizations; but rather than create values and direct human aspirations, organizations, for him, were to represent voluntarily the aspirations of individuals for mutual advancement, self-expression, and reciprocal helpfulness. For Hoover, the operative word was "voluntary." Fausold shows that Hoover's ideas about the need for a society based on disciplined individualism and voluntary association had been expressed and reinforced throughout his professional career and public service. Hoover's various relief activities, his advocacy of voluntary conservation when he was wartime food administrator, and his fostering of trade associations when he was secretary of commerce all are cases in point. By the time he became president, Hoover's commitment to his vision of ordered freedom had become virtually absolute.

Fausold examines the Hoover presidency in detail. He describes its principal events; he surveys the scholarly literature, synthesizing the revisionist scholarship that has rediscovered Hoover's real administrative abilities and reformist goals; and he explicates Hoover's policies and programs, foreign and domestic. Fausold's greatest attention, of course, is given to Hoover's efforts to combat the Great Depression. He shows those efforts to have been imaginative, extensive, and creditable, but he also demonstrates that, with the single exception of the Reconstruction Finance Corporation, they did not compromise Hoover's principals. Hoover's opposition to the employment of the coercive power of the state to enforce cooperative efforts to end the depression or ameliorate its effects was unshakable. In spite of its repeated failings, Hoover steadfastly refused to abandon voluntarism; and after his defeat, he vigorously attacked the New Deal for doing so and thereby undermining liberty.

Fausold acknowledges that the New Deal represents a more creditable model of governing modern society than Hoover's. As he puts it, Hoover risked showing his ideal of ordered freedom to the world and found the world not yet ripe for it. The implication that the American people and their institutions failed Hoover as much as he failed them is troubling, for never have such ideals as Hoover's reflected the American reality. Quakers had discovered in colonial Pennsylvania that ruling meant the sacrifice of their values and that preserving those values meant having to accept political impotence. Hoover's policies were bound to fail. They were rooted in a sectarian concept of human character and social order that bore little relation to the reality of American society.

Hoover's presidency ended in near hysteria, as the president anxiously but unsuccessfully sought to ensure his successor's support of the policies and programs he thought necessary for ending depression while preserving liberty. Afterwards, it would be for Franklin D. Roosevelt to exercise the coercive powers of government to enlist the cooperative responses of real human beings in reordering a worldly society.

THOMAS M. HILL

Kansas City
Missouri

FISHER, LOUIS. *Constitutional Conflicts between Congress and the President.* Pp. xviii, 372. Princeton, NJ: Princeton University Press, 1985. $40.00. Paperbound, $8.95.

This book is a major revision of a 1978 work entitled *The Constitution between Friends: Congress, the President, and the Law.* In a period when publishers are cautiously constructing their lists a book must be very good indeed to merit republication and expansion within seven years. It is no less impressive that this book is actually in its third incarnation, since the first version, *President and Congress*, was published in 1972 by Free Press. These materials clearly deserve to be kept current, as there are few other concise compilations of legal and historical materials surrounding the presidency and its relationships with Congress. Each version of the book was written to digest the legal and constitutional practices of different presidents. This book is an appropriate introduction to the prevailing legal and constitutional setting of the separation of powers in the age of President Ronald Reagan. It puts into historical perspective the limits of presidential powers with respect to Congress.

Certainly, for an American, the understanding of how Congress and the president are intertwined is a pivotal element in grasping the central feature of national political life. Foreigners, for whom American national leadership is frequently a mystery, will get an accurate presentation of the legal-constitutional nature of the American presidency from reading this book.

Some of the mystery surrounding the presidency, will remain, however. This book does not explain the enormous success of President Reagan in obtaining his tax cuts, nor his continuing success in federal budget cutting and military expansion. These topics and the substantial ideological shifts in American political life represented by President Reagan are not fit topics for the Fisher book. The policies and politics of the presidency are not within the scope of this study. Instead, Fisher concentrates on the more permanent features of the relationships between the president and Congress. The result is a magisterial collection of major constitutional precedents that is a repository of insight on the growth and development of presidential powers. Even though the American Congress is probably the world's most powerful legislature, we must agree with Fisher that there has been a "general drift of authority and responsibility to the President over the past two centuries." Fisher suggests that Congress has more constitutional power to resist and correct the president than it has the courage and confidence to employ. In many ways Fisher provides ample illustrations of the available constitutional resources that Congress could employ to resist further expansion of presidential powers. Unfortunately, there are larger political and social forces at play that support the efforts of the president to push Congress further into the shadows. The massive military buildup since 1980 was subject to congressional powers, but Congress went along, even though Secretary of Defense Weinberger happened to discover a loose $4 billion of unallocated military funds in 1985.

But there is no doubt that this book is an indispensable guide to the constitutional and legal rules that govern the struggles between the president and Congress. It is a noble addition to a tradition first developed by Edward S. Corwin several decades ago. His book, *The President: Office and Powers,* became such a classic that it was often cited by the Supreme Court itself as a guide to the interpretation of the Constitution. Doubtless, Fisher's book will enjoy a similar reputation. It is the most expert study of the topic of presidential relations with Congress. It will not be soon surpassed, but it will also not help stem the tide of expanding presidential power. President Reagan has, in his own way, added to the powers of his office. Congress has not developed additional powers or enhanced public regard, although it has, as this book documents, slowed Reagan's plans to cut back on environmental and welfare

programs and to conduct clandestine warfare.

JAY A. SIGLER

Rutgers University
Camden
New Jersey

KNACK, MARTHA C. and OMER C. STEWART. *As Long as the River Shall Run: An Ethnohistory of Pyramid Lake Indian Reservation.* Pp. xvii, 433. Berkeley: University of California Press, 1984. $28.50.

Martha C. Knack is associate professor of anthropology and ethnic studies at the University of Nevada, Las Vegas. She is the author of *Life Is with People,* the result of fieldwork with the Utah bands of the Southern Paiutes. Omer C. Stewart is emeritus professor of anthropology at the University of Colorado. He has authored the book *Northern Paiute Bands.* Hence both qualify as eminent authorities on the subject.

This collaborative ethnohistory of the Paiute Native Americans of Nevada is the result of Knack and Stewart's research while serving as expert witnesses in a Supreme Court case involving these peoples' claims against the state of Nevada. It is a superbly researched and written work, but it admittedly has a strong bias in favor of the Paiutes, whom they know and admire.

The Paiutes were bands, not one big tribe, of nomadic peoples whose history goes back to 2000 B.C. They developed and maintained an archaic desert culture based on common ownership of land, hunting, fishing, and food gathering. This prehistoric culture could coexist with Spanish culture, British fur traders, and even American miners; but it conflicted with Anglo-American agriculture, which stressed farming and private ownership of land. In a classic confrontation, the Westerners thought in terms of the biblical injunction to till the soil, manifest destiny and the advance of progress and civilization.

The Paiutes, to the contrary, wanted to preserve their natural existence and looked upon the westward movement of the white people as aggression and exploitation.

This controversy has continued into the twentieth century. The Newlands Reclamation Project was established to provide irrigation for desert agriculture. This conflicted with the fishery requirements of the Pyramid Lake Reservation, home of the Paiutes, who greatly prize the Lahontan cutthroat trout. So it was that in 1983 the litigation between the tribe and the project reached the Supreme Court. The Court ruled it was "unrealistic" to return the fishing rights; Knack and Stewart, in turn, view that decision as a "bitter blow" to justice.

Since history is not a morality play but a story of power relationships, the past has been probably decided irrevocably in favor of agriculture. Native Americans, as minorities, do have certain rights but to reverse the decision of history is not possible, even though desirable.

FREDERICK H. SCHAPSMEIER
University of Wisconsin
Oshkosh

LAWSON, STEVEN F. *In Pursuit of Power: Southern Blacks and Electoral Politics, 1965-1982.* Pp. xix, 391. New York: Columbia University Press, 1985. $30.00.

A host of writers have chronicled and analyzed the birth and maturing of the civil rights movement from World War II to 1965, but scholarly and popular authors have paid substantially less attention to later efforts to continue and extend the quest for justice and equality. In comparison with the glory years of the movement, the past two decades seem relatively drab, devoid of charismatic leadership or electrifying events, and depressing as a series of conservative or reactionary politicians has dominated the presidency, Supreme Court, and Senate.

Welcome evidence that obituaries for civil rights activism are premature comes in Stephen F. Lawson's story of the Voting Rights Act from its controversial inception in 1965, through its survival despite the black power movement and urban violence of the late 1960s, and through its time of testing in the 1970 and 1975 congressional debates over extending and revising the act, to its maturity in the overwhelming, bipartisan extension of the act in 1982 for 25 years.

Using a wide array of published works and unpublished studies, papers, oral histories, and interviews, Lawson presents a carefully balanced history of the political development and impact of the Voting Rights Act. Supporters and opponents of the law explain their positions, as do varying factions on each side. The bill has had some obvious successes. For instance, the portion of the adult black population registered to vote increased from 40 percent in 1965 to 60 percent in 1982; in the same time span, the number of black elected officials increased from 100 to 2500. These successes, however, do not overshadow the bill's favoring middle- and upper-class blacks over lower-class blacks, or its inability to provide an economic foundation for black political power, or its lack of success in totally ending discrimination, especially discrimination in the form of barriers to effective representation such as at-large elections and multimember districts.

Lawson shows the importance of political continuity and change. The traditional American commitment to the right to vote helped protect the act when other civil rights programs declined. The Supreme Court and an entrenched Justice Department bureaucracy beat back attempts by presidents and opponents in Congress to gut enforcement and key provisions of the law. But important changes came after 1970 as attention shifted from registering black voters to securing effective representation, the Supreme Court strengthened the preclearance provisions of Section 5, and increasing numbers of black voters helped persuade southern congressmen to support the act.

In Pursuit of Power is a masterful synthesis of a wide range of topics and sources and a pioneering, optimistic history of blacks' gaining and effectively using the ballot despite their minority status and local, state, and national opposition. Its limits are more organizational than interpretive or substantive. As a monograph, it must be supplemented by studies of other aspects of race relations and Southern white political participation. Detailed coverage of congressional deliberations and overlapping chronological and topical discussions hinder both its narrative flow and analysis. Its major flaw is excessive attention to the first 4 of the 17 years it covers—118 of 303 pages of text—especially since Lawson has already dealt with these years, 1965-68, in *Black Ballots: Voting Rights in the South, 1944-1969.*

ROBERT G. SHERER

Wiley College
Marshall
Texas

LOWI, THEODORE J. *The Personal President: Power Invested, Promise Unfulfilled.* Pp. xiii, 221. Ithaca, NY: Cornell University Press, 1985. $19.95.

The subject of this mature and sophisticated book by the John L. Senior Professor of American Institutions at Cornell is the decline in the role of the two major political parties; the failure of Congress to maintain its constitutional role in governance; the development of a presidency that interacts routinely with the mass electorate—a "plebiscitary presidency"; and the perceived need to develop more than two parties to rejuvenate the American system of government.

What stimulating reading this was for one whose half-minor in political parties under Thomas S. Barclay at Stanford, in the years 1948-51, began with Edgar Eugene Robinson's *The Evolution of American Political Parties* (1924), and ended with an attempt to master Howard Penniman's rendition of Edmund McChesney Sait's *American Political Parties and Elections* (1948). In the year of Robert M. LaFollette, Robinson judged that the "party is the power that accomplishes results in government." Said Sait by way of Penniman in the year of Henry Wal-

lace, "No one will dispute the potential usefulness of minor parties. They are in a position to think more of principles than of power." In 1984, Lowi finds present parties irrelevant and feels that "a system of three, or even four or five, parties is in itself the reform most needed."

For more than a century in America there was an established system of practices, habits, customs, and morality under the Constitution. With Franklin Roosevelt in 1932 came a governmental revolution that ended federalism, but not the ever-growing state governments. Roosevelt's communication skills left a legacy of "massifying" presidential politics. With Eisenhower came the election of presidents through mechanisms outside the parties. Kennedy, Johnson, Nixon, Carter, and Reagan then sought office with the help of highly personal support organizations.

Government, once Congress centered, is now thoroughly president centered. Party regularity is weak; legislation influenced by political action committees flourishes. Watching the polls, a president anxious to improve public opinion ratings may well resort to a dangerous foreign-policy fix.

Some quotations display Lowi's mature erudition: "Since building up the presidency has not met the problem of presidential capacity to govern, the time has come to consider building it down." "Liberalism is concerned with conduct deemed harmful in its consequences, and conservatism is concerned mainly with conduct deemed good or evil in itself."

Lowi virtually repudiates single-minded reliance on James Barbour's "psychology/character" appraisal of presidential behavior, favoring an "institutionalized approach." That is, there are "tremendous historical forces lodged in the laws, traditions, and commitments of institutions." Similarly, I found it sensible to bypass much of Doris Kearns's psychoanalytic approach to Lyndon Johnson when I was structuring my assessment, *The Presidency of Lyndon B. Johnson* (1983).

Lowi is adventuresome about recent presidents, being especially kind to Nixon. But

President Reagan is exposed as the quiet developer of the largest government we have ever had and of one of the most prominent presidencies. The recent officeholders— other than Ford—have allegedly acted in the spirit of "L'état, c'est moi." In my probably old-fashioned view, the expressed hope for salvation in third-party formation is not solidly based in the national record, the nature of our politics, or constitutional realities, for their most appealing issues may get absorbed. Such a victory leads but to oblivion.

The Personal President is, overall, a historically based, remarkably nonpartisan, up-to-the-minute, and pioneering appraisal of the American presidency of the late 1980s.

VAUGHN DAVIS BORNET

Southern Oregon State College
Ashland

MATTHEWS, RICHARD K. *The Radical Politics of Thomas Jefferson: A Revisionist View.* Pp. ix, 171. Lawrence: University of Kansas Press, 1984. $22.50.

The usual accounts of Jefferson as a typical Enlightenment liberal, differing only in details from his rival Hamilton and his friend Madison, are, Matthews asserts, mistaken. Hamilton was the spokesman for capitalism and possessive individualism. He thought that human nature is selfish, that all social relations are basically market relationships, and that the national goal should be wealth and empire.

Jefferson thought people are innately cooperative. His ideal, as Leo Marx noted in his *Machine in the Garden* (Oxford University Press, 1964), was a pastoral society with a bountiful agriculture as its economic base, some trade and manufacturing but not enough to destroy the beautiful garden with urban blight, and no greedy goal of increasing the gross national product forever. In this pastoral world men would live in peace and freedom and have leisure for intellectual pursuits, artistic creation and the pleasures of country life.

In Matthews's view, Jefferson was a democratic humanist—he had faith in the natural goodness of all men. He believed in participatory democracy, in which every citizen should take full part in government; in a mild communitarian anarchy, with a large measure of economic equality and a minimum of government; and permanent revolution such that political and economic institutions should be remodeled every 20 years.

Matthews's interpretation is more than an academic exercise. Jefferson's philosophy, he notes, disentangled from the liberalism of Hamilton and Madison, "becomes free, once again, to captivate and ignite the American imagination and to offer a legitimate alternative to the 'American Way.' "

In prepublication reviews, C. B. McPherson, who admires Jefferson, writes: "This is a remarkable study which will upset all received ideas of Jefferson as a democratic theorist"; and the conservative historian Forrest Mac-Donald comments: "Matthews has demonstrated, with Jefferson's own words, that the man was precisely the kind of wild-eyed political quack that Hamilton understood him to be." But both agree that Matthews has described Jefferson's principles accurately. I would add only that Matthews has found Jefferson more consistent than he was; he often changed his mind.

RICHARD SCHLATTER

Rutgers University
New Brunswick
New Jersey

MAZUZUN, GEORGE T. and SAMUEL WALKER. *Controlling the Atom: The Beginnings of Nuclear Regulation.* Pp. x, 500. Berkeley: University of California Press, 1984. No price.

BERTSCH, KENNETH A. and LINDA S. SHAW. *The Nuclear Weapons Industry.* Pp. 410. Washington, DC: Investors Responsibility Research Center, 1984. No price.

These two volumes should be read together. They provide an interesting contrast to each other as well as a kind of continuity essential to the beginning of an understanding of the nuclear dilemma in which we find ourselves.

In times like these—with the nuclear arms reduction talks underway in Geneva with little promise of success, continued European and Soviet deployment of missiles, Star Wars research to develop antimissile defense systems, a new arms race—both nuclear and conventional—begun under the euphemism of "modernization" of forces, and a failed nuclear energy industry in the United States—books like these help us understand the helplessness if not the hopelessness of our situation.

A triad of agencies sits astride our civilian and military nuclear programs: the Nuclear Regulatory Commission; the Department of Energy, concerned with military nuclear manufacturers; and the Department of Defense, concerned with military applications. These books document the fact that we live under the overpowering influence of the industrial-military complex.

Controlling the Atom, according to Mazuzun and Walker, is a "public history" of regulatory authority development and of the responsibility for regulation being divided between government and private industry. While the private sector was reluctant at first, the Atomic Energy Commission's promotional efforts under the Eisenhower administration in particular bore fruit.

It is ironic that Eisenhower warned us about the military-industrial complex as he left office, because it was during his tenure that private industry became a full partner in atomic energy matters militarily, as well as in the privately owned nuclear power industry.

The Atomic Energy Commission, congressional committees, scientists and engineers, free-enterprise-oriented executive officers and appointees, and the general public all fell victim to the exaggerated promise of a new source of energy, to a changing and fluctuating international nuclear arms race with its attendant testing, and to technologies being developed and used ahead of a clear understanding of their environmental or human effects. Clearly, here was another example of political decision-making processes usurping technical and scientific areas of responsibility.

Mazuzan and Walker describe carefully the resulting atomic energy regulations that were acceptable to industry; the heavy subsidizations by government of insurance risks and investment costs of the free-enterprise sector; the loosening of licensing procedures; and the development of reactor-site criteria responsive to private industry desires.

Radiation hazards protection during the period from 1946 through 1962 suffered because of the bomb-testing programs, but it suffered too from the age-old struggle between federal and state regulatory conflicts. During this period there were two major failures: a failure to make adequate provisions for the health and safety of atomic workers, including military personnel as well as uranium miners; and a failure to develop adequate technologies for the disposal of nuclear waste. The government, the military, and private industry could not or would not face the reality of the potential dangers of nuclear activities. Even today the nuclear-winter scenario is viewed by too many as a remote possibility. And today the country is awash with huge quantities of undisposed nuclear waste materials.

The Nuclear Weapons Industry is a major reference work that displays clearly how far we have come in developing the industrial-military complex in the last 39 years.

While contributions of political action committees to officeholders—a large percentage of which went to members of the Armed Services Committees of both houses of Congress—have been growing apace, the symbiotic relationship between the Pentagon and these defense contractors should occasion increased concern.

The revolving door still turns. Between 1977 and 1981, 18 of these defense contractors hired 3562 military and civilian—but mostly military—Pentagon officials, while sending 149 of their administrators to Pentagon offices. And the full extent of this exchange is not known.

There is little comfort in these two volumes, but, then, nobody promised us a rose garden.

JACK L. CROSS

Texas A&M University
College Station

MOFFETT, GEORGE D., III. *The Limits of Victory: The Ratification of the Panama Canal Treaties.* Pp. 263. Ithaca, NY: Cornell University Press, 1985. $24.95.

When President Jimmy Carter submitted the Panama Canal treaties to the Senate in September 1977, he hoped for an expeditious ratification that would lay the foundation for a new, post-containment foreign policy for the United States. As former White House assistant George Moffett skillfully argues in *The Limits of Victory,* the succeeding eight months of debate over the "75-year-old, largely outmodeled canal" accomplished just the opposite.

In April 1978, the Carter administration gained ratification of the treaties at the cost of having undermined its own political future and having discredited its foreign policy agenda. The New Right, invigorated by the ratification struggles, would henceforth set the framework for international policy debate in the United States.

To explain how this happened, Moffet draws upon a wide range of domestic secondary sources as well as government papers and the files of business groups such as the U.S. Chamber of Commerce and the Council of the Americas. He asks why the treaties nearly failed to secure Senate approval after 13 years of U.S. negotiations with Panama under four different Republican and Democratic presidents.

Support for the Treaties in the United States was superficial, Moffett contends. Despite endorsement of them by major newspapers, leading business and labor leaders, churches, civic groups, and even the Joint Chiefs of Staff, a campaign led by "relatively untested" organizations "largely outside the political mainstream" could delay ratification and almost prevent it. Moffett thinks that treaty opponents could have killed ratification had they known how to exploit the administration's failure to prove the canal's long-term fiscal viability.

The Limits of Victory attaches great importance to the canal's symbolic representation of U.S. preeminence in world affairs. Only opponents of the treaties, Moffett argues, could generate an intense public following in an era of apprehension over declining U.S. power.

He faults earlier presidents for failing to educate the public about the changing international circumstances that made the treaties imperative. To the Carter administration fell the full burden of persuading a fearful society that relinquishing control of the Panama Canal was a positive act in defense of U.S. interests.

Despite an enormous educational campaign and generally careful work with the Senate, the Carter administration changed few opinions about the treaties. Moffett's thorough analysis of polling supports his thesis that symbolic attachment to the canal far outweighed factual arguments about the national interest.

Ratification, Moffett contends, was an issue without a constituency. The commitment of enlightened church and civic leaders was not enough to overcome popular suspicion of the treaties. Multinational corporations, for whom ratification created "a rare coincidence of idealism and economic self-interest," remained convinced that their Latin American investments would survive any outcome for the treaties in the Senate. Consequently, large corporations offered ratification only "moral support matched by almost total political passivity."

A timely and careful work, *The Limits of Victory* raises a host of intriguing questions about the relationship between domestic society and international affairs. Many of Moffett's arguments have strong implications for current U.S. policy in Central America.

ARTHUR SCHMIDT

Temple University
Philadelphia
Pennsylvania

MORRIS, MILTON D. *Immigration—The Beleaguered Bureaucracy.* Pp. x, 150. Washington, DC: Brookings Institution, 1985. $22.95. Paperbound, $8.95.

Despite concluding that full control over the flow of immigrants into the United States is impossible, Milton Morris's tone is anything but alarmist: "the country is not about to be engulfed by a great alien tide." He acknowledges the existence of problems, including—most obviously—the influx of illegal immigrants, but focuses most of his attention on those difficulties that arise from the conception of America's immigration policy and reside within the bureaucracy that administers it. The fact that many more immigrants enter the United States than the law allows is due, Morris asserts, to a legal limit that is the product of political considerations that have no reference to the nation's labor needs or its absorptive capacity.

Confusion is built into the administrative structure that oversees immigration: six separate bureaucracies share responsibility. With effective examples, Morris details the failure of these bureaucracies even to maintain records that are current and usable. But the bureaucrats are not entirely to blame; underfunded and overworked, they are further hampered by the absence of clearly defined policy objectives. Morris notes that "what appear to be administrative failures often are the result of the failure of policymakers to make critical policy choices." His point is a good one, although he unfairly faults Congress for being too tight-fisted in budgeting the immigration bureaucracy. A chart on page 132 indicates that from fiscal 1977 through 1982 Congress actually appropriated more money than the Immigration and Naturalization Service requested.

A few flaws also appear in Morris's historical review of immigration and its regulation by the government. His description of the national origins system established in 1924 is incomplete, omitting the quota formulation that was implemented in 1929. Nor did the Gentlemen's Agreement "terminate" Japanese immigration. And to characterize the rate of immigration in the 1950s as "high"—relative to what?—is surely misleading.

These are minor points, however. Morris's book, though brief and written in uninspired prose, is very useful. It covers the issue of immigration thoroughly, reviewing the principal grounds of debate, describing the problems that have defied solution, and ana-lyzing the administrative machinery that has attempted to cope with them. Ten tables and figures further clarify Morris's presentation. Most important of all, Morris concludes with seven specific recommendations for addressing the problems he identifies, recommendations that appear both sensible and realistic.

DALE R. STEINER

California State University
Chico

STEINBERG, PETER L. *The Great "Red Menace": United States Prosecution of American Communists, 1947-1952.* Pp. xiv, 311. Westport, CT: Greenwood Press, 1984. $35.00.

DWYER, WILLIAM L. *The Goldmark Case: An American Libel Trial.* Pp. 304. Seattle: University of Washington Press, 1984. $16.95.

With over 80,000 members in 1945, the American Communist Party (CPUSA) should have enjoyed considerable influence in the postwar years. Yet the period following the war was a disastrous one for American Communists. By the late 1950s, after more than a decade of anti-red hysteria and federal prosecution, the party had only a few thousand members, and the *Daily Worker,* the party newspaper, had so few remaining subscribers that it ceased publication.

How American Communists were prosecuted, what effect that prosecution had on the party, how the party responded, and what contributed to the political atmosphere of the time are the subjects of Peter Steinberg's book. Unlike many contemporary historians of McCarthyism, Steinberg does not see the 1950s' Red Scare as taking place within a political environment in which the absence of a viable political Left exaggerated the power and influence of the far Right. Indeed, his main thesis is that "the development of a national hysteria with its integral fear of communism cannot be understood without considering the interaction of the left—particularly the American communists—

with the rising forces of reaction." Specifically, Steinberg argues that the CPUSA's postwar destruction can in large part be traced to the party's decision to return to orthodox Marxism-Leninism and its rejection of the popular front revisionist notion that socialism could peacefully be achieved through the building of broad coalitions with liberals and progressives. That decision, he maintains, was disastrous, for it drastically narrowed the party's base of support and caused self-destructive sectarian strife, not only within the party itself but within the Left as a whole. Moreover, according to Steinberg, the CPUSA's return to a hardline, combative position was used by a group of nonelected government officials, located chiefly in the Federal Bureau of Investigation, the Justice Department, and military intelligence, as justification for mounting a secret but highly effective campaign to destroy the party.

Steinberg's argument that the CPUSA ultimately fell victim to internal sectarianism and external bureaucratic repression is a convincing one and places *The Great "Red Menace"* among a number of post-Watergate histories that have used similar arguments to explain not only the decline of the Old Left but of the New Left as well. Yet less convincing is his contention that the Left was a viable force in the postwar years. To show that it contributed to its own destruction is one thing. To prove it was politically influential is quite another.

Communism in the United States also plays a part in William Dwyer's *Goldmark Case: An American Libel Trial.*

Among the many issues currently before American legal reformers, two of the most widely debated concern the limitations and strengths of trial by jury and the fairness of current laws that narrowly define what is and is not libelous when the claimant is a public official or candidate for elective office. For that reason alone, Dwyer's account of the Goldmark case, offering as it does a review of a celebrated libel trial and a passionate defense of the American jury system, is both timely and relevant.

The case revolved around a series of scurrilous attacks made on the character and family of John Goldmark, a rancher, Harvard Law School graduate, and three-term Washington state legislator, when in 1962 he once again sought the Democratic nomination from rural Okanogan County. As he prepared for what he believed would be a lightly contested primary fight, Goldmark came under attack by the newly resurgent far Right for being under Communist Party influence. The outcome was that Goldmark lost the primary badly and decided to sue his chief accusers for libel and defamation of character.

Dwyer, who was Goldmark's counsel, provides a vivid picture of the courtroom drama that subsequently took place. Quoting heavily from the trial transcript, he skillfully reveals both the substance of the evidence presented and the legal and political issues raised by the trial. In what must be regarded as a strategic blunder, the defendant's lawyers chose not to base their defense on the fair comment privilege—which protects critical expressions of opinion about public officials if they were offered in good faith, even if such expressions were defamatory or injurious—but on proving that Goldmark and his wife were under Communist Party discipline, thus making the trial a forum for the expression and evaluation of the radical Right's notions on how Communists in our midst could be identified. That, despite a parade of so-called experts on communism, the jury was able to perceive the groundlessness of the defense claims Dwyer takes as proof of his belief that juries are able to determine right from wrong no matter how complex the issues involved.

Although detailing Goldmark's vindication in a trial by a jury of his peers, Dwyer raises a prickly issue that he leaves unresolved. Had the case been tried after the Supreme Court's 1964 ruling on *Sullivan* v. *The New York Times*—which declared that libel claimants must prove actual malice or reckless disregard of the truth—Goldmark may not have been able to salvage his reputation. For that reason *The Goldmark Case* may prove considerably more provocative than even its author intended.

RICHARD A. MECKEL

Brown University
Providence
Rhode Island

SOCIOLOGY

BELLAH, ROBERT N., RICHARD MADSEN, WILLIAM M. SULLIVAN, ANN SWIDLER, and STEVEN M. TIPTON. *Habits of the Heart: Individualism and Commitment in American Life.* Pp. xiii, 355. Berkeley: University of California Press, 1985. $16.95.

"What then is the American, this new man?" In the 200 years since J. Hector St. John de Crèvecoeur asked that question, commentators have exhibited little retinence in identifying the major components of American character and society. From Crèvecoeur's emphasis on the environment as an emancipator from want to Michael Kammen's focus on paradox and biformities, a plethora of theories has emerged. Despite interpretative differences, the most astute analyses of national character form an ongoing dialectic. *Habits of the Heart* aspires to embellish that discussion further by investigating areas of ultimate concern: who we are as Americans, what our character is.

Utilizing a sociology supplemented by history, Robert Bellah and his colleagues investigate the evolution of contemporary American mores within a framework sensitive to change over time. Although oral interviews constitute their primary empirical base, the authors draw on a wide array of secondary sources. *Habits of the Heart* examines ideology, marriage, family, mental health, religion, politics, and volunteerism. Ultimately, however, the discussion always returns to the influence of individualism on public and private life.

During the colonial era and beyond, it is suggested, both the biblical and republican traditions tied individual interests to the welfare of the community. Family, church, and town connected the private and public spheres of American life. By the late nineteenth century, however, the rise of national corporations undermined localism. Communities of memory lost cohesion, and mental health first appeared as a widespread concern. Public decisions were increasingly the domain of bureaucratic managers and experts. In contemporary America, individualism finds its chief expression in utilitarian and expressive modes that encourage privatism. Like Christopher Lasch, Bellah and his colleagues believe a therapeutic sensibility envelops contemporary society. From a therapeutic vantage point, familial, religious, and civic obligations acquire importance only to the extent that the individual derives satisfaction from them. Lamenting the decline of American civic life, the authors offer several stratagems for reintegrating the private and public spheres, including promoting awareness of "our intricate connectedness and interdependence."

Habits of the Heart is intelligent, challenging, provocative, and, despite its diverse parentage, felicitous. One wishes that the authors demonstrated more concern with the representativeness of their 200 interviewees. The voices recorded in this volume were largely white and middle class. Perspectives reflective of the working class, racial minorities, and white ethnics might have received greater attention. The authors could also more overtly confront the argument that the contemporary decline of public life derives from a cyclical rather than a linear progression. Perhaps American society resembles a pendulum swinging back and forth between periods of privatism, such as the 1920s and the present, and interludes of heightened public consciousness, such as the 1930s and the 1960s. Nevertheless, this volume merits the accolade it self-consciously pursues: *Habits of the Heart* enriches our discussion of national character.

WILLIAM M. SIMONS

State University of New York
Oneonta

GAYLIN, WILLARD. *The Rage Within: Anger in Modern Life*. Pp. 224. New York: Simon & Schuster, 1985. $16.95.

The topic that Willard Gaylin tackles in this book is an interesting one. Unfortunately, his treatment of it falls very far short of a useful analysis for a number of reasons. First, Gaylin considerably overstates his case. Second, he seems to be giving the reader a view of modern life as experienced in New York City, but under the guise of something more universal. Third, he seems ignorant of many relevant areas of research that would have expanded the conceptual basis of this treatise. Finally, he really has nothing constructive or realistic to say about changing the situation as he sees it.

The book starts off with fairly conventional ideas about physiological anger, its adaptive value in earlier, more physically dangerous times, and its often dysfunctional nature in a more civilized society. However, apart from Gaylin's assertion of the prevalence of anger in modern life and his somewhat one-sided view of it, we are given no evidence for the claimed all-pervasive and all-consuming nature of the phenomenon. Gaylin is inclined to see red under the bed.

There is a lot of Gaylin himself in this book and that is at once a strength and a weakness. It is a strength on those occasions when he allows us the privilege of very frankly sharing moments of his experience and learning about ourselves through him. More important, however, it is a weakness in that it is obvious that Gaylin's evident personal anger is somewhat idiosyncratic and is pervaded by the experience of living and working in New York, a city that is not typical of the United States, let alone anywhere else.

As a consequence, many issues that the book should have been addressing, such as individual differences, cultural factors in the broadest sense, gender factors, developmental factors, and the influence of the media in shaping our view of the world—and hence our emotional reactions to situations and events—are almost totally ignored.

Because of this blinkered approach, Gaylin makes statements that are stunning in their naiveté. For example, he tells us that he has "the nagging feeling that political indignation represents only a trivial amount of the anger generated." A whistle-stop tour of Northern Ireland, Iran, South Africa, and the Middle East would soon cure that myopia!

Gaylin, however, does not need to leave town to display his ignorance for he is quite clearly unaware of well-known research carried out by Stanley Milgram on the characteristic behavior of New Yorkers. Gaylin states that this uncivil behavior "has no rationale in either logic or adaptation." Milgram's view is quite contrary and the reader is left with the impression that Gaylin's background reading was somewhat less than thorough. This view is reinforced by his comments on other areas of research in the social sciences, particularly prejudice and relative deprivation, that indicate an unacceptable and, indeed, quite truculent ignorance.

Throughout this book, Gaylin often appears to be railing against the human condition. When he finally tells us at the end of the book how we should go about tackling the problem, the limitations of his own premises finally drag him into wistful, pistol-packing incoherence. For an individual whose political system has proved capable of rejecting so many wrongs, it is curious that politicians escape scot-free in this tirade while social scientists are castigated for neglect.

KEN HESKIN

Trinity College
Dublin
Ireland

HAUSFATER, GLENN and SARAH BLAFFER HRDY, eds. *Infanticide: Comparative and Evolutionary Perspectives*. Pp. xxxix, 598. Hawthorne, NY: Aldine, 1984. $34.95.

As is the case with most foci that become targeted for scientific investigation, there is an initial phase in which the more a problem is investigated, the more we discover we need to know. The phenomenon of infanticide is no exception and, as also might be expected, the question of definition has to be resolved. This, along with other points, is discussed in the succinct but comprehensive introduction and overview by Hrdy and Hausfater to this collection of papers that resulted from a multidisciplinary conference proposed by Wenner-Gren in 1982. The most widely accepted definition states that "infanticide is any behavior that makes a direct and significant contribution to the immediate death of an embryo or newly hatched or born member of the perpetrator's own species." But Hausfater and Hrdy point out that they are not alone in believing that certain constraints and biases are imposed by this gloss; the same argument is expanded in the article by Mildred Dickemann, "Concepts and Classification in the Study of Human Infanticide: Sectional Introduction and Some Cautionary Notes." Rather than focus only on elimination of an embryo or newborn, the field is broadened to address the whole range of time when the young are dependent on adults, thus taking in pedicide—killing of children—as well as feticide or infanticide. It also covers "any form of lethal curtailment or parental investment in offspring brought about by conspecifics" including

curtailment of parental investment through destruction of gametes . . . or reabsorption of foetus. . . . At this level of generality, contraception, abortion, direct killing of an infant, or nutritional neglect . . . are seen as related phenomena, differing only in the stage of the reproductive continuum at which curtailment of parental investment occurs (p. xv).

The last phrase, "parental investment," is significant for it signals an important assumption of the editors and most of the contributors to the 28 papers that make up this volume. Grounded in the seminal work on sociobiology done by E. O. Wilson, there is an omnipresent concern with cost-benefit analysis, whether in agreement or reactive. While this model has utility, it is a blatant product of the current economically grounded milieu. It also gives the appearance of quantitative rigor but is fraught with hidden biases, ranging from the relatively simple temporal issues—short versus long term—to fundamental epistemological questions.

Putting aside this concern, however, this volume is an exciting collection of papers, with provocative data that will attract those from a wide range of disciplines. Though the section on human infanticide that would be of particular interest to this journal's readers is the shortest, the preceding three sections— "Background and Taxonomic Reviews," "Infanticide in Nonhuman Primates: A Topic of Continuing Debate," and "Infanticide in Rodents: Questions of Proximate and Ultimate Causation"—address general issues with new and unusual perspectives that compel one to reexamine any assumptions about the givens of so-called natural systems. Debates arise—and the contributors to the volume are far from consensus in their positions—on such basic questions as, Is infanticide pathological behavior or is it linked to some aspect of natural selection? Who, predominantly, kills and is killed— males, females, siblings, or newcomers? How are fertility or fecundity rates affected by infanticide? Why are certain modes of infanticide favored, and under what conditions do such modes vary within the same residential group or species? Which sex, if either, is the prime target, and does this vary under specific conditions? How is one to study specifically human infanticide when the target population is knowledgeable and capable of the frequent necessity to conceal the deed? How does the supply of food, the availability of living space, the stress of crowding, and invasion by others affect an increase or decrease in infanticide? How do irrational species weigh individual, band, and species costs and benefits?

It would be a mistake to bypass this book because it addresses the hominids so briefly. Further, even in that brief section on hominids, there is a wealth of insight. Johansson looks at demographic data from preindustrial Europe and modern Third World countries and notes that when males and females contribute equally to family maintenance, male and female mortality ratios are almost equal. But female mortality jumps sharply when male labor becomes the major subsistence focus of the family. Scrimshaw's attempt to determine the rationales for infanticide support this finding, but it also leads one to note the extent to which, say, physical incapabilities—which, of course, do not reflect the ability of the individual to make other contributions—are a basis for infanticide when adults cannot afford long-term risk taking. Daley and Wilson report the finding—surprising to me—that, in contemporary Western societies, intrahousehold lethal child abuse is most frequently directed toward male offspring and the abuser is most likely to be the stepfather. One might compare the ubiquitous Western myth of the wicked stepmother and her female dependents.

I would like to offer one last note in a review too brief to do justice to the sterling qualities—and some notable weaknesses—of this book. It has an excellent 67-page bibliography and is profusely and clearly illustrated with figures, graphs, tables, and maps. Given the quality of the papers, the excellent editing, and the first-class production mechanics, this volume is overall one of the best bargains to come out of any publisher in a long time.

M. ESTELLIE SMITH
State University of New York
Oswego

MUDD, JOHN. *Neighborhood Services: Making Big Cities Work.* Pp. xv, 230. New Haven, CT: Yale University Press, 1984. No price.

In this book John Mudd, a former director of New York City's Mayor's Office of Neighborhood Government, describes the process through which that city developed a new administrative system of district manager cabinets to increase the quality of public service delivery in its neighborhoods. The initial planning took place during the administration of Mayor John Lindsay, and, in 1975, led to the incorporation into the city charter of the district managers and their respective cabinets. Mudd considers this development as the inception of a rather unique strategy for furthering the caliber of city government within its constituent local communities.

In the first part of his book Mudd suggests that administrative changes and established institutional policies aimed to improve efficiency and responsibility often did not function satisfactorily in New York City. He observes that bureaucratic policy measures came to mean red tape, that professional expertise brought with it disregard for the judgment of clients, and that specialization per se tended to lead to the fragmentation of policies and solutions. In general, he views a straightforward functional specialization in bureaucratic structures as a root cause of the decreasing cohesion within territorial units in America.

In an early chapter, "Strategies of the Past," previous attempts to counter bureaucratic problems through a gradual strengthening of central management are discussed. Approaches of this nature are shown to be ultimately self-defeating. Mudd also is critical of the Model Cities Program, with its intention to fuse decentralized citizen participation in planning with central mayoral control over administrative matters. He argues that this particular approach tended—in a variety of ways—to isolate big-city mayors from the agencies created to improve the quality of management in neighborhoods.

In the remainder of the book, then, the reader will find a detailed discussion of the planning and subsequent formation of the district manager cabinets in the city of New York. A final chapter attempts to evaluate the cabinets' impact on the actual functioning of city administration. Special attention is paid in this chapter to the balance of power between the mayor's office and the respective neighborhoods, with a specific focus on the potential complimentariness of the processes of centralization and decentralization as an integral, interdependent aspect of the growth of big-city government.

This book is, in many ways, an insider's account. It will appeal especially to those persons who work in or are associated with the management of large cities. As such, it seems a worthwhile effort. But its primary contribution is—to me at least—of an applied nature. The case of New York City is dealt with thoroughly and competently. However, the degree to which its lessons can be generalized to the problems of growth of other major American cities remains an open question.

JETSE SPREY

Case Western Reserve
Cleveland
Ohio

NASAW, DAVID. *Children of the City at Work and at Play.* Pp. x, 244. Garden City, NY: Doubleday, Anchor Press, 1985. $18.95.

How did the children of working-class immigrant parents and migratory farm workers adapt to the city life of the early twentieth century? *Children of the City* portrays these youths' after-school lives, particularly their business enterprises. Before the advent of public welfare, poverty-stricken families often needed the supplementary income produced by their sons—and occasionally daughters. These youths usually earned money as street traders, by blacking boots, peddling candy, and hawking newspapers. Despite their varying origins, they displayed a remarkable cross-cultural commonality: whether Italians or Jews in New York, Irish in Boston, Poles in Chicago, blacks in Cincinnati, or American-born everywhere, this cohort revealed similar behavior. All used the city streets, not only as playgrounds and social centers, but also as workplaces.

Among the street traders, Nasaw features the newsboys, basing his account of their working lives on documents and reports he unearthed in 32 cities and 20 states. This newsboy cohort spawned a disproportionately large number of celebrities, such as Senator Jacob Javits, Justice Earl Warren, heavyweight boxer Jack Dempsey, diplomat Ralph Bunche, and corporate executive David Sarnoff.

This outcome was hardly accidental. Working experiences had put money into the newsboys' pockets, enabling them to buy the tempting goods and services that the era's technology was developing—penny arcades, nickelodeons, and abundant inexpensive food purveyed in candy stores and restaurants. The money was earned as profit because, as genuine entrepreneurs, the newsboys bought papers from publishers and sold them to the public. They soon learned that profits could be enhanced by hard work, resourceful planning, and aggressive marketing, lessons they could apply in their adult careers. Many old-stock Americans regarded foreigners as radical and un-American. As a result of their juvenile working experiences, however, these youngsters became ardent supporters of America and capitalism alike. After all, their hopes for the future far exceeded their parents' expectations for themselves.

Nasaw is consciously revisionist when he challenges the view that children raised in the city streets were unhappy. He finds them alive and high spirited. Of course, the streets were safer at the turn of the century than they are today. Inadvertently, he also raises questions about the theory that immigration was restricted early in this century partly because out-of-town visitors saw big cities being overrun by young aliens. By way of contrast, he finds adult immigrants relatively inconspicuous, for they usually confined themselves to their own enclaves, out of sight.

Children of the City should appeal to the general public partly because Nasaw has culled interesting materials from countless oral histories, biographies, and memoirs, especially those of media celebrities, and has fit them into an attractive mosaic that offers sidelights on how immigrants and their children helped create Hollywood's film industry. He has also reproduced 68 photographs, many never before printed, and integrated them into the text.

This book will provide possible new insights for specialists in immigration history, municipal history, and child development. It shows how the period's teenage culture helped shape contemporary American civilization.

FREDERICK SHAW

Baruch College
New York City

SECUNDA, VICTORIA. *By Youth Possessed: The Denial of Age in America.* Pp. xxii, 258. New York: Bobbs-Merrill, 1984. $15.95.

This book is about two different issues, the "denial of age" and the "tyranny of norms," which are constantly confused in the narrative. Granted that in order to be culturally fixated on youth a culture must have age-specific norms that constitute the categories of youth, middle-age, and so forth. Still, they are not the same thing. Secunda treats them so, however, because both require that we generalize about people, and this is Secunda's fundamental gripe, a source of the considerable energy that animates the book. The "we" who generalize are social scientists; and, while I appreciate the reminder that to generalize is to run risks with reality, not to mention with individuals' lives, I also note that Secunda constructs her argument by quoting study after study by—guess who?—social scientists.

The denial of age is by now an old story, sociologically speaking. It is a story that Secunda recounts here in bits and pieces, without the awareness that she has amassed enough contradictions to make something more interesting out of her material. It is clear that every age group in this society has more or less severe problems. What is intriguing is the interdependence, the systemic nature of these problems. What is missing is some grasp of the nature of the system. What is this dance we are all dancing, and where is the music coming from? Secunda is stuck again and again with nonsolutions to these problems. Her call for a "rearrangement of personal priorities" makes sociological generalization look good.

The discussion of the potential damage of normative expectations to those who do not fit the mold is more promising, and the argument has particular force when applied to schooling. Again, however, Secunda misses the systemic level on which we encounter a mass, bureaucratic institution the functions of which include holding and processing batches of children and not encouraging each tender flower to bloom on its own schedule.

Secunda's goal is what she calls "age indifference." "Age obsession," she writes, "a cultural waste product of the baby boom generation, is the primary roadblock to age indifference." For me, the issue is not age indifference but the internalized drivenness of all age groups and the manipulation of irrational norms in the service of a life-denying capitalism of the spirit. This particular book is not important, but the issues encountered in it are.

JOEL S. MEISTER

University of Arizona
Tucson

TAUB, RICHARD, D. TAYLOR, and JAN DUNHAM. *Paths of Neighborhood Change: Race and Crime in Urban America.* Pp. xii, 264. Chicago: University of Chicago Press, 1984. $25.00.

In this analysis of eight Chicago neighborhoods, Taub, Taylor, and Dunham present evidence challenging the strict determinism of classical theories of urban change. While they acknowledge the importance of ecological variables in providing the context for neighborhood change, they argue that neighborhoods do not necessarily follow a cycle of decline and deterioration based on processes of invasion and succession. Neighborhoods decline, gentrify, or stabilize in the presence of variable crime rates and minority populations. Sorting out the complex interrelationship among crime, race, and neighborhood change provides the thesis for this book.

The first half of the book introduces this general theoretical question, outlines the study's methodologies, and describes the neighborhoods that comprise the Chicago data. Although the data for this report come from a variety of sources—archival, field research, and other observational methods—Taub, Taylor, and Dunham rely primarily on a Chicago Neighborhood Study based on telephone interviews. Neighborhoods were selected on the degree to which they supported variation in rates of crime, racial change, and market rates of appreciation in housing. The eight neighborhoods selected are divided into three groups: the neighborhoods representing various stages in the typical pattern of growth, change, and decline are Back of the Yards, Austin, and South Shore; those harboring largely working- and middle-class white residents that have resisted racial penetration are East Side and Portage Park; and those supporting a racial mix that diverge from classical predictions of racial tipping are Beverly, Hyde Park-Kenwood, and Lincoln Park. Brief histories of each neighborhood are provided, along with numerous descriptive statistics comparing variation in measures of social cohesion, crime, racial integration, and neighborhood evaluation among these communities.

The remainder of the book is devoted to an analysis of three models of neighborhood change employing both individual and contextual variables; the former are often absent in studies of neighborhood decline. The first model is one of investment decision making based on Granovetter's threshold model of collective action. This model assumes that the perception that other neighborhood residents are investing will, at some threshold point, prompt an individual to make housing improvements. Relative to the strength of the market and the level of deterioration of housing, the principles of investment emerging from the Chicago data are described variably as "capitalizing on a good situation" or "making the best of a bad situation." Thus, while a strong market for housing may encourage investment in the least deteriorated areas, where rehabilitation yields high returns on investment, it may deter investment in the most deteriorated neighborhoods, where housing is easily sold without improvements. Such outcomes—as the authors rightly note—have significant implica-

tions for the formulation of effective urban housing policies.

The second model—"a revised theory of racial tipping"—builds on Schelling's bounded-neighborhood model. In examining expectations of neighborhood tipping, the authors find that the housing market affects both residents' interpretation of and their reaction to racial concentration. Highly competitive markets show no relationship between racial concentration and expectations of tipping, while in weaker markets expectations of tipping are increasingly sensitive to racial concentration. Reactions to crime and neighborhood deterioration have indirect effects on tipping. Those living in deteriorated areas are more likely to view their neighborhood as unsafe; this, in turn, contributes to expectations that their neighborhood will tip.

A final model explores in greater detail the relationship between crime and other causes of urban change. Drawing on Campbell's discussion of subjective social indicators, the authors find that residents are willing to put up with high levels of threatened crime if their neighborhood has other amenities. Based on this weighing of costs and benefits, residents decide whether or not to stay or invest in their neighborhoods. The authors conclude by noting that racial issues have only indirect effects on urban change. "Decisons contributing to neighborhood change are made largely on the basis of the crime problem and the deterioration problem; . . . the resident, whether black or white, is aware that these problems tend to be more severe in areas of high minority concentration."

The major shortcoming of this book is its lack of balance. In the first half of the book the Chicago neighborhoods are described and compared in roughly 50 tables, none of which contains even the simplest of inferential statistics. The three models of neighborhood change, by contrast, are relatively sophisticated. And given this degree of sophistication, more formal modeling techniques would have provided a clearer picture of the intricate relationship among crime, race, and neighborhood change. Nevertheless, the message emerging from these data is an important one: the same measures intended to reverse neighborhood decline may have opposite effects in different areas, and different racial groups may respond to similar conditions in the same way.

LEE J. CUBA

Wellesley College
Massachusetts

ECONOMICS

BARNES, DONNA A. *Farmers in Rebellion: The Rise and Fall of the Southern Farmers Alliance and People's Party in Texas.* Pp. x, 226. Austin: University of Texas Press, 1984. $19.95.

GARDNER, BRUCE L. *The Governing of Agriculture.* Pp. xxi, 148. Lawrence: Regents Press of Kansas, 1981. $19.95. Paperbound, $9.95.

Both of these books deal with the insistence of a segment of the rural population for government intervention in the affairs of agriculture for special benefit to farmers. *Farmers in Rebellion* treats the historical origins of this special-interest agitation and *The Governing of Agriculture* presents economic arguments against federal management of agriculture.

Barnes, a sociologist at the University of Southern Mississippi, traces the historical origins and development of the Texas Farmers Alliance from its inception in 1877 until its fusion with the Populist Party in 1896. This account adds much knowledge of the farmers' protest movement of this period in Texas as distinct from Populism. The Texas Alliance struggled internally between advocates of self-help techniques—sponsoring co-ops and involvment in the bulk marketing of cotton—and those political activists who eventually led the movement into a third party to rally behind the silver crusade of William Jennings Bryan.

One of the most novel ideas to emerge from the Texas Alliance was that of the subtreasury plan. It called for the creation of federal subtreasuries—warehouses—so that the federal government could initiate a commodity loan program to help farmers financially as well as to provide for a flexible money supply. It anticipated the commodity dollar concept of Cornell University's George Warren and the non-recourse loans of the New Deal era's Commodity Credit Corporation.

Farmers in Rebellion is a valuable and interesting work, but it could have been better had it eschewed the historiographic disputation—the first 50 pages—reminiscent of doctoral dissertations.

Gardner, an agricultural economist at Texas A & M, presents a strong case against federal management of agriculture. He amasses considerable economic evidence to indicate that federal intervention invariably interferes with free-market equilibrium and that such interference leads to even more serious dislocations. Short-run political expediency and complicated formulas—which disguise their real intent—to either subsidize producers or curtail production, he contends, lead only to costly confusion that solves nothing. *The Governing of Agriculture* would be more useful if it were updated to include an assessment of the farm program of the Reagan administration.

After reading these two books, one is struck by the fact that farming is a business. No commercial venture can be guaranteed profits by the federal government. After the demise of the Alliance-Populist movement agriculture attained its golden age without federal assistance. Can history repeat itself?

EDWARD L. SCHAPSMEIER

Illinois State University
Normal

BESEN, STANLEY M., THOMAS G. KRATTENMAKER, A. RICHARD METZGER, Jr., and JOHN R. WOODBURY. *Misregulating Television: Network Dominance and the FCC.* Pp. viii, 202. Chicago: University of Chicago Press, 1984. $24.00.

From 1978 to 1980 Stanley M. Besen and his coauthors served on the staff of the Network Inquiry of the Federal Communications Commission (FCC). Their experience enabled them to analyze and assess all aspects of the relationship between the FCC and the television networks. As a result of their investigation, they advocate the repeal of most federal regulations, and they propose a set of network regulatory policies that are designed to operate more effectively within the ever-burgeoning television environment and its new cable, satellite, subscription, and videocassette landscape.

Using the tools of legal and economic analysis and rooting their interpretations in the history of FCC and network involvement, the authors demonstrate that federal regulations and judicial decisions have solidified the dominance of the three major networks—American Broadcasting Company (ABC), Columbia Broadcasting System (CBS), and National Broadcasting Company (NBC)—and created substantial barriers for broadcasters interested in launching other networks. They state that limiting a viewer's choice of information and entertainment by restricting the sources of communication seriously fails to serve the public interest. Throughout the book, there is a refrain that more networks would not only increase the viewing options of people but also force the Big Three to be more creative and challenging in their programming. The authors repeatedly point to the deregulation of radio networks in 1977 as being a model of what they would like to see happen to television networks.

Much of the considerable merit of *Misregulating Television* derives from the methodical examination of the existing and proposed regulations of network entry, structure, and behavior. The analysis is systematic and rigorous; the authors establish and define three specific standards "to measure television network commercial practices and FCC regulations affecting them." The standards around which most of the remainder of the book revolve are "competition," "diversity," and "localism." The authors keep referring to these criteria in discussing current policies and proposals for the future. Their treatment of the nonsensical and counterproductive Prime Time

Access Rule, which was promulgated in 1970 to limit network programming to three hours of prime time in the 50 largest markets, is particularly successful. The rule fails to foster competition, diversity, localism, or anything else, and it deserves to be repealed immediately.

The illuminating aspect of *Misregulating Television* notwithstanding, the book is not without fault. A principal weakness is a plodding style of prose that frequently obscures the meaning of statements. For example, at one point the writers attempt to clarify a point, and they offer an additional sentence:

Put another way, we conclude that no government regulation of network business practices or organization is defensible if, in the absence of that regulation, viewers would then receive the maximum number of signals consistent with any limitations imposed by the physical properties of the electromagnetic spectrum and the need to dedicate parts of the spectrum to competing uses; the industry would operate within that allocation system in a competitive fashion; and influence over program choice would be wielded by the largest number of viewers and stations (p. 29).

Yes, that is the clarification.

Although one is forced to reread many statements two or three times to understand what the authors are saying—or trying to say—*Misregulating Television* is a valuable volume in the field of communications policy. It is comprehensive in its treatment of regulatory policies vis-à-vis the networks, and it is convincing in articulating exactly why the present system is woefully ineffective in serving the public and in recognizing the rich promise of the television technology emerging today. In short, the book is a blueprint for the future and deserves study and action.

ROBERT SCHMUHL

University of Notre Dame
Indiana

BOSWORTH, BARRY P. *Tax Incentives and Economic Growth.* Pp. xi, 208. Washington, DC: Brookings Institution, 1984. $26.95. Paperbound, $9.95.

PECHMAN, JOSEPH A., ed. *Options for Tax Reform.* Pp. ix, 149. Washington, DC: Brookings Institution, 1984. Paperbound, $9.95.

These two books provide well-articulated analyses of important current issues affecting the federal tax system. After a comprehensive review of the literature, Bosworth concludes that no definitive evidence exists concerning the cause of the decline in labor productivity that the U.S. economy experienced during the 1970s. Thus, despite its scapegoat role, excessive government in the form of fiscal and regulatory policies cannot be identified as the culprit. The supply-side fiscal policies of the 1980s are analyzed and placed within the overall perspective of postwar macroeconomic policy. An appropriate mix of fiscal and monetary policies are recommended for the attainment of economic growth, but such policies would differ considerably from those of Reaganomics. In general, they would yield a more restrictive fiscal approach and a more expansionary monetary approach than have characterized the policies of the Reagan administration.

Separate chapters deal with the effects of the federal tax system on incentives for saving, investment, and work effort. The book demonstrates the complexity and uncertainty that surround efforts to understand the forces influencing aggregate economic performance and the economic growth process. The argument is made that it is easier to design tax policies to affect investment than it is to affect saving, but that the former—if poorly designed—can seriously distort investment decisions. Tax reform, as such, is briefly considered and is viewed as leading to an endorsement of a comprehensive personal income tax over a personal consumption tax.

Meanwhile, the entire topic of the book edited by Pechman is tax reform. This book contains papers and discussant comments from a conference on the topic sponsored by the Brookings Institution. In the first paper, following an introduction by the editor summarizing the volume, Richard Goode discusses the lessons we have learned—or, perhaps, should have learned—from seven decades of federal income taxation. The next paper considers the matter of getting tax reform legislation through the political process, as the subject is viewed by Senator Slade Gorton. Michael Graetz, in turn, examines various alternatives for improving the existing income tax structure. Congressman Richard Gephardt then summarizes the Bradley-Gephardt tax proposal for income tax reform, which he has coauthored in Congress. This is followed by Gordon Henderson's evaluation of the personal consumption tax as a replacement for the income tax as well as supplemental value-added and national retail sales taxes as federal revenue sources. The final paper, by Henry Aaron and Harvey Galper, provides arguments in favor of a graduated personal consumption tax. The discussant comments from recognized tax experts such as Charles McLure, Emil Sunley, and Daniel Halperin add a further useful dimension to the papers.

In sum, these two excellent books complement each other very nicely. Yet, if the reader has time for only one of them, either would stand in its own right as an informative scholarly analysis of current issues affecting federal taxation.

BERNARD P. HERBER

University of Arizona
Tucson

GOODE, RICHARD. *Government Finance in Developing Countries.* Pp. xii, 334. Washington, DC: Brookings Institution, 1984. $31.95. Paperbound, $11.95.

Government finance is carried out to achieve multiple objectives: providing collective goods and services, promoting growth and development, ensuring stable growth, and facilitating equitable distribution of income and wealth. These objectives are achieved through fiscal instruments of government spending on goods and services and raising revenue.

These objectives are not easy to realize since fiscal instruments must be applied in such a way that they do not retard investment, saving, consumption, or growth in revenue; discourage the desire to work; restrict domestic production; or impede exports. Conflicts by necessity arise since different interests are served by the objectives. Also, economic, political, social, and demographic conditions prevailing in a country make it difficult to realize these objectives. In developing countries, especially, the latter pose particular challenges to governments in deciding on policies for spending on goods and services and for raising revenue.

This is the thrust of Richard Goode's discussion on government finance in developing countries. The book considers the use of various fiscal instruments to advance objectives of growth and development, economic stability, and equitable distribution and evaluates their suitability to achieve these objectives in developing countries.

Methods of evaluating priorities for spending, and various forms of revenue collection are discussed. Goode considers the advantages and disadvantages of the policies and he considers the compromises that must be made in implementing each policy. Of particular concern is inflation, its impact on the effectiveness of revenue creation, and the impact of revenue creation on inflation.

Also discussed are problems encountered in implementing policies in developing countries, given constraints in financial resources, manpower, education, institutional support, information systems, and administrative capability.

The description of fiscal instruments is related to experiences of specific countries. Insight is provided into how governments have adapted fiscal policies to their special circumstances. Their successes and failures are related as guides for what fiscal policies will work in developing countries.

Goode's major criticism of government finance in developing countries is that policymakers too often make policy for political expediency and pay little attention to how policies can be carried out effectively and efficiently. They fail to analyze adequately the means of financing expenditures and the distribution of benefits.

Another criticism is that developing countries are impatient for growth and try to imitate methods that are used in developed countries. Goode emphasizes that fiscal instruments must be designed with consideration of the administrative capability and compliance capacities of a country. He recommends incremental reform rather than sudden comprehensive reform.

The book clearly conveys that government finance in developing countries is no easy task. It entails balancing different forces that act upon one another. Goode does not attempt to provide all the answers, but he does provide sufficient information so that a reader will be in a better position to judge which fiscal policy is the most appropriate to follow. It is a comprehensive book, with substantial material to be digested slowly.

JOHN C. BEYER

Robert R. Nathan Associates, Inc.
Washington, D.C.

McCRAW, THOMAS K. *Prophets of Regulation: Charles Francis Adams, Louis D. Brandeis, James M. Landis, Alfred E. Kahn.* Pp. xii, 387. Cambridge, MA: Harvard University Press, Belknap Press, 1984. $20.00.

Business regulation, as well as deregulation, is a timely topic today, as it has been for a decade or so. The subject has assumed outstanding importance in three other periods: the 1870s, the Granger years; the early 1900s, the Progressive era; and the 1930s, the New Deal period. On each occasion one man in particular has so strongly influenced the regulatory movement as almost to personify it. Having observed this fact, Thomas K. McCraw, of the Graduate School of Business Administration, Harvard University, has derived the happy idea of writing a history of regulation and organizing it around the careers of the four preeminent regulators. "My approach," McCraw explains, "fluctuates between the lives of men, economic theory, and historical incident." The execution is as excellent as the conception. McCraw writes extremely well, making complex issues understandable and interesting for the ordinary reader as well as the expert.

The four men he writes of varied considerably in their methods and the areas in which they applied them. As originator and head of the Massachusetts Board of Railroad Commissioners, Charles Francis Adams (1835-1915) favored the use of publicity and persuasion rather than adversary proceedings. Louis D. Brandeis (1856-1941), a determined trustbuster who considered bigness bad in itself, became the philosopher of Woodrow Wilson's New Freedom and the chief architect of the Federal Trade Commission. James M. Landis (1899-1964), as principal founder and first chairman of the Securities and Exchange Commisison, was careful to enlist the cooperation of brokers, bankers, and corporation executives. Alfred E. Kahn (b. 1917), while on the New York Public Service Commission, revolutionized public-utility rate making by basing it on marginal costs. Then, as chairman of the Civil Aeronautics Board (CAB), he liberalized its policies, largely deregulating the airlines, which the CAB previously had cartelized.

It is meaningless, McCraw concludes, to say that regulation in the United States has been either a failure or a success. It has succeeded fairly well in its objectives when the right person and the opportune moment have met. Kahn, the only economist among the four regulators, seems the most successful; certainly he contributed the most to economic efficiency. Among the other three, all lawyers, Brandeis appears to have had the least understanding of economics. He imagined that investment bankers, through representation on interlocking directorates, exercised more control over business than they actually did. Nevertheless, his book *Other People's Money* (1913) had a signifi-

cant effect on both the making of public policy and the writing of American history.

RICHARD N. CURRENT
University of North Carolina
Greensboro

NELSON, JOEL I. *Economic Inequality: Conflict without Change.* Pp. ix, 280. New York: Columbia University Press, 1982. No price.

Perhaps a better title for this work might have been *Conflict without Change: Economic Inequality.* The main thesis of this book is that two sociological views of the United States—the consensus, or liberal, view and the conflict view, which is more Marxian—do not adequately represent the United States. A synthesis of these two views is presented by Nelson, and it is applied to analyze, among other things, economic inequality.

The consensus view holds that a free-enterprise system, with a democratically elected government, will move naturally to eliminate inequality, by means of:

—the economic mobility of labor, in which skills are rewarded and people move easily up the economic ladder;

—economic growth, giving labor more income even when its relative share is unchanged; and

—democratic governments that eliminate racial and economic barriers, and a welfare system that helps those who somehow do not benefit from economic mobility of labor or from economic growth.

The conflict view holds that government and the economy are controlled by an economic elite that will not give up any of its wealth to the working class, unless labor militancy forces them to do so and thereby causes fundamental changes in the economic structure. Monopolistic capitalists have been able to buy off labor through economic growth. Since there is no guarantee that economic growth will continue, any long stagnation will lead to conflict between labor and a monopolistic capitalist class and to greater inequality.

Nelson's synthesis claims that the economic and political system in the United States has elements of conflict—such as strikes, monopolistic control—but that the system does not seem headed for revolutionary structural change, contrary to what proponents of the conflict view claim. He supports his theory with the following arguments:

1. Strikes occur when the economy is growing, when high demand, low inventory, and high surplus allow owners to raise wages. Thus the strike is for short-term wage gain, not structural reform.

2. Since the mid-1960s, the United States has seen much lower economic growth rates, contradicting the consensus claim of the growing economic pie.

3. Corporations are designed to maximize profits, not to maximize worker welfare; thus the consensus view of an invisible hand reducing inequality is wrong.

4. Government programs have done little to reduce inequality because government acts as neither a benevolent equalizer, as in the consensus view, nor a vehicle for the elite, as in the conflict view, but as an independent agent interested in controlling as much power as possible. Thus a large antipoverty program will create a lot of bureaucrats but provide little aid to the poor.

5. There has been little change in the distribution of income over the last 20 years, and little change in factor shares and the distribution of wealth for over 50.

The conclusions Nelson draws are that "as long as institutions hitch their star to economic growth, inroads into inequality will not necessarily be made." And as long as there is no trend toward structural revolution, we cannot expect to see a reduction in inequality.

We have one minor and two more significant critiques of this book. First, the empirical evidence, while very broad, is not always convincing, and is sometimes contradictory, as the following examples show.

1. Nelson claims that "post transfer income inequality [was] virtually unchanged" between 1950 and 1970, yet he also claims in several places that "the [welfare] funds unquestionably provide relief from the hardships of poverty."

2. Although Nelson claims that strikes and labor militancy occur only during economic booms, some of the most severe labor actions occurred during the depression of the 1930s.

3. Nelson claims that higher wages in core industries represent "no loss of profit" and that wages can be raised "without unduly eroding corporate profits." Although "unduly" may be in the mind of the beholder, this seems a contradiction.

4. Nelson seems to overstate the strength of oligopolies. Although large corporations certainly have greater market control than smaller ones, they do not have unlimited power, subject as they are to foreign competition and government regulations. The severe restructuring in the auto industry in the late 1970s and early 1980s, and the difficulties of several large utility companies in recent years, are two counterexamples.

Overall, the empirical evidence is not wholly convincing, but certainly not entirely wrong.

More significant, we feel more attention should have been paid to the structurally unemployed, to those who work only part-time or not at all, and to the increasing number of female-headed families below the poverty line. These issues do not fit neatly into an argument over factor shares or labor militancy. Although Nelson deals with these issues to some extent in his case study of black Americans, this coverage could have been more thorough.

Finally, there is no sense of a theory of "conflict without change" in this book. Rather it is a collection of evidence supporting the notion that there are elements of consensus and conflict in our society, and since these elements have existed together for some time, they can be expected to continue coexisting.

Notwithstanding these criticisms, we found the book to be a serious attempt to get away from the easy—albeit different—answers to the problems of inequality presented by many Marxists and free-marketeers. For this Nelson ought to be thanked, and praised.

PHILIP LAREN
DEBORAH S. LAREN

University of Michigan
Ann Arbor

PASCALL, GLENN. *The Trillion Dollar Budget—How to Stop the Bankrupting of America.* Pp. xxii, 328. Seattle: University of Washington Press, 1985. $19.95. Paperbound, $9.95.

President Reagan entered office in January 1981 pledging to cut both taxes and government spending. He was distinctly successful—more so than most at the time had thought possible—in cutting tax rates. But he was far less successful in cutting federal spending. In retrospect, the tax-cut program had great political appeal. Nearly all individuals and groups stood to gain from it. The spending-cut program inherently lacked a similar appeal. It lacked balance. A balanced program would have called for significant cuts in all three of the major categories of spending: defense, transfer payments, and discretionary domestic programs. In the end, however, none of the cuts came in defense and none came in non-means-tested transfers such as Social Security, Medicare, and the federal military and civil service retirement programs. The president opposed cuts in defense and his political opposition opposed cuts in middle-class entitlements. So all the cuts of 1981, such as they were, came in the domestic budget and the means-tested entitlements of the poor.

The result of 1981's mix of successes and failures is today's problem of the budget deficit. The deficit problem is like the weather: most of us are aware of it but no one seems to be able to do anything about it. Glenn Pascall's book sizes up the full dimensions of the problems and points the way toward a solution.

Pascall advises us to forget about cutting the discretionary domestic spending programs. As a result of earlier decisions, these programs, which embodied "the creative imagination of government," already "are being ground to bits between two millstones: military spending and middle-class welfare." His strategy instead is to go after the millstones and cut them down to size.

Most of the book is given to detailed analysis of defense spending and middle-class transfers. He makes a convincing case—if one needs to be convinced—that the security value received by Americans per dollar of defense spending is not high. The cap for the leg of a stool that cost $1100 and the coffee pot that cost $7600, both for airplanes, are outrages that the public understands. Middle-class welfare is more complex because the public is both the bad guy and the good guy—but statesmanlike solutions are possible.

The book ends with a detailed listing of spending-cut proposals that would save from $145 billion to $198 billion. The suggestions are only indirectly Pascall's; all come from 1 or more of 10 reputable governmental or private sources. Policy analysts know what ought to be done. What remains is for the rest of us to inform ourselves. Pascall's book, full of despair and hope, is a good place to start.

RICHARD SYLLA
North Carolina State University
Raleigh

ROBERTSON, JAMES OLIVER. *America's Business.* Pp. x, 277. New York: Farrar, Strauss & Giroux, Hill & Wang, 1985. $17.95.

For the student or general reader seeking an authoritative introduction to American business history, as well as for the professional wishing a reliable review of this segment of his or her field, Robertson's book probably is without peer. Divided into four largely chronological sections, the narrative begins in 1565 and is brought down to 1984. Most big businesses and their leaders pass here in review, but the trucking industry is among some notable exceptions.

From the beginning of American colonial history, Robertson observes, business was a concern of settlers and their financial sponsors. After providing for their own subsistence, colonists shipped abroad products of the field and forest to reimburse their promoters or for personal gain. The colonies were the offspring of an empire whose directing minds believed that colonies existed for the primary benefit of the mother country. With the winning of independence, however, restraints on manufacturing were lifted or broken and American business moved into textiles and other lines of manufacturing and into construction of canals, turnpikes, and railroads. From these modest beginnings America was to emerge in our own day as the leading industrial power of the world.

But in the new nation, absolute freedom and independence were no more possible for business than for the individual, and the problem of public control of business was ever present. Until the adoption of the Fourteenth Amendment, in 1868, control was exercised largely at state and local levels. Soon thereafter, however, a series of Supreme Court decisions defined corporations as persons within the meaning of the new amendment and made interstate commerce the special province of the federal government. After surviving strikes by organized labor and a number of panics, businesses shortly undertook many mergers and formed large conglomerates, national and multinational, and problems of control became acute. Indeed, big business operations became so intricate and complex that legislative control and its enforcement could scarcely keep up with the new developments. Moreover, the law of supply and demand gave way to a law of oversupply and a demand created partly by built-in obsolescence of manufactured products. This

consumer-oriented approach sought to show the benevolence of business in providing many good things of life and the employee wages to buy them. When Calvin Coolidge said that "the business of America is business" and Charles E. Wilson declared that "what is good for General Motors is good for America," they very nearly summed up the business philosophy of our time.

JENNINGS B. SANDERS

Kensington
Maryland

SINGER, S. FRED, ed. *Free Market Energy: The Way to Benefit Consumers.* Pp. 430. New York: Universe Books, 1984. $19.95

This new addition to the burgeoning field of regulatory literature presents the case for further deregulation of America's sources of energy. In its approach, the book reflects the thrust of policymakers in the Carter and Reagan administrations whose objectives have met with considerable success in wider areas of social and economic deregulation.

The authors are scientists and economists; their conclusions and arguments follow the rigor of their respective disciplines. Lester Lave's article on the relationship between coal and the Clean Air Act, for example, carefully documents the unanticipated consequences of environmental legislation and argues for the addition of economic incentives in the form of effluent fees as a more viable method of increasing regulatory efficiency. Similarly, Walter J. Mead and Gregory G. Pickett advocate loosening up the bidding for oil and gas leases on federal lands as a way of increasing the efficient allocation of these resources, and reducing government's role in the process.

The theme of maximizing efficiency through economic incentives, and the elimination of command-and-control regulation, prevails throughout the book, whether the authors are addressing nuclear power, coal, oil, natural gas, or emergency management. Several of the authors attribute intrusive regulatory policies in the energy area to these factors: (1) the crisis mentality that followed the oil embargo and shortages of 1974; and (2) notions of redistributive justice through resource allocation that led to the development of the regulatory process in the energy field.

These themes are somewhat stretched to their limit in Bernard L. Cohen's study of regulatory excess in the nuclear power industry. He correctly points up the excessive confusion, poor mangement, frequent design changes, and legal wrangling that have virtually destroyed the business of building nuclear reactors in the United States. From there, he unfortunately makes the leap from data to rhetoric in blaming the media and citizens groups for distorting the risk factor and obstructing the construction of nuclear facilities. To the contrary, the data show that the troubles of the nuclear industry come from poor performance on a variety of levels: an ossified regulatory agency steeped in minutiae and too weak to stand up to industry in situations of real risk such as those at Diablo Canyon and Three Mile Island, among others; an industry that could not police itself; and an insensitivity to public concerns on the part of both the agency and the industry that led to the current negative image of nuclear power. This important source of energy deserves better treatment. The strong and effective nuclear regulatory systems in Germany, France, and Japan indicate that the presence of a governmental counterpoint to industry helps—not hinders—the development of nuclear power.

For its genre, *Free Market Energy* represents an interesting, if conventional, treatment of the argument for the government to abdicate its role in allocating energy resources. For those who accept that premise, there is more than adequate documentation; those who do not will not find the other side of the coin discussed in anything but a dismissive style. Questions of equity, redistributive justice, the management of risk, and the public sector's role in those issues are not addressed substantively. Nevertheless, the articles are well written and challenge the reader to think about problems that were not even in the forefront of the public agenda 20 years ago.

SUSAN J. TOLCHIN

George Washington University
Washington, D.C.

OTHER BOOKS

ALEXANDER, HERBERT E. and GERALD E. CAIDEN. *The Politics and Economics of Organized Crime.* Pp. viii, 175. Lexington, MA: Lexington Books, 1985. $20.00.

ALI, TARIQ, ed. *The Stalinist Legacy.* Pp. 551. New York: Penguin Books, 1985. Paperbound, no price.

ASIWAJU, A. I., ed. *Partitioned Africans: Ethnic Relations across Africa's International Boundaries, 1884-1984.* Pp. xii, 275. New York: St. Martin's Press, 1985. $29.95.

BALFE, JUDITH H. and MARGARET JANE WYSZOMIRSKI, eds. *Art, Ideology, and Politics.* Pp. xii, 369. New York: Praeger, 1985. $39.95.

BARANSKI, ZYGMUNT G. and JOHN R. SHORT, eds. *Developing Contemporary Marxism.* Pp. viii, 308. New York: St. Martin's Press, 1985. $27.50.

BENJAMIN, ROGER and STEPHEN L. ELKIN, eds. *The Democratic State.* Pp. vii, 275. Lawrence: University Press of Kansas, 1985. $29.95. Paperbound, $12.95.

BERGAN, FRANCIS. *The History of the New York Court of Appeals, 1847-1932.* Pp. viii, 354. New York: Columbia University Press, 1985. $35.00.

BERRIDGE, G. R. and A. JENNINGS, eds. *Diplomacy at the UN.* Pp. xvii, 227. New York: St. Martin's Press, 1985. $27.50.

BIEN, JOSEPH. *History, Revolution and Human Nature: Marx's Philosophical Anthropology.* Pp. 228. Amsterdam: B. R. Gruner, 1985. Paperbound, $20.00.

BOYLE, FRANCIS ANTHONY. *World Politics and International Law.* Pp. x, 366. Durham, NC: Duke University Press, 1985. $32.50. Paperbound, $14.75.

BRAHAM, RANDOLPH L., ed. *Perspectives on the Holocaust.* Pp. xvi, 501. New York: Columbia, 1984. $40.00.

BRASS, PAUL. *Ethnic Groups and the State.* Pp. 341. Totowa, NJ: Barnes and Noble Books, 1985. $27.50.

BROWN, ARCHIE, ed. *Political Culture and Communist Studies.* Pp. xii, 211. Armonk, NY: M. E. Sharpe, 1985. $30.00. Paperbound, $14.95.

BROWN, ROBERT. *The Nature of Social Laws.* Pp. ix, 270. New York: Cambridge University Press, 1984. $39.50.

BROWN, THOMAS. *Politics and Statesmanship: Essays on the American Whig Party.* Pp. v, 330. New York: Columbia University Press, 1985. $32.50.

BUTLER, EAMONN. *Hayek: His Contribution to the Political and Economic Thought of Our Time.* Pp. 168. New York: Universe, 1985. $15.00. Paperbound, $7.95.

CAMPBELL, BERNARD. *Human Evolution.* Pp. xxvi, 477. Hawthorne, NY: Aldine, 1985. $39.95. Paperbound, $16.95.

CIRINCIONE, JOSEPH, ed. *Central America and the Western Alliance.* Pp. xix, 238. New York: Holmes and Meier, 1985. $26.50.

CLAPHAM, CHRISTOPHER and GEORGE PHILIP, eds. *The Political Dilemmas of Military Regimes.* Pp. 282. Totowa, NJ: Barnes and Noble Books, 1985. $28.50.

COLTON, TIMOTHY J. *The Dilemma of Reform in the Soviet Union.* Pp. xi, 115. New York: Council on Foreign Relations, 1984. Paperbound, $6.95.

DELBRUCK, HANS and WALTER J. RENFROE, Jr. *History of the Art of War within the Framework of Political History: The Modern Era.* Pp. xi, 487. Westport, CT: Greenwood Press, 1985. $75.00.

DEMIRCHIAN, K. S. *Soviet Armenia.* Pp. 98. Moscow: Progress, 1984. Distributed by Imported Publications, Chicago, IL. $5.95.

DRYAKHLOV, NIKOLAI. *The Scientific and Technological Revolution: Its Role in Today's World.* Pp. 264. Moscow: Progress, 1984. Distributed by Imported Publications, Chicago, IL. Paperbound, $2.95.

DUNCAN, HUGH DALZIEL. *Communication and Social Order.* Pp. lii, 475. New

Brunswick, NJ: Transaction Books, 1985. Paperbound, $14.95.

EBERTS, RANDALL W. and JOE A. STONE. *Unions and Public Schools.* Pp. xvi, 195. Lexington, MA: D. C. Heath, 1984. $24.00.

EITZEN, D. STANLEY. *In Conflict and Order: Understanding Society.* Pp. xvi, 605. Rockleigh, NJ: Allyn and Bacon, 1985. Paperbound, no price.

FRIEDMAN, JULIAN R. and MARC I. SHERMAN, eds. *Human Rights: An International and Comprehensive Law Bibliography.* Pp. xxviii, 868. Westport, CT: Greenwood Press, 1985. $75.00.

FRISCH, MORTON J., ed. *Selected Writings and Speeches of Alexander Hamilton.* Pp. xiv, 524. Washington, DC: American Enterprise Institute, 1985. Paperbound, no price.

GAWALT, GERARD W., ed. *The New High Priests: Lawyers in Post-Civil War America.* Pp. xiv, 214. Westport, CT: Greenwood Press, 1984. $29.95.

GOLDSTEIN, STEVEN M., ed. *China Briefing, 1984.* Pp. x, 125. Boulder, CO: Westview Press, 1985. $22.00. Paperbound, $12.50.

GOLDWIN, ROBERT A. and WILLIAM A. SCHAMBRA, eds. *How Does the Constitution Secure Rights?* Pp. xiv, 125. Washington, DC: American Enterprise Institute, 1985. Paperbound, no price.

HAGOPIAN, MARK N. *Ideals and Ideologies of Modern Politics.* Pp. viii, 263. New York: Longman, 1985. Paperbound, $12.95.

HAINES, DAVID W., ed. *Refugees in the United States: A Reference Handbook.* Pp. xviii, 243. Westport, CT: Greenwood Press, 1985. $39.95.

HENIG, JEFFREY R. *Public Policy and Federalism: Issues in State and Local Politics.* Pp. xiii, 401. New York: St. Martin's Press, 1985. $32.50.

HILVERT, JOHN. *Blue Pencil Warriors: Censorship and Propaganda in World War II.* Pp. vi, 258. New York: University of Queensland Press, 1984. $27.95.

HOLLIST, W. LADD and F. LAMOND TULLIS, eds. *An International Political Economy Yearbook.* Vol. 1, *An International Political Economy.* Pp. xii, 300. Boulder, CO: Westview Press, 1985. $32.85. Paperbound, $14.85.

ISAAK, ALAN C. *Scope and Methods of Political Science.* Pp. xv, 305, Homewood, IL: Dorsey Press, 1985. Paperbound, $18.00.

JOHNSON, JAMES TURNER, ed. *The Bible in American Law, Politics, and Political Rhetoric.* Pp. vii, 204. Philadelphia: Fortress Press, 1985. No price.

KAMARCK, ANDREW M. *Economics and the Real World.* Pp. x, 165. Philadelphia: University of Pennsylvania Press, 1983. $16.50.

KAPLAN, HOWARD B. *Patterns of Juvenile Delinquency.* Pp. 160. Beverly Hills, CA: Sage, 1984. $15.95. Paperbound, $7.95.

KAUFMANN, WILLIAM W. *The 1986 Defense Budget.* Pp. 59. Washington, DC: Brookings Institution, 1985. Paperbound, $6.95.

KETTL, DONALD F. *The Regulation of American Federalism.* Pp. xviii, 195. Baton Rouge: Louisiana State University Press, 1983. $20.00.

KING, JOHN LESLIE and KENNETH L. KRAEMER. *The Dynamics of Computing.* Pp. xii, 283. New York: Columbia University Press, 1985.

KWAK, TAE-HWAN, WAYNE PATTERSON, and EDWARD A. OLSEN, eds. *The Two Koreas in World Politics.* Pp. xx, 404. Boulder, CO: Westview Press, 1984. $25.00.

LAUFFER, ARMAND. *Understanding Your Social Agency.* 2nd ed. Pp. 168. Beverly Hills, CA: Sage, 1984. Paperbound, $9.95.

LEE, ALFRED McCLUNG. *Terrorism in Northern Ireland.* Pp. viii, 253. Bayside, NY: General Hall, 1983. $23.95. Paperbound, $9.95.

LEVINSON, RISHA W. and KAREN S. HAYNES. *Accessing Human Services: International Perspectives.* Pp. 320. Beverly Hills, CA: Sage, 1984. $28.00. Paperbound, $14.00.

LEWYTZKYJ, BORYS. *Who's Who in the Soviet Union*. Pp. xi, 428. New York: K. G. Saur, 1984. $128.00.

LIDZ, CHARLES W. et al., eds. *Informed Consent: A Study of Decisionmaking in Psychiatry*. Pp. xv, 365. New York: Guilford Press, 1984. $30.00.

MAJKOWSKI, WLADYSLAW. *People's Poland: Patterns of Social Inequality and Conflict*. Pp. xvii, 234. Westport, CT: Greenwood Press, 1985. $35.00.

MAMONOVA, TATYANA. *Women and Russia: Feminist Writings from the Soviet Union*. Pp. xxiii, 273. Boston: Beacon Press, 1984. Paperbound, $9.95.

MANDEL, ERNEST, ed. *Ricardo, Marx, Sraffa*. Pp. xvi, 286. New York: Schocken Books, 1985. $30.00. Paperbound, $11.50.

MASHAW, JERRY L. *Bureaucratic Justice*. Pp. x, 238. New Haven, CT: Yale University Press, 1983. Paperbound, no price.

MASTNY, VOJTECH. *Power and Policy in Transition*. Pp. ix, 271. Westport, CT: Greenwood Press, 1984. $29.95.

McKELVEY, JEAN T. *The Changing Law of Fair Representation*. Pp. iv, 298. New York: ILR Press, 1985. $25.00. Paperbound, $12.95.

MEIER, KENNETH J. *Regulation: Politics, Bureaucracy, and Economics*. Pp. xviii, 334. New York: St. Martin's Press, 1985. $32.50.

MENDELSOHN, M. S. *The Debt of Nations*. Pp. vi, 67. New York: Priority Press, 1984. Paperbound, $7.00.

MILLER, TRUDI C., ed. *Public Sector Performance*. Pp. ix, 276. Baltimore, MD: Johns Hopkins University Press, 1984. $27.50. Paperbound, $12.95.

MITZMAN, ARTHUR. *The Iron Cage*. Pp. xxx, 337. New Brunswick, NJ: Transaction Books, 1985. Paperbound, $12.95.

MORAN, FERNANDO et al. *Third World Instability: Central America as a European-American Issue*. Pp. xii, 155. New York: Council on Foreign Relations, 1985. No price.

MORTON, HENRY W. and ROBERT C. STUART, eds. *The Contemporary Soviet City*. Pp. xiv, 262. Armonk, NY: M. E. Sharpe, 1984. $30.00. Paperbound, $14.95.

NASH, HENRY T. *American Foreign Policy: A Search for Security*. Pp. xvi, 382. Homewood, IL: Dorsey Press, 1985. Paperbound, $20.00.

NEFF, WALTER S. *Work and Human Behavior*. Pp. xv, 345. Hawthorne, NY: Walter de Gruyter, 1985. $39.95. Paperbound, $14.95.

PERELOMOV, L. and A. MARTYNOV. *Imperial China: Foreign Policy Conceptions and Methods*. Pp. 199. Moscow: Progress, 1983. Distributed by Imported Publications, Chicago, IL. $5.95.

PONOMAREV, BORIS, ed. *The International Working Class Movement*. Pp. 699. Moscow: Progress, 1984. Distributed by Imported Publications, Chicago, IL. $11.50.

PUGH, D. S., D. J. HICKSON, and C. R. HININGS, eds. *Writers on Organization*. Pp. 234. Beverly Hills, CA: Sage, 1985. $25.00. Paperbound, $10.00.

QUIGLEY, JOHN M. and DANIEL L. RUBINFELD, eds. *American Domestic Priorities: An Economic Appraisal*. Pp. xv, 398. Berkeley: University of California Press, 1985. $32.50. Paperbound, $9.95.

RAPP, GEORGE, Jr. and JOHN A. GIFFORD, eds. *Archaeological Geology*. Pp. xvii, 435. New Haven, CT: Yale University Press, 1985. $35.00.

RIEMER, NEAL. *The Future of the Democratic Revolution: Toward a More Prophetic Politics*. Pp. x, 305. New York: Praeger, 1984. $39.95.

RIGBY, ANDREW. *Initiation and Initiative*. Pp. 217. New York: Columbia University Press, 1984. $22.00.

RIST, RAY C., ed. *Policy Studies*. Pp. 722. New Brunswick, NJ: Transaction Books, 1985. No price.

ROWLAND, WILLARD D., Jr. and BRUCE WATKINS., eds. *Interpreting Television: Current Research Perspectives*. Pp. 293. Beverly Hills, CA: Sage, 1984. $28.00. Paperbound, $14.00.

SAFRAN, WILLIAM. *The French Polity.* Pp. xvii, 314. New York: Longman, 1985. Paperbound, $14.95.

SAIVETZ, CAROL R. and SYLVIA WOODBY. *Soviet-Third World Relations.* Pp. xiii, 254. Boulder, CO: Westview Press, 1985. $32.50. Paperbound, $14.95.

SCAMMELL, MICHAEL. *Solzhenitsyn.* Pp. 1051. New York: W. W. Norton, 1984. $29.95.

SCHAPIRO, LEONARD and JOSEPH GODSON, eds. *The Soviet Worker from Lenin to Andropov.* Pp. xii, 326. New York: St. Martin's Press, 1984. $29.95.

SHAW, TIMOTHY M. and OLAJIDE ALUKO, eds. *Africa Projected: From Recession to Renaissance, by the Year 2000?* Pp. xv, 217. New York: St. Martin's Press, 1985. $22.50.

SHEEHAN, HELENA. *Marxism and the Philosophy of Science.* Pp. xii, 438. Atlantic Highlands, NJ: Humanities Press, 1985. $34.95.

SHUBIK, MARTIN. *Game Theory in the Social Sciences: Concepts and Solutions.* Pp. ix, 514. Cambridge, MA: MIT Press, 1985. Paperbound, $12.95.

SONNENFELDT, HELMUT, eds. *Soviet Politics in the 1980's.* Pp. x, 247. Boulder, CO: Westview Press, 1985. Paperbound, $22.50.

STANILAND, MARTIN. *What is Political Economy? A Study of Social Theory and Underdevelopment.* Pp. xi, 229. New Haven, CT: Yale University Press, 1985. $18.50.

STRAUSSMAN, JEFFREY D. *Public Administration.* Pp. x, 422. New York: Holt, Rinehart and Winston, 1985. No price.

TÄGIL, SVEN, ed. *Regions in Upheaval.* Pp. 314. Kristianstad, Sweden: Kristianstads Boktryckeri AB, 1984. No price.

TAYLOR, SAMUEL H. and ROBERT W. ROBERTS. *Theory and Practice of Community Social Work.* Pp. xiii, 442. New York: Columbia University Press, 1985. $22.50.

TAYLOR, THEODORE W., ed. *Federal Public Policy.* Pp. iv, 327. Mt. Airy, MD: Lomond, 1984. $27.50. Paperbound, $13.50.

TIKHVINSKY, S. L., ed. *Manzhou Rule in China.* Pp. 358. Moscow: Progress, 1983. Distributed by Imported Publications, Chicago, IL. $7.95.

TOLCHIN, SUSAN J. and MARTIN TOLCHIN. *Dismantling America: The Rush to Deregulate.* Pp. 323. New York: Oxford University Press, 1985. Paperbound, $7.95.

TOUVAL, SAADIA and I. WILLIAM ZARTMAN, eds. *International Mediation in Theory and Practice.* Pp. ix, 274. Boulder, CO: Westview Press, 1985. Paperbound, $24.00.

TURNER, BRYAN S. *Capitalism and Class in the Middle East.* Pp. vi, 229. Atlantic Highlands, NJ: Humanities Press, 1984. $33.25.

ULYANOVSKY, R. A. et al. *Fighters for National Liberation.* Pp. 175. Moscow: Progress, 1984. Distributed by Imported Publications, Chicago, IL. $5.95.

VAUGHAN, ELIZABETH. *The Ordeal of Elizabeth Vaughan: A Wartime Diary of the Philippines.* Pp. xxii, 312. Athens, GA: University of Georgia, 1985. $24.95.

WEINBERG, ALVIN, MARCELO ALONSO, and JACK N. BARKENBUS, eds. *The Nuclear Connection.* Pp. 295. New York: Paragon House, 1985. $27.95. Paperbound, $19.95.

WESSELL, LEONARD P., Jr. *Prometheus Bound: The Mythic Structure of Karl Marx's Scientific Thinking.* Pp. xii, 312. Baton Rouge: Louisiana State University Press, 1984. $32.50.

WIARDA, HOWARD J. and HARVEY F. KLINE, eds. *Latin American Politics and Development.* Pp. xiv, 672. Boulder, CO: Westview Press, 1985. $48.50. Paperbound, $20.00.

INDEX

Publisher's Note: The following information is printed in accordance with U.S. postal regulations: Statement of Ownership, Management and Circulation (required by 39 U.S.C. 3685). 1A. Title of Publication: THE ANNALS OF THE AMERICAN ACADEMY OF POLITICAL AND SOCIAL SCIENCE. 1B. Publication No.: 026060. 2. Date of Filing: September 30, 1985. 3. Frequency of Issue: Bi-monthly. 3A. No. of Issues Published Annually: 6. 3B. Annual Subscription Price: paper-inst., $50.00, cloth-inst., $66.00; paper-ind., $26.00, cloth-ind., $39.00. 4. Location of Known Office of Publication: 3937 Chestnut Street, Philadelphia, PA 19104. 5. Location of the Headquarters or General Business Offices of the Publishers: 3937 Chestnut Street, Philadelphia, PA 19104. 6. Names and Complete Addresses of Publisher, Editor, and Managing Editor: Publisher: The American Academy of Political and Social Science, 3937 Chestnut Street, Philadelphia, PA 19104; Editor: Richard D. Lambert, 3937 Chestnut Street, Philadelphia, PA 19104. Managing Editor: None. 7. Owner (if owned by a corporation, its name and address must be stated and also immediately thereunder the names and addresses of stockholders owning or holding 1% or more of total amount of stock. If not owned by a corporation, the names and addresses of the individual owners must be given. If owned by a partnership or other unincorporated firm, its name and address, as well as that of each individual must be given.): The American Academy of Political and Social Science, 3937 Chestnut Street, Philadelphia, PA 19104. 8. Known Bondholders, Mortgagees, and Other Security Holders Owning or Holding 1% or More of Total Amount of Bonds, Mortgages or Other Securities: None. 9. For Completion by Nonprofit Organizations Authorized to Mail at Special Rates (Section 423.12, DMM only): Has not changed during preceding 12 months.

	Av. No. Copies Each Issue During Preceding 12 Months	Actual No. of Copies of Single Issue Published Nearest to Filing Date
10. Extent and Nature of Circulation		
A. Total no. copies printed (net press run)	9142	9232
B. Paid circulation:		
1. Sales through dealers and carriers, street vendors and counter sales	164	60
2. Mail subscription	5626	5263
C. Total paid circulation (sum of 10B1 and 10B2)	5790	5323
D. Free distribution by mail, carrier or other means: samples, complimentary, and other free copies	125	133
E. Total distribution (sum of C and D)	5915	5456
F. Copies not distributed:		
1. Office use, left over, unaccounted, spoiled after printing	3227	3776
2. Return from news agents	0	0
G. Total (sum of E, F1 and 2—should equal net press run shown in A)	9142	9232

11. I certify that the statements made by me above are correct and complete. (Signed) Ingeborg Hessler, Business Manager.

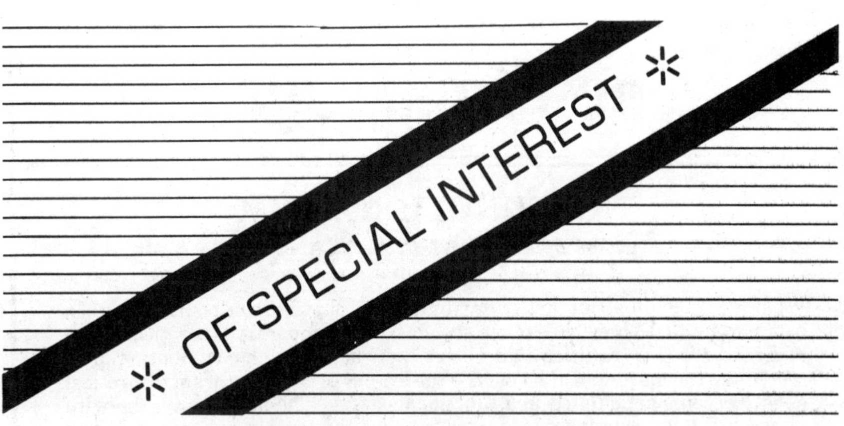

GOVERNMENT MINISTERS IN THE CONTEMPORARY WORLD

by JEAN BLONDEL,
University of Essex

Governments have grown in scope, and spread geographically, to the point where a new phenomenon has emerged—rule by a political class of ministers regarded as the main instruments. Yet ministerial careers and the structure of ministerial careers have been largely neglected areas of study in political science. Jean Blondel's new book is a major, comparative study of the world's government ministers since 1945, which examines both their similarities and differences.

Party structures, legislative behavior, even bureaucratic arrangements vary from country to country, but the nature of the job and the status of ministers is largely uniform, making it possible to study and tackle fundamental questions and assumptions of ministerial government.

This volume builds an analytical framework in order to probe the very foundation of the "ministerial profession" and explore important questions concerning political executives. Do social, economic, cultural or institutional factors contribute to the making of good or bad ministers? Are we justified in complaining about bad government? And, does high ministerial turnover contribute to bad government?

CONTENTS: The Study of Ministerial Careers // **I. Background** // The Social Background of Ministers / The Routes to Ministerial Office // **II. The Duration of Ministers in Office** // A Short Ministerial "Career" / Ministerial Duration and the Impact of Institutions / Patterns of Ministerial Duration / The One-Year Ministers // **III. Ministers in Government** // Amateurs and Specialists / The One-Post Ministers, Those who are Mobile, and Those who Come and Go / Long-Lasting Ministers / Conclusion

Political Executives in Comparative Perspective: A Cross-National Empirical Study, Volume 3
1985 / 304 pages / $32.00 (h) / $16.00 (p)

SAGE PUBLICATIONS, INC.
275 South Beverly Drive,
Beverly Hills, California 90212

SAGE PUBLICATIONS LTD
28 Banner Street,
London EC1Y 8QE, England

SAGE PUBLICATIONS INDIA PVT LTD
M-32 Market, Greater Kailash I, New Delhi 110 048, India

new from sage!

NEOFUNCTIONALISM
edited by JEFFREY C. ALEXANDER,
University of California, Los Angeles

What is important about these contributions is that using the point of view of a common tradition they have taken account of contemporary theoretical development. It is this tradition that allows the whole of each contribution to be more than the mere sum of its parts—the lessons of twenty years of theoretical debate become articulated in a functionalist way. The idea of a system with interrelated and relatively autonomous parts; the tension between ends and means; the reference to equilibrium; the distinction between personality, culture, and society; and the sensitivity to differentiation as a master trend and a commitment to independent theorizing—and many other basic fundamentals of "functional" thinking—permeate each essay.

Jeffrey Alexander points out, "Ideological critique, materialist reference, conflict orientation, and interactional thrust can in this way emerge as relatively coherent variations on a theme rather than as a collection of eclectic, completely diverse essays in sociological theory."

In the quest for scientific accumulation, such coherence is a definite advantage. But there are more substantive advantages: within a neofunctionalist framework, materialist reference is never separated from culture or personality systems, ideological criticism of society occurs within a multifaceted understanding of social differentiation. Also, thinking about conflict is intertwined with theories of integration and societal solidarity.

Alexander views functionalism as not just a set of concepts, methods, models or ideologies—but as a tradition. **Neofunctionalism**, which represents the author's sense of the future direction of this tradition as well as the discovery of its past, will be of major interest to social and political theorists, sociologists, and political scientists.

CONTENTS: Introduction: Neofunctionalism J.C. ALEXANDER // **I. Interpretation and Theoretical Boundaries** // 1. The Practical Groundwork for Critical Theory: Bringing Parsons to Habermas (and vice-versa) D. SCIULLI / 2. Prolegomena to Any Future Theory of Societal Crisis M. GOULD / 3. Predicting Technological Innovation: A Dialectical Reinterpretation of the Four-Function Paradigm I. ROSSI // **II. Explanation and Social Change** // 4. Systematic Qualities and Boundaries of Societies: Some Theoretical Considerations S.N. EISENSTADT / 5. Evaluating the Model of Structural Differentiation in Relation to Educational Change in the Nineteenth Century N.J. SMELSER / 6. Uneven Structural Differentiation: Toward a Comparative Approach P. COLOMY / 7. Modernity and Its Discontents: Revitalization Syndromes in Action-Theoretical Perspective F.J. LECHNER // **III. Politics and Responsibility** // 8. Totalitarian and Liberal Democracy: Two Types of Modern Political Orders J. PRAGER / 9. Beyond Parsons' Theory of the Professions B. BARBER / Commentary—Differentiation, Consensus, and Conflict: Reflections on Neofunctionalism in Smelser, Colomy, Lechner, and Barber R. MUNCH

Key Issues in Sociological Theory, Volume 1
1985 (September) / 256 pages (tent.) / \$28.00 (h) / \$14.00 (p)

SAGE PUBLICATIONS, INC.
275 South Beverly Drive,
Beverly Hills, California 90212

SAGE PUBLICATIONS LTD
28 Banner Street,
London EC1Y 8QE, England

SAGE PUBLICATIONS INDIA PVT LTD
M-32 Market, Greater Kailash I, New Delhi 110 048, India

CAREERS, COLLEAGUES, AND CONFLICTS
Understanding Gender, Race, and Ethnicity in the Workplace
by ARMAND LAUFFER, *University of Michigan*

**Published in cooperation with the
University of Michigan School of Social Work**

This volume is an indispensable guide to strategic career planning and effective working relationships with colleagues. Topics include satisfaction, motivation, and effort on the job (task, roles, responsibilities); gender, class, culture, and identity in the workplace; professionalism and deprofessionalization; interpersonal conflict; and conflict management. Each chapter includes a set of exercises designed to promote self-study and analysis, and an extensive bibliography. A unique blending of real-life, on-the-job experience with theoretical perspectives drawn from psychology, sociology, political science, and anthropology. Readers are directed toward an assessment of their own interests and the requirements of the workplace.

CONTENTS: Introduction / 1. Getting Turned on to Work / 2. Rubbing Shoulders and Rubbing Wounds / 3. Climbing the Ladder and Crossing the Bridge / 4. Claiming Professional Status / 5. Becoming a Colleague and Entering the Agency's Culture / 6. Getting the Job Done and Getting Along / Epilogue

Sage Human Services Guides, Volume 43
1985 (November) / 176 pages / $9.95 (p) (20407)

HOW TO CONDUCT SURVEYS
A Step-by-Step Guide
by ARLENE FINK & JACQUELINE KOSECOFF
Adjunct Associate Professors of Medicine and Public Health,
University of California, Los Angeles

Concise and clearly written, this practical guide examines the nitty-gritty of interview and questionnaire surveys. It takes the reader through the step-by-step process of deciding informational needs and hypotheses, choosing a questionnaire or interview format, designing a data collection method, choosing a sample, analyzing the findings, and reporting the results.

"The methods in this book are to help you organize a rigorous survey and evaluate the credibility of other ones," Fink and Kosecoff point out. "We have aimed for simplicity not for embellishment." Open-ended items versus forced choices, self-administered surveys, pilot testing, sample size and response rate, probability versus nonprobability sampling, statistical significance, visual presentations, and many more subjects are discussed.

How to Conduct Surveys is geared for everyone who needs to learn how to do a simple survey, regardless of his or her statistical knowledge. Didactic examples, helpful practice exercises with answers, and informative appendices with rules for performing technical computations make this book appropriate for both self-teaching and classroom use.

CONTENTS: Preface / 1. Conducting Surveys: Everyone Is Doing It / 2. The Survey Form: Questions, Scales, and Appearance / 3. Getting It Together: Some Practical Concerns / 4. Sampling / 5. Survey Design: Environmental Control / 6. Analyzing Data from Surveys / 7. Presenting the Survey Results / Appendix

1985 (July) / 120 pages / $12.00 (p)